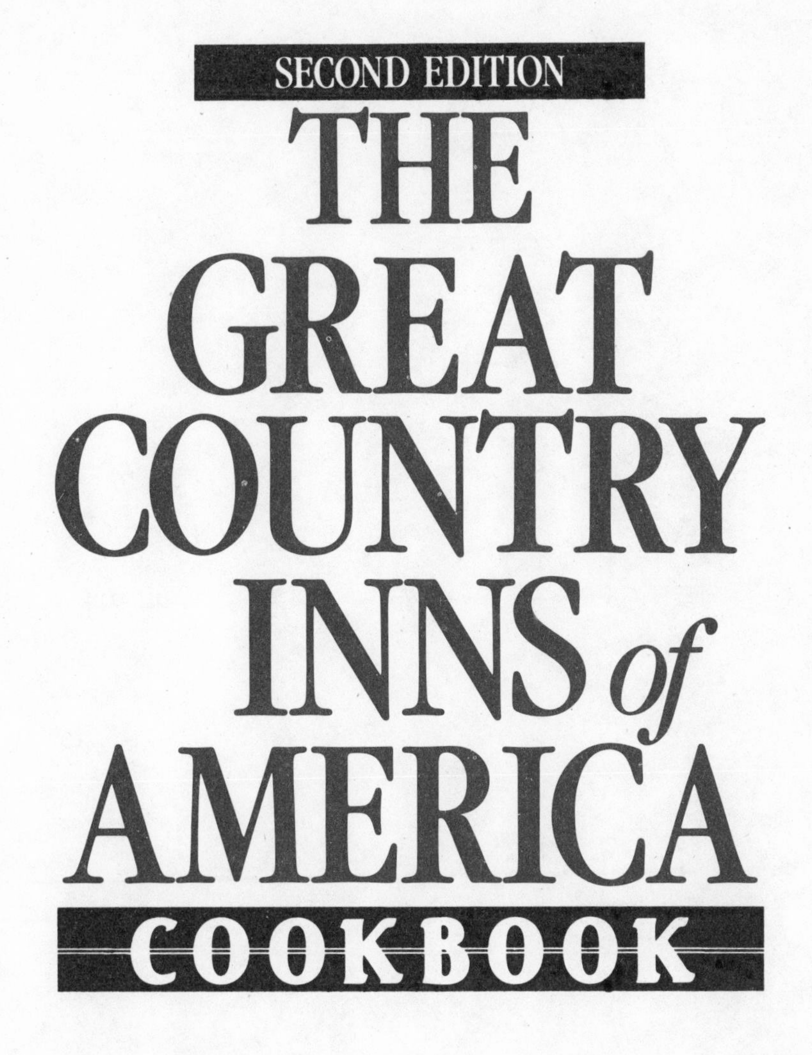
SECOND EDITION
THE GREAT COUNTRY INNS of AMERICA
COOKBOOK

SECOND EDITION

THE GREAT COUNTRY INNS *of* AMERICA COOKBOOK

James Stroman

ADAMS PUBLISHING
Holbrook, Massachusetts

Published by: Adams Media Corporation
260 Center Street, Holbrook, MA 02343

ISBN: 1-55850-165-7

Printed in the United States of America

J I H G F E D C B

To all the chefs and innkeepers
across the country who so generously
donated their recipes

Contents

The Inns and Their Recipes

New England

CONNECTICUT

MAINE

RHODE ISLAND

VERMONT

Middle Atlantic

The South

VIRGINIA

WEST VIRGINIA

The Midwest and Plains States

ILLINOIS

INDIANA

IOWA

KANSAS

MICHIGAN

MINNESOTA

MISSOURI

NEBRASKA

NORTH DAKOTA

OHIO

SOUTH DAKOTA

WISCONSIN

The Rocky Mountains and Southwest

ARIZONA

COLORADO

IDAHO

TEXAS

The Crystal River Inn	Asparagus Vinaigrette, 50 Rice and Pecans, 143
The Delforge Place	Fresh Peach Soup, 121 San Saba Pecan French Toast, 245
Excelsior House	Breakfast Casserole, 239 Baked Yams, 140
Mayan Ranch	Oatmeal Banana Cookies, 370 Picadillo, 206 Texas Style Chili, 207
Raumonda	Columbus Potato Soup, 106 Cranberry Ring, 64
White House Inn	Zucchini Muffins, 358

UTAH

Greene Gate Village Inn	Quick Granola, 265 Bread Sticks, 334
Old Miner's Lodge	Barbecued Flank Steak, 204 Cinnamon Syrup, 402 Champagne Punch, 408 Red Cabbage Salad, 43
Pah Tempe Hot Springs Resort	Lentil Soup, 108
Snowed Inn	Very Special Vegetables, 11
Washington School Inn	Cottage Cheese Dip, 3 Zucchini Brownies, 385

WYOMING

Country Fare Guest House	Crab Quiche, 269
The Historic Hotel Higgins	Baked French Toast, 246
The Irma	Hot Buttered Rum Mix, 409 Lemon Chicken, 165
Lost Horizon	Chicken and Walnuts, 169 Szechwan Shredded Beef with Broccoli, 205
Savery Creek Ranch	Spinach Soup, 90
Spahn's Bighorn Mountain Lodge	Creamy Eggs, 231
Sundance Inn	Tom Thumb Tarts, 383

The West

ALASKA

CALIFORNIA

HAWAII

OREGON

WASHINGTON

1
Appetizers

Washington School Inn is a perfect example of what preservationists call "adaptive use." A schoolhouse built in 1889, the building was fully restored as an inn, opening in June, 1985. Its location in the old town of Park City, Utah, puts it close to the magnificent skiing opportunities for which this area is noted. The inn offers its visitors deliciously prepared food, and afternoon goodies are always available to hungry skiers returning from the slopes.

Cottage Cheese Dip

2 cups cottage cheese
4 scallions, sliced fine
6 to 8 radishes, diced
6 tablespoons mayonnaise
2 teaspoons Ranch Dressing mix (dry)
1/4 teaspoons toasted sesame seeds

Combine all ingredients and serve with assorted raw vegetables. Makes 2 cups.

Note: For a smoother consistency, place all ingredients except the sesame seeds in a food processor and blend. Stir in the sesame seeds.

Washington School Inn

P.O. Box 536
Park City, Utah 84060
(801) 649-3800

Ham and Cheese Dip

1/2 teaspoon garlic powder
1/2 cup sour cream
1 tablespoon prepared mustard
1 tablespoon Worcestershire sauce
2 tablespoons Parmesan cheese
1 pound cream cheese, softened
2 large slices Swiss cheese, cut in pieces
1 teaspoon chopped parsley
1 teaspoon chopped chives

Combine all ingredients in a food processor and blend untill smooth. Makes about 2 cups.

Here is an inn in a delightful part of Vermont where winter's cast is pure white, summer is a velvetlike green, and fall colors unbelievable. Skiers of yesteryear were carried to the slopes by horse and sleigh; although the many guests now use more modern modes, the inn itself has maintained the original warmth and simplicity of a family-run country inn.

The Village Inn

Box 215
Landgrove Road
Londonderry, Vermont 05148
(802) 824-6673

Yes Bay Lodge offers rustic elegance in a wilderness setting, 50 miles northwest of Ketchikan. The area is noted for outstanding salmon and trout fishing. The Hack family provides warm hospitality and personal service.

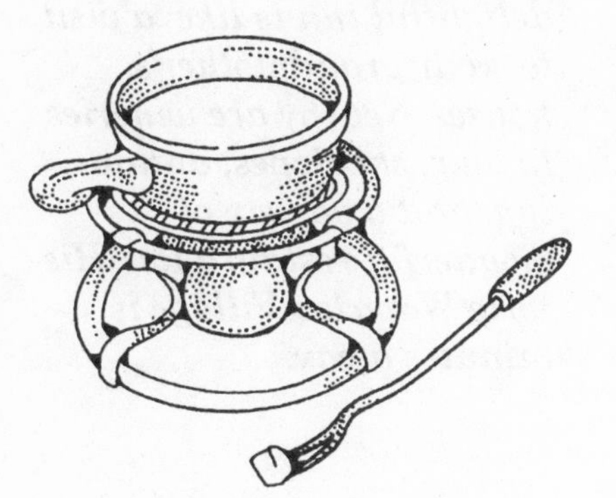

Smoked Salmon Dip

8 ounces cream cheese, softened
1 cup mayonnaise
2 teaspoons lemon juice
1 pound smoked salmon, flaked
Garlic salt to taste

Combine all ingredients and mix well. Thin with sour cream if needed. Makes 2 1/2 cups.

Yes Bay Lodge

Yes Bay, Alaska 99950
(907) 247-1575

Curry Vegetable Dip

8 ounces cream cheese, softened
1 cup mayonnaise
3 tablespoons lemon juice
3 tablespoons ketchup
3 tablespoons honey
10 drops Tabasco sauce
1 1/2 teaspoons curry powder
3 tablespoons grated onion

Combine all ingredients. Serve with assorted raw vegetables. Makes 2 cups.

Whistling Swan Inn

P.O. Box 791
Stanhope, New Jersey 07874
(201) 347-6369

Tucked away in the Skylands of northwestern New Jersey, you will find the Whistling Swan Inn, a ten-bedroom family home built circa 1900. All the rooms have private baths and a full buffet style breakfast is served in the dining room. A stay at this delightful inn is like a visit to your grandmother's house. Nearby are wineries to tour, ski slopes, antiquing, and a variety of wonderful restaurants. Historic Waterloo Village is minutes away.

Greenvale Manor is in the historic Northern Neck of Virginia, on a peninsula overlooking the Rappahannock River and Greenvale Creek. The manor house was built in 1840 and is filled with antiques. On warm days, guests enjoy breakfast on the sunny veranda with its gorgeous water views, and later in the day on weekends, a cookout with locally caught steamed crabs is enjoyed by all. With crackling fires during the colder months, Greenvale Manor is a special year-round getaway for "lovers" of all ages.

Corned Beef and Horseradish Dip

1 12-ounce can corned beef
1 5-ounce jar horseradish
1 cup mayonnaise
1 medium onion, chopped fine
Worcestershire sauce, to taste
Pepper to taste
Chopped parsley, for garnish

Combine all ingredients. Mix well and refrigerate for several hours or overnight. Sprinkle with parsley and serve with crackers. Serves 8 to 10.

Greenvale Manor Inn

P.O. Box 7
Mollusk, Virginia 22517
(804) 462-5995

Chutney Cheese Spread

1 pound cream cheese, softened
1/2 cup chopped chutney
1/2 cup toasted almonds
1/2 teaspoon dry mustard or curry powder
Chopped toasted almonds and chopped parsley, for garnish

Using an electric mixer, whip the cream cheese. Add other ingredients, except garnish. Form into two balls. Roll in the chopped almonds and finely snipped parsley.

Storybook Inn

28717 Highway 18
P.O. Box 362
Skyforest, California 92385
(714) 336-1483

The Storybook Inn is a quiet, refined inn located on the renowned "Rim of the World" highway. It was restored to its natural beauty in 1986 by Kathleen and John Wooley. A complete gourmet breakfast is served; an evening social hour offers delicious California wines and tasty hors d'oeuvres. The Storybook provides a unique country inn experience high in the mountains near famous Lake Arrowhead, California's answer to the Swiss Alps.

Owned and operated by Carl and Vita Hinshaw, Chalet Suzanne was born some fifty years ago of Yankee ingenuity and Southern hospitality. Carl's mother, Bertha, was a gourmet cook, collector and world traveler who had her own way of coping with the double disaster of her husband's death and loss of the family fortunes in the 1930s. To support her son and daughter, she turned her home into an inn and dining room, ignoring the gloomy predictions of friends. For ten days, nothing happened, then came her first guests, a family of five. A few days later, she was in business. The Chalet continued to grow and is now world famous for its soups and other delicacies. Its award-winning restaurant has been voted one of Florida's top 10 for 23 consecutive years and has been featured in every major food and travel magazine and guide.

Bleu Cheese Mousse Dean

1 1/2 envelopes unflavored gelatine, 1 1/2 tablespoons
1/4 cup cold water
6 egg yolks
2 cups heavy cream
3/4 pound bleu cheese
3 egg whites, stiffly beaten
2 tablespoon poppy seeds

Sprinkle the gelatine over the cold water to soften. Combine the egg yolks and 1/2 cup of the cream in a small heavy saucepan. Over low heat, cook and beat with whisk until the mixture is creamy and slightly thickened. Add the gelatine and beat until it is dissolved. Pour the mixture into a large mixing bowl and set aside. Press the cheese through a sieve or process in a blender or food processor until smooth; add to the gelatine mixture. Cool until the mixture is partially set. Whip the remaining cream and fold it into the cheese mixture; then fold in the egg whites and poppy seeds. Turn mixture into an oiled 2-quart mold. Chill. To serve, unmold on a serving plate. Garnish with endive and serve with raw vegetables, toast rounds, and crackers. Serves about 35.

Chalet Suzanne

P.O Box AC
Lake Wales, Florida 33859
(813) 676-6011

Cold Cauliflower Nivernais

3 or 4 heads cauliflower, broken into flowerets
2 1/2 cups mayonnaise
3/4 cup sour cream
7 tablespoons Dijon mustard
2 tablespoons chopped parsley
Pimento, red bell pepper, or chopped parsley for garnish

Boil the caulifloweret in salted water for seven minutes; they should be slightly crisp. Drain immediately and submerge in iced water to cool quickly. Drain again. In a separate bowl, place the mayonnaise, sour cream, mustard, and parsley. Combine until light and creamy. Toss with cauliflower and chill. Garnish with strips of pimiento, red bell pepper, or chopped parsley.

Three Village Inn

150 Main Street
Stony Brook, New York 11790
(516) 751-0555

Stony Brook is an old shipping and fishing village nestled in the hills of the North Shore of Long Island, with its own harbor and with the Sound immediately adjacent. Three Village Inn offers modern comfort in an atmosphere of 1800. It is housed in the Jonas Smith Homestead built in 1785. Good food, good drink, and a good night's rest are assured. Head Chef Nelson Roberts and his wife, Monda, place a great deal of emphasis on the food served. In good weather, many guests enjoy the In-and-Out dining room where an outdoor grill allows diners to watch their meals being prepared while they relax on the lawn.

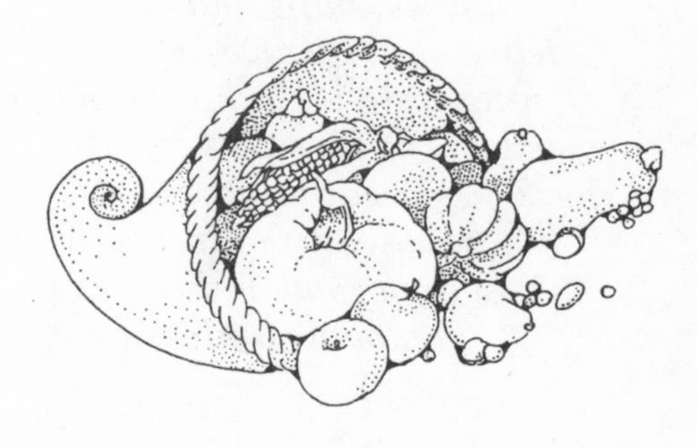

Park City is one of the most beautiful mountain resorts in America. The Snowed Inn is pure Victorian elegance with all the modern conveniences of a fine hotel. There are ten elegantly appointed suites and glorious food is served in the relaxing dining room.

Very Special Vegetables

1 pound cream cheese, softened
1/2 cup snipped chives
Worcestershire sauce
Salt
White pepper
Snow pea pods, blanched
Celery
Cucumber
Zucchini

Blend the cheese, chives, Worcestershire sauce, salt, and pepper to taste in a food processor. Prepare the vegetables—slit open the pea pods, remove strings from celery stalks, and slice cucumber and zucchini lengthwise and remove the seeds. Stuff the mixture into the vegetable "boats" and slice into appetizer-size pieces. Makes about 2 cups of filling.

Snowed Inn

3770 North Highway 224
Park City, Utah 84060
(801) 649-5713

Roasted Red Bell Pepper Terrine

3 1/2 pounds red bell peppers
4 tablespoons hot water
salt and pepper to taste
1 cup plus 1 tablespoon heavy cream
2 tablespoons unflavored gelatin
1 tablespoon sugar
2 tablespoons cognac

Quarter the peppers and remove seeds and white flesh. Broil skin-side up until blackened and flesh is cooked. Shock in ice water. Remove and discard blackened skin. Puree flesh and heat in the top of a double boiler with the salt, pepper, and sugar.

While the puree is heating, add gelatin to boiled hot water and whip carefully until it is dissolved. Add to the heated pepper puree and cool to room temperature.

Add the cognac. Whip the heavy cream until firm. Fold the cream into the pepper mixture; pour into mold lined with aluminum foil strips. Chill 4-6 hours at 35-40 degrees. Serves 8 to 10.

Old Lyme Inn

P.O Box 787
Old Lyme, Connecticut 06371
(203) 434-2600

The warm exterior of a fine old nineteenth-century home, typifying New England's charming colonial residences, welcomes travelers and diners to the elegance of the Old Lyme Inn. Situated on the main street in Old Lyme's historic district, the Inn represents the classic traditions of excellence in dining and lodging that are the very heart of this small Connecticut town. Built in the 1850s, the inn remained a private residence and working farm of some 300 acres for over a century. Today, it retains its historic grandeur. White tablecloths, single rose centerpieces, and antique furniture are just a few of the accoutrements of a memorable dining experience . An innovative menu based on the best of America's produce and culinary talent offers diners sophistication in food uniquely prepared and graciously presented.

Quiet, intimate, romantic, and special are just a few of the adjectives that describe The Glenborough Inn.

Hot Artichoke Dip

1 14-ounce can artichokes, broken up
1/2 cup mayonnaise
1 4-ounce çan chopped green chilies
1 cup grated Parmesan cheese

Combine all ingredients and bake in a shallow 4-cup dish for 15 minutes at 350 degrees. Serve with crackers.

The Glenborough Inn

1327 Bath Street
Santa Barbara, California 93101
(805) 966-0589

Old English Fondue

Here is another delicious appetizer from The Storybook Inn.

8 ounces cream cheese
2 5-ounce jars Old English sharp cheddar
1 can minced clams
1 4-ounce can minced Ortega chilies
1/2 cup chopped green onion
1 tablespoon Worcestershire sauce

Combine all ingredients. Heat at 350 degrees F. until bubbly (20 to 30 minutes). Serve with corn chips or other chips as desired, or serve in a hollowed-out round loaf of sour dough bread, using the bread as dippers. Serves 8 to 10.

Storybook Inn

28717 Highway 18
P.O. Box 362
Skyforest, California
(714) 336-1483

At The Checkerberry Inn, the visitor will find a unique atmosphere, unlike anywhere else in the midwest. The individually decorated rooms and suites will please even the most discerning guests. Every room has a breathtaking view of the unspoiled rolling countryside. A top-rated restaurant serves only the freshest foods using herbs and other ingredients from the local countryside.

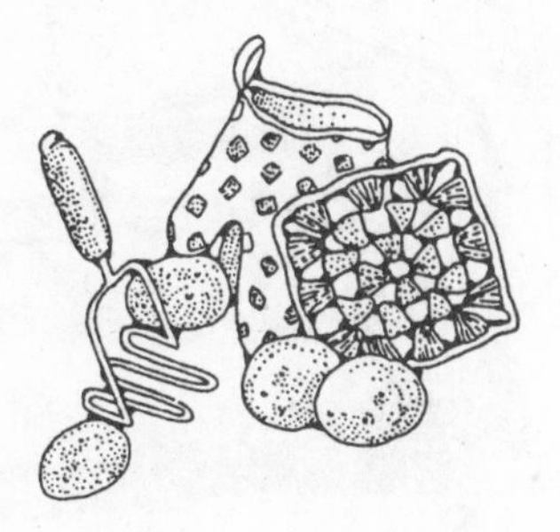

Caviar-Stuffed Potatoes

10 small red potatoes
Oil
1/2 cup sour cream
1/2 cup buttermilk
1/4 cup chopped fresh chives
4 tablespoons virgin olive oil
1 clove garlic, minced
1/4 pound extra sharp Cheddar cheese, shredded fine
Salt
White pepper
1 small jar lumpfish caviar

Coat potatoes with oil and roast at 325 degrees until soft-baked (about 35 minutes), turning every 10 minutes. Let cool to room temperature. Mix sour cream and buttermilk with chives and salt to taste and refrigerate until ready to use. Mix olive oil with garlic and let stand at room temperature for 1 hour.

When potatoes are cool to the touch, slice off 1/2 inch of one end and carefully scoop out the insides, keeping the shell intact. Place potato insides in a small bowl and mix with the olive oil mixture, cheese, and salt and pepper to taste. Carefully flatten the opposite ends of the potato shells so they will stand upright. Fill with the potato mixture and refrigerate for several hours but not overnight. When ready to serve, heat potatoes for 10 to 15 minutes in a 350 degree oven until evenly hot (or heat in a microwave). Warm the sour cream mixture but do not let it boil. Top each potato with approximately 4 tablespoons of the sour cream mixture and a small spoonful of caviar.

Serves 4.

Note: This recipe allows two extra potatoes, in case one or two of the shells tear during preparation.

The Checkerberry Inn

62644 County Road 37
Goshen, Indiana
(219) 642-4445

Mushrooms Pennsylvania

1 pound fresh mushrooms, cleaned and quartered
2 ounces sun-dried tomatoes, sliced and soaked in white wine overnight
6 tablespoons butter
1 cup Madeira
3/4 cup heavy cream
1 tablespoon finely chopped shallots
Ground white pepper
2 scallions, sliced
4 garlic croutons

Croutons

4 3/4-inch slices French bread, cut on the diagonal
4 ounces melted butter
2 or 3 garlic cloves, finely chopped
Paprika
Chopped parsley
Grated Parmesan cheese

To prepare the croutons, butter one side of each bread slice, top each slice with chopped garlic, and sprinkle with parsley, cheese and paprika. Bake at 400 until golden brown.

To prepare the mushrooms, heat a heavy skillet and melt the butter. When the butter sizzles, add the mushrooms and saute to cook through. Drain the sun-dried tomatoes and add to the pan. Add Madeira and shallots, reduce by two-thirds. Pour in the heavy cream, add pepper to taste. Allow the sauce to reduce to a slightly thick consistency. Place one crouton on each serving plate and divide the mushrooms evenly over the croutons. Top each dish with a few of the scallion slices. Serves 4.

The Golden Plough

P.O. Box 218
Lahaska, Pennsylvania 18931
(215) 794-4004

The slogan for The Golden Plough Inn is: "A stay in the country for days full of pleasures and nights to remember." This inn is definitely for those who appreciate the finer things in life surrounded by a unique combination of country hospitality and romantic comfort. It is located in Buck County's most picturesque area where every season is a delightful experience. Innkeeper Earl Jamison is proud of his family's 200-year history of innkeeping , and is committed to quality and fine service.

This beautiful inn offers comfort and charm in a traditional setting. Built in 1873, the inn is included in the National Register of Historic Places. The 18-room inn boasts a handsome red brick exterior, high ceilings, shutters, a massive, beautifully carved front door, walnut paneling, and parquet floors. After a restful night, guests enjoy a full breakfast including omelettes, quiches, homemade breads, and other luscious foods prepared and supervised by Innkeeper Mildred Cameron. The inn is only minutes away from the Missouri River, which offers boating, fishing, and riverfront parks.

Tortilla Rolls

1 package large tortillas
8 ounces cream cheese, softened
1 2 1/4-ounce can chopped black olives
1 4-ounce can chopped green chilies
1 1/2 cups grated Cheddar cheese
1/2 cup sour cream

Mix all ingredients and spread on tortillas. Roll like a jelly roll, wrap, and refrigerate overnight. Slice into 1/2 inch slices and serve with a bowl of salsa. Makes about 12 dozen.

The Mulberry Inn

512 Mulberry Street
Yankton, South Dakota 57078
(605) 665-7116

Empanaditas

Pastry
2 cups sifted flour
1 teaspoon seasoned salt
1 teaspoon chili powder
2/3 cup shortening
5 tablespoons cold water

Filling
1/3 pound cooked chicken
2/3 cup chopped toasted walnuts
2 tablespoons diced canned green chilies
2 tablespoons diced onion
1/2 teaspoon chili powder
1/4 teaspoon salt
1/4 cup mayonnaise

Pastry
Sift the flour with the salt and chili powder into a bowl. Cut shortening using two knives or a pastry blender until the mixture resembles coarse meal. Add water, a little at a time, and toss with a fork until the dough can be formed into a ball, as for pie crust. Pat into a ball and chill.

Filling
Cut the chicken into small pieces and mix well with the remaining ingredients. Roll the pastry on marble or a lightly floured board to about 1/8-inch thickness. Cut into rounds, using a 1 3/4-inch cutter. Spoon a little filling into each round and fold over, making small turnovers. Press edges together with the tines of a fork to seal. Prick the top of each turnover. Bake on an ungreased cookie sheet until golden brown, about 10-12 minutes at 450 degrees. Makes 5 dozen.
Note: These turnovers freeze well, but will take longer to bake if they are frozen.

Coleen's California Casa

P.O. Box 9302
Whittier, California 90608
(213) 699-8427

Here the visitor enjoys a tranquil homelike atmosphere on a hillside overlooking Los Angeles. Guests enjoy the quiet peacefulness of a rural area. The dining room serves freshly prepared dishes prepared by owner Coleen Davis herself. You can hike in Sycamore Canyon, tour the Whittier College campus, and walk "around the circle" to enjoy the hillside view. As twilight falls, enjoy wine and cheese on the luxurious deck and see the lights of the city flickering below.

Located in the northern tip of Custer State Park, this resort inn overlooks scenic Black Elk Wilderness Area and is bordered by the spired granite rock formations that highlight the Needles Highway. The original lodge burned down from unknown causes and in 1936 the present lodge was constructed. The fresh pine-scented air, the crystal clear waters of Sylvan Lake, and the magnificent view of Harney Peak from the rock patio of this historic lodge are amenities unique to Sylvan Lake Resort. There is gourmet dining in the Lodge's Lakota Dining Room.

Bacon Wrapped Chestnuts

1 pound bacon, strips cut in half
3 8-ounce cans whole water chestnuts
1/2 cup brown sugar
1/2 cup ketchup

Wrap a piece of uncooked bacon around each chestnut and secure with a toothpick. Place in a baking dish and bake at 350 degrees for 30 to 45 minutes or until bacon is done. Drain off bacon fat. In another bowl, mix brown sugar and ketchup. Pour over chestnuts. Bake for another 30 minutes. Serve hot. Serves 8 to 10.

Sylvan Lake Resort

Box 752
Custer, South Dakota 57730
(605) 574-2561

Chicken Liver Pate

1 pound chicken livers
4 anchovies
1 cup cream
1/2 cup flour
3 tablespoons butter, softened
1 teaspoon salt
1/8 teaspoon celery salt
1 teaspoon pepper
1 egg
1/4 teaspoon onion powder
Raw bacon slices

Using a food processor or blender, grind the chicken livers and anchovies. Add the cream. Blend together the flour and butter to make a paste, then add to the food processor. Add the salt, celery salt, pepper, egg, and onion powder and mix well. Line a one-quart dish with raw bacon slices. Pour in the liver mixture. Fold bacon slices over the top. Place the dish in a deep pan of hot water. Bake at 350 degrees for 1 1/4 hours. Let cool and chill before unmolding and serving with melba toast or crackers. Serves 12 to 16.

Redfish Lake Lodge

P.O. Box 9
Stanley, Idaho 83278
(208) 774-3536

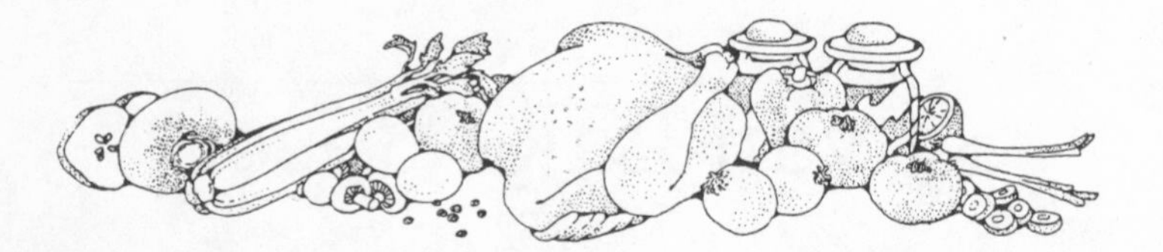

Redfish Lake Lodge is located at the headwaters of the main fork of the Salmon River in the heart of the Sawtooth National Forest and bordering the Sawtooth wilderness area. The dining room offers an excellent menu with a mountain atmosphere. The inn was built for the sportsman, nature lover, photographer, horseback rider and naturalist— in short, for the person who wants to turn his back upon the grinding roar of the civilized world and seek peace and quiet in untouched mountain country.

Norma and Johnny Crow have lived on the Silver Leaf Farm in Hickman County Tennessee. for several years. In 1972, they purchased the adjoining 160 acres and the log house built in 1815. Norma's dream was to have a country inn, make each guest feel at home, and serve them the best in home style cooking. Her dream came true. Luscious food pours forth from Norma's kitchen. This recipe following is from her cookbook, Norma's Favorite Recipes and Reflections.

Chafing Dish Meatballs

1 pound ground beef
1/2 cup biscuit mix or dry bread crumbs
1/3 cup minced onion
1/4 cup milk
1 egg
1 tablespoon snipped parsley
1 teaspoon salt
1/8 teaspoon pepper
1/2 teaspoon Worcestershire sauce
1/4 cup shortening
1 12-ounce bottle chili sauce
1 10-ounce jar grape jelly

Mix the ground beef, biscuit mix, onion, milk, and egg and add the seasonings. Shape into 1-inch balls. Melt the shortening in a skillet; brown the meatballs. Remove from the skillet and drain off fat. Heat the chili sauce and the jelly in the skillet until the jelly is melted, stirring constantly. Add the meatballs and stir to coat with sauce. Simmer for twenty minutes. Serve hot in a chafing dish. Makes 5 dozen meatballs.

Silver Leaf, A Country Inn

Route 1, Box 122
Lyles, Tennessee 37098
(615) 670-3048

Country Style Terrine

1 1/2 pounds pork
3/4 pound veal
3/4 pound lamb
1 1/2 pounds pork fatback
1 pound duck liver
2 eggs
2 tablespoons brandy
4 tablespoons salt
4 teaspoons cracked black pepper
1 1/2 cups minced onion, sauteed in butter
12 cloves garlic, minced and sauteed in butter
4 tablespoons parsley, chopped
1/4 teaspoon each: allspice, ground clove, nutmeg, curry, dry mustard, cayenne pepper
2 ounces toasted hazelnuts, chopped
4 ounces diced ham
1 pound bacon

Ground the first five ingredients in a meat grinder with a medium die. Then combine the remaining ingredients, except the bacon, with the ground meat. Line two terrine molds with the bacon and spoon the mixture into the molds. Place the molds in a baking pan and pour in boiling water to reach halfway up the sides of the molds. Bake at 300 degrees for 90 minutes, or until the internal temperature reaches 140 degrees. Let the terrines cool overnight before unmolding and serving. Serves 16 to 20.

The Inn at Long Last

P.O. Box 589
Chester, Vermont 05143
(802) 875-2444

The Inn at Long Last is one of Vermont's very best and offers one of the most distinctive menus in New England. The inn is housed in a gracious plantation-style home on the Village Green. It is old-fashioned in comfort and young in spirit. The 35 guest rooms are filled with colonial antiques. The grounds include a heated pool, tennis courts, and a gracious patio.

Located on the beautiful campus of Dartmouth College, The Hanover Inn reflects the growth and changes of the college.

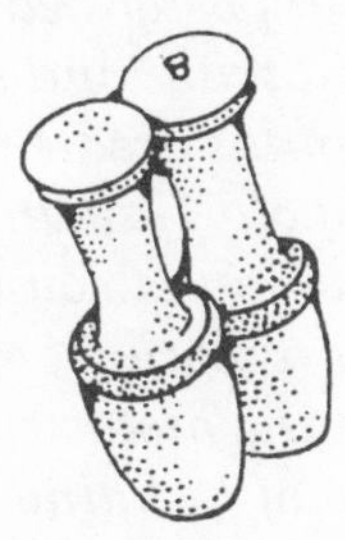

Ivy Grill East of Buffalo Wings

2 pounds chicken wings
Salt and pepper to taste
1 cup soy sauce
1 1/2 tablespoons Tabasco sauce
1 tablespoon honey

Arrange the chicken wings on a jelly-roll pan or in a shallow casserole. Season with salt and pepper. Bake for 1/2 hour at 375 degrees. Drain and cool. Set aside or refrigerate for up to a day.

When ready to serve, fry until crisp in 1 tablespoon of oil or bake for 15 minutes at 425 degrees. The wings should be crispy. Drain off fat. Place wings in a bowl and toss with a sauce made by combining the soy sauce, Tabasco, and honey. Accompany with Cucumber Dip and celery sticks. Serves 6 to 10.

Cucumber Dip
2 large cucumbers, peeled, seeded, and chopped fine
1 cup sour cream or plain yogurt
1 teaspoon lemon juice
Salt and pepper to taste

Combine all ingredients and blend well.

The Hanover Inn

P.O. Box 151
Hanover, New Hampshire 03755
(603) 643-4300

Calamari with Lime and Ginger

3 tablespoons sesame oil
3 tablespoons peanut oil
Salt and pepper
3 pounds calamari, cleaned, gutted, and sliced 1/4 inch thick
1 scallion, sliced 1/4 inch thick
2 ounces fresh ginger, peeled and diced small
3 limes, peeled and sectioned (save juice that comes out during peeling and sectioning)

When ready to serve, heat two heavy saute pans and add both oils. Season the calamari. Saute on high heat to retain tenderness and crispiness. Cook only a few seconds. Turn off heat. Add scallions ginger and lime juice. Transfer to a heated serving plate. Decorate with the lime sections and serve immediately. Serves 6.

The Plantation Inn and Gerard's Restaurant

174 Lahainaluna Road
Lahaina, Maui, Hawaii 96761
(808) 667-9225

Here, combined are one of America's finest inns and very finest restaurants. Gerard's changing menu and award winning creations have earned it a rating as one of Hawaii's top 10 restaurants in Sheldon Landwehr's prestigious Who's Who in America's Restaurants. *The elegant, intimate French restaurant at the inn is a favorite dining spot for Hawaiian residents and visitors alike. The Plantation Inn blends an elegant turn-of-the-century ambience with the first-class amenities of the finest hotels. Antiques, stained glass, hardwood floors, brass and poster beds, extensive wood trim, and sprawling verandas create the charm of old Hawaii. The inn is in a quiet country setting just a block from the ocean in the historic whaling town of Lahaina, near Kaanapali.*

The Colby Hill has witnessed many changes over the years, as might be expected of a place nearly 200 years old. Originally built to serve as a farm and homestead around 1800, it has since been used as a tavern, a church, meeting house, private school, and now as a charming country inn. Antique furnishings, wide pine board floors that sag and tilt, a fireplace with a bake oven, Indian shutters and delicious food all make Colby Hill a memorable inn.

Smoked Trout Pate

3/4 pound boned smoked trout
1 pound cream cheese, softened
1 bunch scallions, chopped
1/4 tablespoon chopped dill
2 tablespoons lemon juice
1 tablespoon chopped parsley

Combine all ingredients and mix until smooth. Store in an air-tight container overnight. The pate can be molded or served in individual ramekins. Makes about 3 cups.

Colby Hill Inn

The Oaks
Henniker, New Hampshire 03242
(603) 428-3281

Smoked Salmon Mousse

1 tablespoon finely chopped shallots or green onions
2 tablespoons unsalted butter
2 or 3 ounces smoked salmon, boned and flaked
1/4 cup softened cream cheese
1/4 cup sour cream
1/4 cup unsalted butter, softened
2 tablespoons lemon juice
1 tablespoon vodka
1/4 cup heavy cream, whipped

Saute the shallots in the two tablespoons butter until golden. Add the salmon, mix, and remove from heat. Place the mixture in a blender, add the cream cheese, sour cream, and butter, and blend well. Add the lemon juice and vodka. Blend until smooth. Remove the mixture to a bowl and fold in the whipped cream. Refrigerate for a couple of hours or up to two days. Serve cold, but not too chilled, on crackers or warm french bread. Makes about 1 1/2 cups.

Chalet de France

Star Route Box 20-A
Kneeland Post Office
Eureka, California 95549
(707) 442-0333

This inn is a deluxe wilderness retreat in the heart of northern California's Redwood Country and Wild Rivers region. A traditional hand-crafted eighteenth century Swiss-Tyrolian chalet perched atop a 3000 foot mountain, overlooking views of 40 miles or more. This 160-acre hideaway features strictly gourmet cuisine, spectacular mountain vistas, breathtaking sunsets, and the coastal expanse of the Pacific Ocean.

Holmes Retreat, with the Holmeses as hosts,is situated on the banks of Mink Creek, in an area that is a haven for songbirds and hummingbirds.

Hot Crab Spread

1 tablespoon milk
8 ounces cream cheese, softened
3 tablespoons chopped onion
1 tablespoon horseradish
1/4 teaspoon salt
1 or 2 dashes Tabasco sauce
8 ounces cooked crabmeat, cut into 3/4 inch cubes
1/3 cup sliced almonds

In a bowl, mix the first 6 ingredients. Fold in the crabmeat. Transfer to a 6 x 4 x 2-inch baking dish. Sprinkle the top with the almonds. Bake at 350 degrees F. until the mixture bubbles. Serve with crackers. Makes 2 cups.

Holmes Retreat

178 North Mink Creek Road
Pocatello, Idaho 83204
(208) 232-5518

Hot Crab-Cheese Canapes

1/2 cup Old English Sharp Cheddar Cheese
1/2 cup butter or margarine
1 6-ounce can crabmeat
1 tablespoon mayonnaise
1 teaspoon lemon pepper
1 teaspoon garlic salt
1 teaspoon seasoned salt
Dash pepper sauce
Dash Worcestershire sauce
12 English muffins

Cut the cheese and butter or margarine into pieces and place in the bowl of a food processor along with the crabmeat, mayonnaise and seasonings. Blend until smooth. Split the muffins and spread with the mixture. Cut each split muffin into 4 or 6 wedges and heat under the broiler until warm. You can also freeze the wedges until needed and broil them without thawing first. Makes 8 or 12 dozen.

Cedar Grove Mansion

P.O. Box B
Vicksburg, Mississippi 39181
(601) 636-1605

One of the South's largest and loveliest historic mansions, Cedar Grove is exquisitely furnished with many original antiques, including gaslit chandeliers, gold leaf mirrors, and Italian marble mantels. The mansion was built by John A. Klein as a wedding present for his bride. They returned from their European honeymoon with many architectural amenities today enjoyed by visitors from around the world. Guests stay in luxurious guest rooms or suites, all with private baths. The grounds are enhanced by magnificent formal gardens and gazebos. The formal dining room, still in use today, was the setting for many special occasions. Confederate President Jefferson Davis danced in the magnificent ballroom, and a Union cannonball remains lodged in the parlor wall.

Here is a historic country inn offering good food, good friends, and good lodging. It was built in 1898 with a wide old staircase and spacious halls to welcome visitors to its attractive parlors. All rooms have private baths, and there are also family suites. The inn serves regional New England cuisine in its large attractive dining room. Connie and Tom Mazol are the innkeepers.

Deviled Clams

24 littleneck clams on the half shell
6 tablespoons butter
3 tablespoons minced onion
1 garlic clove, minced
1 tablespoon minced parsley
1/4 cup beer
4 slices crisp cooked bacon, crumbled
4 tablespoons bread crumbs

Remove clams from shells and coarsely chop. Cream together the butter, onion, garlic, and parsley. Blend in the beer, then mix in bacon and clams. Fill clam shells with the mixture and sprinkle with bread crumbs. Place on a baking sheet. Bake at 375 degrees for 10 minutes. Serves 4 to 6.

The Bradford Inn

Main Street
Bradford, New Hampshire 03221
(603) 938-5309

Bacon Baked Oysters

1 dozen oysters
3 tablespoons butter, melted
2 tablespoons lemon juice
Dash of salt
Dash of pepper
1/2 cup fresh bread crumbs
1/2 cup crumbled crisp-fried bacon
2 tablespoons bacon fat

Open the oysters and leave in the half shell. Settle each shell into crumpled foil on a baking sheet, to prevent tipping. Combine the butter, lemon juice, and salt and pepper and baste each oyster with the mixture. Combine the bread crumbs, bacon, and bacon fat and top each oyster with this mixture. Bake for 4 to 5 minutes at 425 degrees. Serves 4.

Blue Coat Inn

800 North State Street
Dover, Delaware 19901
(302) 674-1776

Once a private home, the Blue Coat Inn today offers a varied bill of fare in country-style surroundings. The inn takes its name from the uniform worn by Colonel John Haslett's Delaware Regiment of 1776.

The Evergreen Inn and the 1109 Restaurant are side-by-side in two historic mansions. The Swiss-trained owner/chef, Peter Ryter, and his wife Myrna, oversee the restaurant and the inn. Each room at the inn, as well as the restaurant, has a varied, distinct, and elegant style of its own. Visitors enjoy the three near-by lakes and the beautiful scenery.

Oysters Bienvielle

1 pound crabmeat
2 teaspoons minced garlic
Small amount of butter
1 tablespoon Pernod
1/2 cup white wine
2 teaspoons flour
1 cup cream
20 oysters

Saute the crabmeat and garlic in butter over low heat for 1 minute. Add the Pernod and wine and reduce the liquid to about 1/4 cup. Add the flour and then the cream. Transfer the mixture to the bowl of a food processor and blend until well combined. Shuck the oysters and place on a flat pan. Bake for 4 minutes at 375 degrees. Spoon crabmeat mixture onto the oysters and broil until golden brown. Serves 4.

Evergreen Inn

1109 South Main Street
Anderson, South Carolina 29621
(803) 225-1109

Texas Oysters

24 jumbo select oysters
2 jars hot salsa
2 cups finely chopped green onion
2 cups shredded Jack and Cheddar cheese (mixed)
2 cups crushed taco chips

Open the oysters and arrange on a cookie sheet on crumpled foil to keep level. Layer each oyster with a tablespoon or two of each ingredient in the order listed. Broil 3 to 5 minutes until cheese is melted and taco chips are toasted. Or bake 10 minutes at 375 degrees.

The Meadowlark Manor

241 West 9th Avenue
Red Cloud, Nebraska 68970
(402) 746-3550

Visitors to the Meadowlark Inn enjoy Victorian lighting fixtures, windows of leaded and beveled glass, a bay window with star motif, beautifully polished hardwood floors, and a wide front porch with classical columns. The inn was constructed in the early 1900s and is part of the Seward Street Historic District of the Willa Cather Thematic Group. This important property is carefully maintained by the Warner Family, owners / innkeepers at the Meadowlark Manor.

If you want to experience the ambience of southern France without the expense of going there, a visit to L'Auberge Provencale may be your answer. Settled in rolling farm country near the Blue Ridge Mountains, with a flower-lined walkway and sweeping front porch, it is a charming retreat. Owner / chef Alain Borel and his wife Celeste are a perfect team. Chef Borel explains, "Cooking is like breathing in my family. It was always a part of our lives and I never gave any thought to another line of work." He calls his cooking "cuisine moderne." "Classic French cooking is very rich and heavy and nouvelle cuisine is extremely light with small portions,"he explains. The Borels develop the menu together. It changes seasonally to feature the freshest ingredients. Guests can dine in two intimate dining rooms or a solarium with windows providing a lovely view of the countryside.

Mussels with Fresh Herbs of Provence

1 1/2 cups dry vermouth
1 teaspoon chopped shallots
1/2 teaspoon chopped garlic
1/4 teaspoon white pepper
Juice of 1/2 lemon
1 teaspoon chopped fresh tarragon
1 tablespoon chopped fresh mint
1/2 teaspoon chopped fresh parsley
1 teaspoon chopped fresh oregano
1/2 teaspoon chopped fresh thyme
1/2 teaspoon chopped fresh fennel leaf
5 pounds fresh mussels, washed and debearded

In a large stainless steel pot, combine all of the ingredients except the mussels. Bring to a boil. Add the mussels and cover the pot. When the mussel shells open up, remove the pot immediately from the burner. Do not overcook the mussels, since they will become rubbery. Arrange the mussels in serving dishes, discarding any unopened ones. Ladle some of the broth and herbs on top of each serving. Serve immediately. Serves 6 to 8.
Note: Dried herbs are not recommended for this dish.

L'Auberge Provencale

P.O. Box 119
White Post, Virginia 22663
(703) 837-1375

Escargot Montross Inn

10 imported helix snails
1 12 x 16 inch sheet puff pastry
1/4 pound garlic butter
1/2 cup tomato concasse (chopped, seeded, and peeled tomatoes)
Egg wash (1 egg mixed with 1/2 cup water)

Cut ten 1 1/2-inch squares of puff pastry; place a snail on each square and top with a knob of garlic butter. Cut ten more pieces of pastry, approximately 2 1/2 inches square; place each as a lid on each snail. Trim edges and crimp decoratively, then refrigerate until needed. Brush pastry with the egg wash and bake at 400 degrees until golden brown (about 6 minutes).

Sauce
2 cloves garlic, finely chopped
Pinch of chopped shallots
1/2 cup white wine
1 cup chicken stock
1 cup heavy cream
1/4 pound lightly salted butter.

Saute the garlic and shallots for about a minute, deglaze the pan with white wine, bring to a boil and reduce by half. Add the chicken stock and reduce by half, then add the cream and again reduce by half. Remove from the heat and quickly whisk in the butter. Strain the sauce.
To serve, pour the sauce onto serving plates. On each plate, arrange five baked escargot in a circle and place the tomato concasse in the center. Serves 2.

The Inn at Montross

P.O. Box 908
Montross, Virginia 22520
(804) 493-9097

This inn is located in the small colonial town of Montross and is rapidly becoming known for innovative cuisine of a caliber usually found only in big cities. The menu changes seasonally to take advantage of the freshest ingredients available. All desserts are made on the premises; a modest but complementary wine list, featuring, among others, the wines of several Virginia wineries, rounds out the offerings.

2
Salads and Salad Dressings

At the historic Victorian Inn, one is surrounded by the charm and adornments of the Victorian era with all the tranquility and graciousness of yesteryear. The guest rooms are in authentically restored Victorian elegance. The food is just as wonderful, lovingly and graciously prepared.

Green Salad with Hot Sweet and Sour Dressing

2 tablespoons sugar
2 tablespoons water
2 tablespoons vinegar
2 tablespoons catsup
2 tablespoons butter
Salt and freshly ground pepper to taste
Mixed greens—romaine, leaf lettuce, spinach
2 ripe avocados
1 sweet onion, thinly sliced
6 slices bacon, fried crisp and crumbled

In a saucepan, heat the sugar and water until the sugar is dissolved. Stir in the vinegar, catsup, butter ,salt, and pepper. Cook over low heat for 15 to 20 minutes. Put bed of greens on each plate, fan out slices of avocado and a few rings of onion on top. Sprinkle with bacon and top with warm dressing mixture. Serves 4.

Victorian Inn

1229 7th Street
Port Huron, Michigan 48060
(313) 984-1437

Layered Salad

1 10-ounce bag spinach, washed, dried, and stems removed
A little watercress
1/2 10-ounce package frozen peas, thawed
1/2 onion, chopped
1 cup shredded lettuce
1/2 cup shredded Swiss cheese
1 cup crumbled bacon
2 or 3 hard-boiled eggs, chopped

Dressing:
1 cup sour cream
1 cup mayonnaise
Basil, sage, and thyme to taste.

Layer the salad ingredients in a salad bowl in the order given, adding salt and pepper to each layer. Put dressing in the middle and on top. Toss well.

The Inn at Weston

P.O. Box 56
Weston, Vermont 05161
(802) 824-5804

About this peaceful inn and the town of Weston, the travel editor of The Los Angeles Times *said, "You get the idea that Norman Rockwell painted it and somebody came along and copied it." Nestled in the Green Mountains of Vermont, The Inn at Weston is like an old-fashioned Christmas card come to life. Often called the friendliest inn in all of New England, the rambling old frame structure seems to invite the traveler to enter and partake of its special brand of hospitality. Sue and Stu Douglas bought an 1848 farmhouse several years ago. They fixed up the guest rooms, created new ones in the hayloft of the barn, made a dining porch out of the woodshed, and have been making patrons happy with a menu that changes daily ever since.*

Once part of a 1000-acre dairy farm, The Silver Fox Inn remains a gracious country farmhouse. The living room dates back to 1768 and is a comfortable place to enjoy a good book, conversation with guests, and, on chilly evenings, a wood-burning stove.

Spinach Salad with Sweet and Sour Dressing

1 10-ounce bag spinach, washed, dried, and stems removed
2 hard-cooked eggs, chopped
3 slices bacon, cooked and crumbled
4 large mushrooms, sliced
1 small onion, diced
Sweet and sour dressing (recipe below)
Bean sprouts, for garnish

Wash and tear the spinach into bite-size pieces. Place in a salad bowl, add the remaining ingredients, and toss with the dressing. Garnish with bean sprouts. Serves 4.

Sweet and Sour Dressing:
1/2 cup vinegar
1/2 cup sugar
1 tablespoon Worcestershire sauce
1/3 cup catsup
3/4 cup oil
1/4 cup water

Mix all ingredients and chill.

The Silver Fox Inn
RFD 1, Box 1222
Rutland, Vermont 05777
(802) 438-5555

Caesar Salad

Romaine
Croutons
Fresh lemon juice
Freshly ground pepper to taste
Grated Parmesan cheese

Dressing
4 eggs
4 tablespoons minced garlic
7 anchovy fillets
1 1/2 teaspoons dry mustard
2 tablespoons fresh lemon juice
1 tablespoon Worcestershire sauce
Dash of Tabasco sauce
1/2 teaspoon salt
1/2 teaspoon pepper
2 tablespoons red wine vinegar
1 3/4 cups olive oil

To make the dressing, place the eggs, garlic, anchovies, dry mustard, 2 tablespoons lemon juice, Worcestershire sauce, Tabasco sauce, and salt and pepper in the bowl of a food processor. Process for 10 seconds. Add the vinegar and continue to process. With the motor still running, slowly add the olive oil. Makes about 2 cups of dressing.

To make the salad, for each serving toss 4 to 6 tablespoons of the dressing with one large handful of romaine leaves, 1/2 cup croutons, a splash of lemon juice, and several grinds of pepper. Top with the grated Parmesan cheese.

Campbell's on Lake Chelan

P.O. Box 278
Chelan, Washington 98816
(509) 682-2561

Clinton C. Campbell arrived in Chelan from Iowa in 1889—the year of Washington's statehood—lured west by tales of rich mines, homesteading, and the boundless opportunity of the untamed frontier. In 1900, with the help of a loan, Campbell built the hotel he had been planning for years. The opening of the Holden Mine uplake brought new vigor to the valley, and business prospered. Today, the resort inn is managed by Campbell's grandson, Arthur II. Two other grandchildren, Sally and Clinton Campbell, assist in the management. Eight spectacular acres, 1200 feet of sandy beach and lakefront, and a full service restaurant are all features of the historic Campbell Hotel.

Walnut Mandarin Salad

3/4 cup large walnut pieces
2 tablespoons butter
1/4 teaspoon minced or crushed garlic
Orange Vinaigrette Dressing (recipe below)
1 large or 2 small heads chilled lettuce
1/2 cup thinly sliced red onion rings
1 11-ounce can mandarin orange sections, drained

Saute the walnuts in a small skillet with the butter and garlic over moderately low heat for about 5 minutes or until lightly brown, stirring constantly. Cool. Prepare the Orange Vinaigrette Dressing. At serving time, tear the lettuce into bite-size pieces to measure 1 1/2 quarts. Top with the onion rings, drained orange sections, garlic, and toasted walnuts. Pour dressing over the salad and toss lightly. Serves 6.

Orange Vinaigrette Dressing:
1/2 cup oil
3 tablespoons red wine vinegar
3/4 teaspoon salt
1 teaspoon grated orange peel
1 teaspoon basil, crumbled.

Combine all ingredients in a small jar. Cover and shake well to blend. Shake again just before using. Makes 3/4 cup.

The story behind this elegant inn is one of local interest and color. The inn was originally constructed in 1908 as a children's home. Its restoration is the fulfillment of a dream for Francie Morgan, who grew up in the neighborhood and, as a child, played with many of the children who lived at the home. Overnight guests are served a delightful breakfast—in bed, on the balcony, or in the Tea Room. The Sunday Brunch Buffet is a favorite with overnighters as well as short-term guests.

Francie's

104 South Line
Du Quoin, Illinois 62832
(618) 542-6686

Tossed Greens with Gorgonzola, Walnuts, and Pears

2 quarts washed and torn organic greens, such as escarole, Boston lettuce, red oak, arugula, etc.
2 ounces good-quality Gorgonzola cheese
1/4 cup toasted chopped walnuts
1 firm but ripe bosc pear
Pear or Raspberry Vinaigrette (recipe below)

Arrange the greens on individual salad plates, and sprinkle with the cheese and walnuts. Place slices of pear on top. When ready to serve, spoon over the Vinaigrette.

Pear or Raspberry Vinaigrette
2 tablespoons pear or raspberry vinegar
1/4 teaspoon salt
Dash of freshly ground pepper
1/4 cup olive oil

Whisk vinegar, salt, and pepper until blended. Whisk in the olive oil in a thin stream.

Huckleberry Springs

P.O. Box 400
Monte Rio, California 95462
(707) 865-2683

Located on 56 acres above the Russian River, Huckleberry Springs offers a quiet and private escape to the Sonoma Coast and Wine Country. Designed to offer its guests comfort and relaxation after the day's adventures, the inn offers a hillside spa, swimming pool, and gourmet dining in the solarium under the redwoods. The kitchen specializes in a varied cuisine, capitalizing on fresh seasonal produce, seafoods, and the fine wines of Sonoma County Four unique cottages have private baths, skylights, and woodstoves.

This inn is a renovated 1893 building located in the national historic district of the colorful resort town of Park City. The Lodge was established in 1893 as housing for local miners seeking their fortunes from the ore-rich hills of Park City. Today, the spirited warmth and hospitality of Park City's illustrious past live on at the Old Miner's Lodge.

Red Cabbage Salad

1 cup vinegar
1/2 cup oil
1 tablespoon sugar
1 teaspoon dried or 1 tablespoon chopped fresh basil
1/2 teaspoon dry mustard
2 tablespoons fresh lemon juice
Garlic salt and freshly ground pepper to taste
1 head red cabbage, grated or chopped fine

Mix all the ingredients except the cabbage well and then toss with the cabbage. Serve with a slotted spoon. Serves about 6.

The Old Miner's Lodge

P.O. Box 2639
Park City, Utah 84060
(801) 645-8068

Old Fashioned Sweet-Sour Cole Slaw

1 1/2 pounds shredded green cabbage
1 teaspoon salt
2/3 cup sugar
1/3 cup cider vinegar
1 cup heavy cream

Place the cabbage in a covered dish in the refrigerator for several hours. Mix the remaining ingredients in the order given 30 minutes before serving. Combine with the cabbage. Chill and serve. Serves 4.

Brookville Hotel

Box 7
Brookville, Kansas 67425
(913) 225-6666

The Brookville Hotel traces its history to the early 1870s when the railroads spread their tracks out across the prairies to meet the expected rush of cattle from the Texas cattle drives. The town of Brookville was named after a lovely brook that meanders through it. In 1897, the hotel was acquired by Gus and Mae Magnusons. Mrs. Magnusons' tasty cooking started the hotel's reputation for good food; that reputation continues to this day. Its famous chicken dinners were first served in 1915. Today, guests dine at tables dressed with Blue Willow china and laden with platters of crisp fried chicken, along with mashed potatoes, cream style corn, cole slaw with a special sweet-sour dressing, and other goodies, including country style ice cream.

Fred and Evelyn Crider are innkeepers at this delightful manor. It is accurately billed as "a home away from home." The visitor can relax in a quiet, restful country setting away from city noises, busy crowds, and bustling traffic. The inn is nestled among the beautiful Lancaster County farmlands. Step back in time as you travel through Old Strasburg and historic Lancaster. Learn more about history as you tour nearby Gettysburg.

Zucchini Slaw

2 tender large zucchini, unpeeled, thinly sliced
1 small onion, thinly sliced
1/2 cup vinegar
4 tablespoons brown sugar
Salt and freshly ground pepper to taste

Sprinkle the zucchini and onion slices with salt and let stand. Combine the vinegar and sugar. Drain the zucchini-onion mixture and pour over the vinegar-sugar mixture. Season to taste with salt and pepper. Cover and refrigerate for 1 hour or longer before serving. Serves 4 to 6.

The Village of Little Britain

P.O. Box 20
Nottingham, Pennsylvania 19362
(717) 529-2862

Turner Salad

4 cups small broccoli flowerets, blanched if desired
1 cup raisins
1 cup sliced mushrooms
1/2 cup chopped red onion
6 slices bacon, cooked crisp and crumbled
Salt and freshly ground pepper to taste

Dressing
1 egg
1 egg yolk
1/2 cup sugar
1/2 teaspoon dry mustard
1 1/2 teaspoons cornstarch
1/4 cup distilled white vinegar
1/4 cup water
1/4 teaspoon salt
2 tablespoons unsalted butter (softened)
1/2 cup mayonnaise

To make the dressing, whisk together in a small bowl the whole egg, egg yolk, sugar, mustard, and cornstarch. In a saucepan combine the vinegar, water, and salt, and bring the mixture to a boil over moderate heat. Whisk in the egg mixture and cook for 1 minute, whisking until thickened. Remove the pan from the heat and whisk in the butter and mayonnaise. Cover and chill.

Make the salad in a large bowl, combining the broccoli, raisins, mushrooms, onions and bacon. Pour the dressing over the salad and toss well. Add salt and pepper to taste. Serve on a bed of red or green lettuce. Serves 6.

The Sugar Hill Inn

Route 117
Franconia, New Hampshire 03580
(603) 823-5621

The Sugar Hill Inn, tucked away in the beautiful White Mountains, offers its guests the quiet charm of a true country inn. It was built in 1789 by one of Sugar Hill's original settlers and converted to an inn in 1929. Much care and thought was given to restoring old beams, floors, and original fireplaces. The ten rooms in the inn and the six country cottages are individually decorated with fine antiques, hand stenciling, and delicate wallpapers and fabrics. Dinners are served in a dining room enhanced by stenciled Hitchcock chairs, old brass tools, and colorful paintings on velvet.

The Amana Colonies were once a group of seven villages where property and enterprises were owned communally and basic needs were provided by the community. The Ox-Yoke Inn is composed of several houses with several dining rooms serving family-style meals amid the antiques and curios of the colonists. The inn had its origin in 1940 when William and Lina Leichsenring began serving their fine food to local people. The original building, now the Amana Room, is more than 125 years old. It used to be a community kitchen where the people of Amana came for their meals. The Amana Home was constructed of brick made from native clay. The timbers were hewn in the nearby forests and set up on the site without nails of any kind.

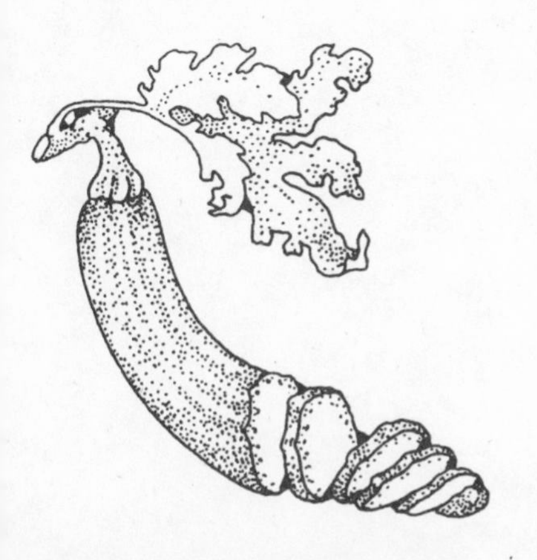

Cucumber Salad

4 medium cucumbers, peeled, seeded and sliced
1 onion, cut fine
2 hard-boiled eggs, sliced
1/2 teaspoon salt
Freshly ground pepper to taste
2 tablespoons vinegar
1/2 cup cream

Mix all ingredients together and serve. Serves 4 to 6.

The Ox-Yoke Inn

P.O. Box 230
Amana, Iowa 52203
(319) 622-3441

Dilled Cucumber Salad

2 large cucumbers, peeled, seeded, and sliced thin
1 teaspoon salt
1 cup plain yogurt
1 tablespoon finely chopped onions
1/2 teaspoon sugar
1 tablespoon finely chopped fresh dill,
  or 1 teaspoon dried dill
Dash of Tabasco sauce
Lettuce leaves, washed and crisped
2 tomatoes, peeled and cut into wedges, for garnish

Toss the cucumbers with the salt and place in a colander for 1 hour. Rinse well and drain thoroughly. Combine the yogurt, onion, sugar, Tabasco sauce and dill in a bowl. Pat the cucumbers dry with paper towels and add to the yogurt dressing. Toss well. Serve on lettuce leaves and garnish with tomato wedges. Serves 4.

There is no such thing as a one-time visitor to The Keeper's House, a delightful island lighthouse inn boasting a magnificent setting on the rockbound coast of Maine. Guests return over and over again. Delicious goodies flow from innkeeper Judith' Burke's aromatic kitchen. This recipe was taken from her popular cookbook, Kitchen With A View.

The Keeper's House

P.O. Box 26
Isle au Haut, Maine 04645
(207) 367-2261

The elegant Vermont Marble Inn stands proudly on the village green in the sleepy town of Fair Haven. At first sight, the Victorian mansion, built in 1867 of Vermont golden marble, is breathtaking, but one step through the towering walnut doors reveals an unexpected intimacy and charm. Dining at the inn is a delight. Great care has been taken to create an inviting and romantic atmosphere in the two stately dining rooms.

Tomato-Avocado Salad

4 ripe tomatoes, preferably plum, peeled and seeded
2 ripe avocados, diced in 1-inch chunks
1 clove garlic, minced fine
6 sprigs cilantro (fresh coriander), chopped
1 large lime
Salt and freshly ground pepper
Thin slices lime, for garnish

Dice the tomatoes into 1-inch cubes. In a large salad bowl, combine all the ingredients except the lime. Split the lime and squeeze the juice over the salad. Add salt and pepper to taste. Mix well. Serve well chilled over a romaine leaf. Garnish with thin lime slices.

The Vermont Marble Inn

On the Town Green
Fair Haven, Vermont 05743
(802) 265-8383

Asparagus Vinaigrette

3 pounds fresh asparagus
1/4 cup white wine vinegar
1 1/2 cups extra virgin olive oil
1 tablespoon capers
1 tablespoon finely chopped fresh parsley
1 tablespoon shallots
1/2 teaspoon sugar
1/2 teaspoon Dijon mustard
Freshly ground pepper to taste

Steam the asparagus until it is brilliant green, 4-6 minutes. Plunge into cold water and let drain in towel. Chill.

Combine remaining ingredients to make the vinaigrette. About 1 hour before serving, toss asparagus in the vinaigrette to marinate. Serve well chilled. Serves 6.

The Crystal River Inn

326 West Hopkin
San Marcos, Texas 78666
(512) 396-3739

The Crystal River Inn is located on the major highway connecting Austin and San Antonio in the lovely little riverside town of San Marcos. The crystal clear headwaters of the San Marcos River are here, along with two theme parks, a major university, and four unusually beautiful historic districts. The inn is located in one of these districts, shaded by pecan trees. It is an 1883 Victorian, with fireplaces in many of the guest rooms, designer decor, antiques, a wicker-strewn veranda, a fountain courtyard, and many special touches. Guests enjoy brandy and chocolates at bedtime; fresh flowers; and, of course, delicious food—fast becoming legendary in Central Texas.

Shaded by a 200-year-old live oak, Barrow House stands in the heart of the historic district of the quaint town of St. Francisville. The original house was a saltbox structure built in 1809 with a Greek Revival wing added just before the Civil War. A large screened porch is "the place to be" for coffee in the morning and drinks in the evening. Rooms are furnished in antiques dating from 1840 to 1870. The inn's candlelight dinners, featuring New Orleans style food, are well-known in the area. Six plantations (open to the public) are close by.

Southern Good Luck Salad

1 can black-eyed peas
Creole Vinaigrette (recipe below)
Several kinds of lettuce including fresh spinach (about 2 heads lettuce) and 1/2 10-ounce bag of spinach
1 2-1/4-ounce can sliced black olives
1 chopped red bell pepper, or a 4-ounce jar chopped pimentos, or 1 diced fresh tomato
2/3 cup chopped roasted pecans
1 bag pork skins, crumbled (available in the snack section of most supermarkets)
Pickled okra (1 per serving), for garnish

Heat the peas. Drain off the liquid, add 1/3 cup Creole Vinaigrette, and marinate for 8 hours or overnight in the refrigerator. When ready to serve, tear the lettuces into bite-size pieces. Combine with olives, peas, bell pepper, and pecans. Add vinaigrette to coat well, and toss. Place on plates and top with crumbled pork skins. Add one pickled okra to each plate. Serves 12 to 15.

Creole Vinaigrette
1/2 cup white wine vinegar
1 1/2 cups salad oil
2 cloves garlic, minced
4 tablespoons water
2 teaspoons soy sauce
2 or 3 teaspoons Creole seasoning
2 teaspoons sugar

Whisk together all ingredients. Makes 2 1/2 cups.

Barrow House

P.O. Box 1461
St. Francisville, Louisiana 70775
(504) 635-4791

Old Time Kidney Bean Salad

2 1-pound cans kidney beans, well-drained
1 cup chopped celery
1 cup chopped sweet pickle or sweet pickle relish
1/4 cup chopped onion
4 hard-cooked eggs, chopped
1/2 cup coarsely chopped pecan meats
4 tablespoons vinegar
2 tablespoons sweet pickle juice
2 teaspoons salt
1 tablespoon prepared mustard
1 tablespoon sugar
Egg slices, for garnish

Combine the first six ingredients. Make a dressing of the vinegar, pickle juice, salt sugar, and mustard and pour over salad. Garnish with egg slices. Serves 8 to 10.

Patchwork Quilt Country Inn

11748 County Road 2
Middlebury, Indiana 46540
(219) 825-2417

This unusual and delightful restaurant is located on a 340-acre working farm where many of the foods served are grown. The inn began in 1962 as a vacation farm for city people. A few years later a new dining room, The Wood Shed, was added. In it there is a display of antique woodworking and logging tools and more than 75 plates from around the world. There is a homespun atmosphere at the Patchwork. The kitchen opens into the dining room; here grand, family-style meals are served amid wonderful surroundings. Handmade quilts and patchwork tablecloths are available for purchase.

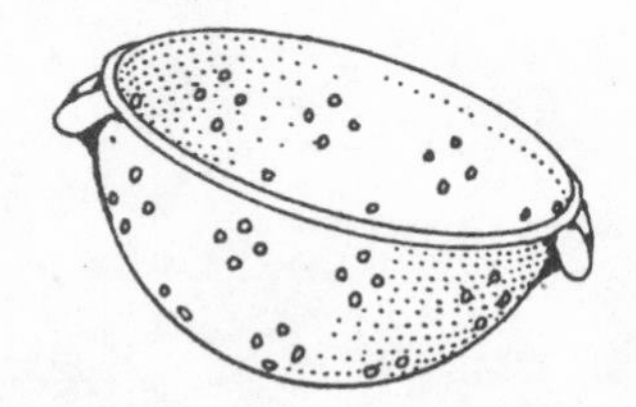

In 1857, Henry Mortimer Robinson fashioned bricks with his own hands and built a mansion with walls that measure 18 inches thick in some places. In 1984, the Conklin Players Dinner Theatre, which is adjacent to The Brick House and occupies two barns belonging to the estate, took possession of the house and began the much-needed restoration process that has resulted in its use as an inn and restaurant. A visit to The Brick House calls to mind the bold pioneer spirit that was so special to the Illinois heartland in the pre-Civil War era when Abraham Lincoln traveled what is now the historic Heritage Trail.

Dillies

1 1-pound can green beans or 3/4 pound fresh green beans
1/3 cup red wine vinegar
1/2 teaspoon Beau Monde seasonings
1/2 teaspoon dill weed
3 tablespoons olive oil
1 tablespoon onion salt

Drain the beans. Heat the vinegar and pour over the beans. When cool, add the Beau Monde seasoning, dill weed, and olive oil. Toss lightly to combine thoroughly. Chill well for several hours, preferably overnight. Just before serving, sprinkle with onion salt.

Note: This salad is better if it is prepared the day before it is scheduled to be served.

The Brick House

Conklin Dinner Theatre
Box 301
Goodfield, Illinois 61742
(309) 965-2545

Rice Salad

2 cups raw long-grain white rice
1/2 cup unsalted butter
Salt and freshly ground pepper to taste
1/2 cup toasted sliced almonds
1 6-ounce jar marinated artichoke hearts, drained and cut lengthwise into quarters
1/2 cup cooked fresh or frozen peas
1/4 cup chopped pimento
1 bunch scallions, thinly sliced
1/2 pound marinated mushrooms, sliced
1/2 cup sliced black olives
1/2 pound salami, diced
1/2 cup chopped fresh parsley
Watercress, for garnish
Cherry tomatoes, for garnish

Vinaigrette Dressing
1 1/2 teaspoons dried basil
1 1/2 teaspoons dried tarragon
1 teaspoon Dijon mustard
1/4 cup red wine vinegar
1/4 cup salad oil
Salt and pepper to taste

Add the rice and salt to a large pot of boiling water. Cook on low heat for 18 minutes. Drain the rice and rinse with warm water. Add butter, salt, and pepper and dry in a 250 degree oven for 30 minutes, stirring occasionally with a fork. Transfer to a large bowl and add the remaining salad ingredients. Combine all the ingredients for the vinaigrette dressing and mix well. Add to the salad and mix well. Pack tightly into an oiled ring mold or bundt pan. Refrigerate overnight. Unmold and garnish with watercress and cherry tomatoes. Serves 12.

The Governor's Inn

86 Main Street
Ludlow, Vermont 05149
(802) 228-8830

The Governor's Inn represents the culinary talents and pleasure-in-sharing personalities of Charlie and Deedy Marble, innkeepers of this historic, village inn. The inn, originally built by Vermont Governor William Wallace Stickney as his private dwelling, stands as a classic example of the fine craftsmanship of the late Victorian period (circa 1890). Now it serves as a haven for enjoying life's pleasures and as a base for exploring Vermont. The recipes we include were taken from the inn's own cookbook, A Collection of Recipes from the Inn's Kitchen, *by Charlie and Deedy Marble.*

At the Frankenmuth Inn, a corner of Germany has been transported to southern Michigan. The inn is noted for its Bavarian dinners and family-style chicken served in a variety of dining rooms, with names such as Wetter Haus, Glockenspiel, Onion Tower, and Austrian. The architecture of the inn is authentic Bavarian.

German Potato Salad

6 boiled potatoes, peeled and sliced
1 small onion
1/2 teaspoon salt
1 teaspoon Accent
2 tablespoons chopped fresh parsley
6 slices bacon, cut up
1/2 cup water
1/2 cup vinegar
3 tablespoons sugar
1 1/2 tablespoons flour
2 tablespoons bacon fat

Combine the potatoes, onion, salt, Accent, and parsley. Let sit for a half-hour. Fry the bacon and drain, reserving 2 tablespoons of the fat. Add 1/4 cup of the water, the vinegar, sugar, and bacon grease. Combine the flour and the other 1/4 cup of water and add to the vinegar-sugar mixture. Add to the potato and toss lightly. Keep warm until ready to serve.

Frankenmuth Bavarian Inn

1 Covered Bridge Lane
Frankenmuth, Michigan 48734
(517) 652-2651

Tabouli Salad

1 cup bulgur (cracked wheat)
1 cup warm water
2 tomatoes, peeled, seeded, and diced
1 bunch green onions, diced
4 tablespoons chopped fresh parsley
Juice from three lemons
1/4 cup olive oil
3 fresh mint leaves, diced
Salt and freshly ground pepper to taste

Soak the bulgur in the water for 1 hour. Add the remaining ingredients and mix well. Add salt and pepper to taste. Serves 6.

Ivy Inn

2355 University Avenue
Madison, Wisconsin 53705
(608) 233-9717

Personal service, charming room accommodations and quiet elegance have made the Ivy a favorite home away from home for over 30 years. Homestyle cooking, including a heart-healthy menu, is served in the colonial dining room. The inn is in a residential setting near some of Madison's finest older homes.

I V Y
I N N

Hilltop House Chicken Salad with Pimiento

3 cups diced cooked chicken
1 4-ounce jar pimientos
4 stalks celery, chopped fine
3 tablespoons pickle relish
1 teaspoon dry mustard
1 1/2 tablespoons vinegar
2 tablespoons sugar
Salt and freshly ground pepper to taste
1 cup mayonnaise
Pineapple rings, for garnish
Toasted coconut, for garnish

Combine all salad ingredients well and serve on a pineapple ring with a bit of toasted coconut sprinkled on top.

Hilltop House

P.O Box 930
Harper's Ferry, West Virginia 25425
(304) 535-2132

Hilltop House was built before the turn of the century and has long been popular with those who love beautiful scenery, atmosphere, and fine food. Purchased in 1955 by a Baltimore attorney, D.D. Kilham, a great-grandson of one of Harpers Ferry's first settlers, Hilltop House is being restored, keeping its original flavor but adding modern conveniences. There is a large dining room that will seat 340 people, and smaller dining rooms as well.

Chutney Salad

2 cups cooked dark meat of chicken, turkey, or lamb, shredded or cut in chunks
1 avocado, diced
1/3 red bell pepper, diced
1/3 green bell pepper, diced
1 fresh jalapeno, chopped fine
3/4 cup diced celery
1 red apple, cored and diced
1 green apple, cored and diced
2 green onions, diced
1 tablespoon chopped cilantro
1 clove garlic chopped fine
1/3 cup cashews

Dressing
3/4 cup mayonnaise
1/4 cup milk
1/8 teaspoon ground cloves
1/8 teaspoon coriander
1/8 teaspoon cumin
1/8 teaspoon turmeric
1/8 teaspoon black pepper
1/2 teaspoon salt

Combine all the ingredients for the dressing. Combine the salad ingredients and coat well with dressing. Serves 6 to 8.

Brookside Farm

1373 Marron Valley Road
Dalzura, California 91917
(619) 468-3043

Brookside Farm is a rambling 1928 farmhouse complete with vintage furniture pieces and co-proprietor Judy Guishard's handmade quilts, rugs, and watercolors, which give each room a distinctive personality. It is set by a soothing oak-shaded babbling brook; the atmosphere is rustic but still sophisticated. Farm animals and gracious flower gardens share the acreage. Delicious foods are prepared by co-owner Ed Guishard, who also teaches cooking classes.

This lovely inn was originally a merchant's house. The back wing was built about 1785 and the larger portion in the 1840s. The Asphodel complex of overnight accommodations, restaurant, and shops is located six miles south of the town of Jackson. Visitors flock here for famous biscuits, Shrimp Fettucine, Crab Corn Soup, and many other delicacies.

Curried Pineapple Chicken Salad

2 frying chickens, roasted
1 20-ounce can drained pineapple
1 cup chopped celery
2 tablespoons curry powder
1/2 cup chopped green onions including tops
1/2 cup golden raisins
1/2 cup broken pecans
Mayonnaise to bind
Salt and pepper to taste

Remove the chicken from the bones and cut in bite-size pieces. Combine the chicken with the remaining ingredients and toss well. Serve very cold on a bed of lettuce.

Inn at Asphodel Village

Route 2
Box 89
Jackson, Louisiana 70748
(504) 654-6868

Chicken and Vegetable Pasta Salad

2 cups corkscrew pasta
1 chicken breast (broiled, baked, or poached) shredded or sliced
1/2 cup shredded carrot
1/2 cup shredded unpeeled zucchini
1/2 cup shredded peeled and seeded cucumber
1/4 cup chopped parsley
1/4 cup diced red bell pepper
1/2 cup chopped fresh basil
Juice of 1 lemon
2 tablespoons olive oil
2 tablespoons rice vinegar
1/4 teaspoon garlic powder
Salt and freshly ground pepper to taste
Salad greens

Cook the pasta, then rinse under cold water to cool. In a large bowl mix the pasta, chicken, carrots, zucchini, cucumber, parsley, red pepper, and basil. Add the lemon juice, olive oil, vinegar, and garlic powder. Season to taste and serve on a bed of salad greens. Serves 2 or 3.

Kawanhee Inn

Route 142, Webb Lake
Weld, Maine 04215
(207) 585-2243

The scenery at this lakeside resort is unsurpassed. On a magnificent mountain lake in the Maine woods, it commands a fantastic view of the mountains and lake. On entering, one is impressed with its appointments, both rustic and refined, including a huge stone fireplace accommodating four-foot logs. The comfortable bedrooms suggest a homey, friendly atmosphere. The inn is noted for its delicious home-cooked food for family dining served in the spacious main dining room or, weather permitting, on the screened porches. All of this is nestled between the cathedral pines on a knoll overlooking Webb Lake.

Note: During winter months, the inn's mailing address is: 7 High Street, Farmington, Maine 04938

Here is an enticing shrimp recipe from Carl and Vita Hinshaw, co-proprietors of the legendary Chalet Suzanne

Shrimp Suzanne with Dill

1/2 cup sour cream
1/2 cup mayonnaise
1/2 cup grated peeled and seeded cucumber
1/3 cup minced onion
1 1/2 tablespoons chopped fresh dill
1 1/2 teaspoons fresh lemon juice
Garlic to taste
Salt and freshly ground pepper to taste
8 drops Tabasco sauce
1/4 teaspoon caraway seeds
1 pound shrimp (25 to 30 count), cooked, peeled and cleaned
Bibb lettuce

Combine all ingredients but the shrimp and lettuce to make a sauce. Stir in the shrimp. Mix well and chill. Serve on a bed of Bibb lettuce, either as individual servings or in a lettuce-lined bowl. Serves 4 to 6.

Chalet Suzanne
P.O. Box AC
Lake Wales, Florida 33859
(813) 676-6011

Crab, Pasta, and Pecan Salad

2 pounds snow crab or back-fin crabmeat, shelled and picked over
1 pound Rainbow rotini, cooked al dente and drained
1/4 cup mayonnaise
2 tablespoons olive oil
4 tablespoons lemon juice
1 teaspoon garlic salt
1 1/2 cups pecan or walnut halves
Salt and freshly ground pepper to taste
Dill, for garnish

Crumble the crab into a large bowl. In a separate bowl, toss the cooled pasta with mayonnaise, oil, lemon juice, and spices. Add the crab and nuts, toss gently, and serve cold. Serves 8.

Holly Inn

P.O. Box 2300
Pinehurst, North Carolina 28374
(919) 295-2300

Amid the majestic loblolly pines of North Carolina's sandhills region sits a charming New England-style village built before the turn of the century by wealthy Bostonian James Tufts. He had famed landscape architect Frederick Law Olmstead design the small resort village. At the heart of the new village, in 1895, Tufts built the Holly Inn; a five-story country inn resembling the ones he had long enjoyed on Cape Cod. For over 90 years, celebrities, presidents, sports figures, and many other guests from around the world have enjoyed the graceful style and hospitality of the Holly Inn.

This delightful inn and the village of Redstone were built in 1902 by a financier with a dream. He built a village for the workers in his coal mines, with cottages for families and the inn as a home for bachelor employees. Today, the inn has some of the original hand-pegged oak furniture in the oldest of its 24 rooms. Every room has a view of the colorful mountains and rugged Redstone cliffs. The dining room features massive beams, heavy iron chandeliers, a handsome fireplace, and delicious food.

Horseradish Salad

2 3-ounce packages lemon gelatin dessert
2 3-ounce packages lime gelatin dessert
4 cups hot water
2 cups cold water
4 cups crushed or chopped pineapple
2 cups mayonnaise
2 cups coarsely chopped walnuts
2 14-ounce cans sweetened condensed milk
4 cups cottage cheese
4 tablespoons prepared horseradish
Lime slices, for garnish
Parsley or lettuce, for garnish

Combine the gelatin dessert mixes and hot water in a large bowl and stir until dissolved. Add the cold water and cool until slightly thickened. Add the remaining ingredients and blend well. Pour into molds. Chill. Unmold. Garnish with lime slices and parsley or leaf lettuce.

The Redstone Inn

0082 Redstone Boulevard
Redstone, Colorado 81623
(303) 963-2526

Cranberry Ring

2 cups cranberries
1 1/4 cups water
1 cup sugar
1 3-ounce package strawberry or cherry gelatin dessert
3/4 cup diced celery
1/2 cup chopped pecans
1/4 teaspoon salt

Cook the cranberries in the water. When soft, add the sugar and cook for 5 minutes. Add the gelatin dessert to the boiling cranberry mixture and stir until dissolved. Chill. When partially set, add celery, pecans, and salt. Pour into a 4-cup mold and chill. Serve unmolded on crisp lettuce. Serves 6.

Raumonda

P.O. Box 112
Columbus, Texas 78934
(409) 732-5135

Raumonda takes its name from its owners, the Rau family. Their beautifully restored inn, built in 1897, features two-story porches at the front, with some of the laciest mill work to come out of the Victorian period. The Raus offer their guests hospitality reminiscent of the Old South. Meals are served in the formal candlelit dining room from an old-fashioned butler's pantry. Each bedroom is different, with spectacular furnishings. As Buddy Rau's grandmother says, "Raumonda is a house fit for Scarlett O Hara."

Here is an exquisite colonial manor inn in the heart of Santa Fe. With an ideal location just two blocks from the historic Plaza, Grants Corner is nestled among intriguing shops and galleries. Built in the early 1900s as a home for the Windsors, a wealthy New Mexican ranching family, the inn boasts charming guest rooms, each appointed with antiques and treasures from around the world. The recipe following was taken from the Inn's own cookbook, Grant Corner Inn Breakfast and Brunch Cookbook by Louise Stewart.

Ginger Honey Pineapple Boats

1 large pineapple, quartered lengthwise, leaves left on
1/2 teaspoon ground ginger
1/4 teaspoon salt
1/4 teaspoon paprika
1/4 cup vegetable oil
2 tablespoons fresh lemon juice
1 1/2 tablespoons honey
Lime slices for garnish

For each serving, cut the flesh from the pineapple rind in one piece, then slice crosswise into 8 pieces; chill.

In a jar with a lid, place the ginger, salt, paprika, oil, lemon juice, and honey. Shake well to mix. Return the pineapple pieces to the quarters of rind.

Serve each pineapple quarter with 2 tablespoons of the dressing; garnish with lime slices. Serves 4.

Grant Corner Inn

122 Grant Avenue
Santa Fe, New Mexico 87501
(505) 983-6678

Tomato Vinaigrette Dressing

1 egg
1/4 teaspoon dry mustard
1 tablespoon paprika
2 teaspoons salt
6 tablespoons tomato paste
1 tablespoon sugar
1/2 teaspoon chopped fresh basil
1 teaspoon Worcestershire sauce
1 cup vegetable oil
1/3 cup white wine vinegar
1/2 cup warm water

Place the first eight ingredients in a blender and blend on low for 1 minute. Add the oil and vinegar alternately, then add the warm water. Makes 2 cups.

Visitors to The Pine Ridge Inn experience a unique combination of elegance and coziness. Each room is picturesque, from the colorful living room with its museum-quality antiques to the simple comforts of the conference nook; overnight guests choose from a variety of bedroom styles. All guests are treated to gracious hospitality and delicious cuisine, including homemade breads and muffins.

Pine Ridge Inn

2893 W. Pine Street
Mount Airy, North Carolina 27030
(704) 789-5034

Fagleysville Country Hotel was built in 1861 and has always been a "public house" serving food and spirits to locals and those travelling through the hills of eastern Pennsylvania between Philadelphia and Reading. It boasts a 150-year-old bar of hand-carved black mahogany and three dining rooms where guests may enjoy the best in gourmet foods. Owners David Miller (also the Chef) and Mark Lacey have recently renovated several rooms in the hotel.

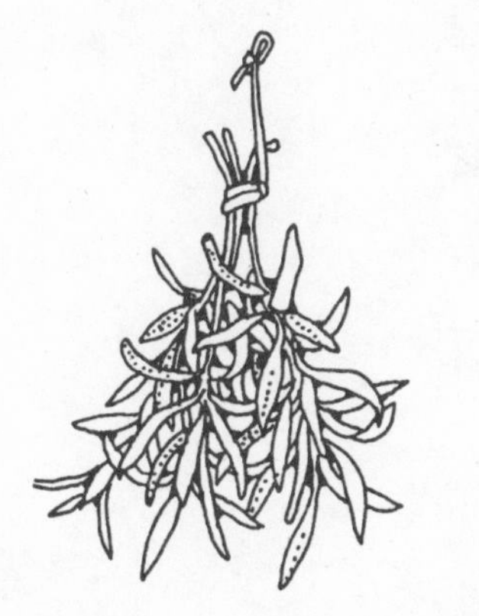

Tarragon Dressing

4 tablespoons lemon juice
4 tablespoons tarragon vinegar
1 tablespoon sugar
1 1/4 teaspoon salt
1/2 teaspoon pepper
1 teaspoon dry mustard
4 cloves garlic
1 egg yolk
1 cup peanut oil
1 teaspoon dried or 2 teaspoons fresh tarragon

Put all ingredients except the peanut oil and tarragon in a blender in the order in which they are listed. Blend on low speed for 10 seconds. Turning the motor to high speed, slowly add the oil and blend until the mixture thickens. Turn off the blender, add tarragon, and blend for 5 seconds. Makes about 1 1/2 cups.

Note: One way to serve this dressing is with tossed mixed lettuce, sliced scallions, and firm white mushrooms. Use approximately 2 tablespoons per serving. The dressing keeps in the refrigerator for several days.

Fagleysville Country Hotel

2485 Swamp Pike
Gilbertsville, Pennsylvania 19525
(215) 323-1425

Celery Seed Dressing

1/2 cup sugar
1 teaspoon dry mustard
1 teaspoon salt
1 tablespoon celery seed
1/4 teaspoon grated onion
1/3 cup distilled white vinegar
1 cup salad oil

Mix all the dry ingredients together. Add the onion. Add a small amount of the oil. Mix well. Gradually add small amounts of vinegar and oil alternately, ending with oil. Mix in either a blender or an electric mixer.
Makes about 1 1/2 cups.

The Golden Lamb

27 South Broadway
Lebanon, Ohio 45036
(513) 932-5065

Ohio's oldest inn, established in 1815, has served the finest foods for more than 150 years. Rustic woods and bricks form the surrounding for a unique dining experience.

Recently designated a Michigan Historical Site, this delightful inn is over 100 years old. It was originally built by a Presbyterian minister and subsequently used as a mission house for early settlers. In 1887, the house was turned into a general store and resort hotel. Located in rural Upper Peninsula Michigan, where the farms are hilly, the barns are small and faded, and the fields always seem to have a deer or two prancing across them at dusk, Helmer House has lovely guest rooms furnished with antiques. The main lodge portion is known for its wrap-around porch which is glassed in and serves as an attractive restaurant.

Sweet and Sour Poppy Seed Dressing

3/4 cup sugar
1 teaspoon dry mustard
1 teaspoon salt
1/3 cup cider vinegar
1 tablespoon onion juice (optional)
1 cup salad oil
1 1/2 tablespoons poppy seeds

In a medium bowl, combine the sugar, mustard, salt, vinegar, and onion juice. Using a portable mixer, gradually beat in the oil until the mixture is thick and smooth. Stir in the poppy seeds. Store in a covered container in the refrigerator. Makes 1 2/3 cups.

Helmer House

McMillan, Michigan
(906) 586-3204

Special Thousand Island Dressing

1 8-ounce package cream cheese
1 pint sour cream
3/4 cup catsup
1/4 cup cider vinegar
1/4 cup salad oil
1 tablespoon Worcestershire sauce
1 tablespoon horseradish
2 dashes Tabasco sauce
1 cup mayonnaise
1/2 cup sweet relish
1 teaspoon paprika
Salt and freshly ground pepper to taste

Cream the cheese in a large bowl; add the sour cream, mixing well. Add remaining ingredients and mix well. Serve on lettuce or boiled shrimp salad. Makes 1 quart.

Walking Horse Hotel

P.O. Box 266
Wartrace, Tennessee 37183
(615) 389-6407

The home of the first World Champion Tennessee Walking Horse is located behind this historic hotel. Guests relax in the antique and lace decor of the hotel's main dining room. Fresh flowers, linens, and candlelight create a warm atmosphere. Homemade breads and desserts, house dressings, and delicious casseroles are just part of the reason people come from miles around to dine here. The inn is listed on the National Register of Historic Places. This recipe is taken from the hotel's own cookbook, Walking Horse Hotel Storybook and Cookbook.

Built around 1899, Red Creek Colonial Inn is about an hour east of New Orleans on the Mississippi Gulf Coast and is situated on eleven acres of magnolias and ancient oaks. The three-story raised French cottage, owned by Mr. and Mrs. Karl Mertz, has six elegant fireplaces and is furnished with handsome antiques. The original house was built by a retired Italian sea captain to entice his young bride away from her family's home in New Orleans. Claudia Mertz describes the 64-foot front porch as a place "where I can eat boiled shrimp and crabs in the shade of magnolias, or just swing to my heart's content, enjoying a tall drink and a thick novel."

Red Creek Remoulade Sauce

1 cup mayonnaise
4 finely chopped hard-boiled eggs
1 teaspoon dry mustard
2 tablespoons finely chopped fresh parsley
1 tablespoon finely chopped green bell pepper
1 teaspoon finely chopped garlic
1 tablespoon anchovy paste
1 teaspoon Worcestershire sauce
6 finely chopped olives
White pepper to taste
1 tablespoon finely chopped capers
1 tablespoon finely chopped fresh chervil
1 tablespoon finely chopped fresh tarragon
1 tablespoon finely chopped gherkins

Place the mayonnaise in a bowl. Add the remaining ingredients and mix well. Serve with shrimp, crab or other seafood. Makes about 1 1/2 cups

---

Red Creek Colonial Inn

7416 Red Creek Road
Long Beach, Mississippi 39560
(601) 452-3080

Buttermilk Dressing

1 cup mayonnaise
1 cup buttermilk

Seasoning Mix
2 tablespoons salt
2 teaspoons parsley flakes
1 teaspoon garlic powder
1 teaspoon pepper
1/2 teaspoon onion powder

To make the Seasoning Mix, combine in a small bowl the salt, parsley flakes, garlic powder, pepper and onion powder. Mix thoroughly. Combine the mayonnaise and buttermilk and add 3 1/2 teaspoons of the Seasoning Mix; mix well. Store the dressing and seasoning mix in airtight containers in the refrigerator. The flavor of the dressing is best after 24 hours. Makes 2 cups dressing.

Westways

P.O. Box 41624
Phoenix, Arizona 85080
(602) 582-3868

Westways was fashioned after the world's finest resorts, with one exception . . they offer only six private guest rooms. The inn's contemporary Spanish design complements the majestic mountains that rise up around it.

After living in Washington D.C. for 12 years, the Stafurskys were ready for a more relaxed environment. To satisfy that urge, they opened the Savannah Inn in 1983—a country inn in a country setting. The structure was built in the late 1700s, and its furnishings date from the eighteenth and nineteenth centuries. The inn serves European-style vegetarian breakfasts adapted to American tastes.

Miso Salad Dressing

3 heaping tablespoons blond miso
1 cup safflower oil
1/3 cup cider vinegar
2 tablespoons tamari
1 very small onion, chopped
2 tablespoons honey
2 tablespoons water, or more

Blend all ingredients in a food processor or blender. Dressing should be the consistency of heavy cream. If it is too thick, add a little water and blend again. This dressing is good on green salads or on fruit. Makes about 2 cups.

Savannah Inn

330 Savannah Road
Lewes, Delaware 19958
(302) 645-5592

Lite Apricot-Sesame Dressing

Here is another delicious New England recipe from the Kawahnee Inn -- a light and zesty apricot-sesame salad dressing.

1 teaspoon cornstarch
1/8 teaspoon garlic powder
1/8 teaspoon ground ginger
1 5-1/2 ounce can apricot nectar
1/4 cup red wine vinegar
1 teaspoon honey
1 teaspoon sesame oil
1 teaspoon toasted sesame seeds

In a small saucepan, combine the cornstarch, garlic powder, and ginger. Stir in the apricot nectar, vinegar, honey, and oil. Cook, stirring constantly, until thick and bubbly. Cook 2 minutes more. Chill. Makes 2/3 cup.

Kawanhee Inn

Route 142, Webb Lake
Weld, Maine 04215
(207) 585-2243

3
Soups

Here is the perfect elegant inn --- and the pride of Macon. Wonderfully preserved Americana is everywhere, and true southern hospitality abounds. The inn dates back to 1847. Its Village Bistro restaurant features international cuisine, with superb meals served in a delightful dining room setting.

Bistro Chowder

1/2 cup chopped carrots
1/2 cup chopped potatoes
1/2 cup chopped celery
4 tablespoons butter
1 cup crabmeat
1 cup diced peeled and deveined shrimp
1 cup cut-up sea scallops
6 cups milk
1 cup heavy cream
1/2 cup condensed chicken broth
1 tablespoon basil
1 teaspoon pepper
Roux made from 1/2 cup butter and 1/2 cup flour (see note).

In a heavy pot, saute the vegetables until tender in the 4 tablespoons butter. Add the seafood, milk, heavy cream, and chicken broth. Cook until almost to the boiling point, then add the basil and pepper and enough roux to thicken. Serves 8.

Note: To make the roux, melt the butter and stir in the flour. Let cook, stirring constantly, for 5 minutes to avoid a starchy taste. Leftover roux may be stored in the refrigerator for a few days.

Victorian Village

1841 Hardman Avenue
Macon, Georgia 31201
(912) 742-2540

Down East Fish Chowder

2 ounces salt pork
1/2 onion, diced
3 cups rich fish stock
2 bay leaves
1 teaspoon thyme
2 potatoes, peeled and diced
1 1/2 pounds haddock fillets
1 to 2 cups half-and-half
2 tablespoons fresh butter
2/3 tablespoon fresh chopped parsley

Saute the salt pork with the onion; add the fish stock, bay leaves, and thyme; add the potatoes and haddock fillets. Simmer until the potatoes are almost tender; add the half-and-half. Continue to simmer; add the butter and chopped parsley. Simmer and serve. Serves 6 to 8.

Note: The chowder is even better the second day.

Dana Place

10 Pinkham Notch Road
Jackson, New Hampshire 03846
(603) 383-6822

This is a beautiful inn which for many years has welcomed interesting people to share its rare charm and superb location within the White Mountain National Forest. It was built along the Ellis River in 1890 as a farmhouse. The Ellis River Trail, popular with Nordic Skiers, runs from Jackson Village five miles along the river to the inn's door. The inn offers enjoyable food in strikingly appointed surroundings.

Yes Bay Lodge offers rustic elegance in a wilderness setting, fifty miles northwest of Ketchikan. The area is noted for outstanding salmon and trout fishing. The Hack family provide warm hospitality and personal service. Meals are served family style.

Halibut Vegetable Chowder

2 carrots, julienne-cut
2 stalks celery, sliced diagonally
1/2 cup chopped onion
1 clove garlic, minced
2 tablespoons oil
1 28-ounce can tomatoes
1 cup water
3 tablespoons minced fresh parsley, divided
1 teaspoon chicken bouillon granules
1/2 teaspoon salt
1/4 teaspoon thyme, crushed
1/4 teaspoon basil, crushed
1/8 teaspoon pepper
1 1/2 pounds halibut, thawed if necessary

Saute the onions, carrots, celery, and garlic in the oil for 5 minutes. Add the tomatoes, water, 2 tablespoons parsley, bouillon, and seasonings. Break up the tomatoes with a spoon. Cover and simmer for 20 minutes. Cut the halibut into 1-inch cubes; add to the chowder. Cover and simmer 5 to 10 minutes or until the halibut flakes easily when tested with a fork. Sprinkle with the remaining parsley. Serves 6 to 8.

Note: The recipe may be halved using a 14 1/2 to 16-ounce can of tomatoes.

Yes Bay Lodge
Yes Bay, Alaska 99950
(907) 247-1575

Crab Bisque

2 cups chopped celery
1 cup chopped onion
1/2 cup butter
3 cups double strength chicken stock
4 cups milk
2 cups cream
1 teaspoon white pepper
1/2 teaspoon salt (optional)
3 tablespoons cornstarch
3 tablespoons water
1 1/2 pounds crabmeat, picked over
Fresh chives or paprika, for garnish

Saute the celery and onion in the butter until tender. Add the chicken stock, milk, cream, white pepper, and salt. Bring to a simmer and thicken with the cornstarch dissolved in the water. Return to a simmer for about 2 minutes. Add the crabmeat, and turn off heat. The heat of the soup will warm the crab. Garnish with fresh chives or shake paprika through a stencil onto the top of the soup for a pretty design. Serves 8.

Glacier Bay Country Inn

P.O. Box 5
Gustavus, Alaska 99826
(906) 697-2288

Situated near the center of a 160-acre homestead, this inn offers the chance to experience Alaskan country living in a true wilderness setting. There are forests of towering spruce, hemlock, and pine; hayfields swaying in the breeze; meadows ablaze with wildflowers; bountiful gardens; meandering creeks; exceptional mountain views; and, deep in the woods, down a narrow winding road, this delightful inviting inn. Marvelous food is one of its features. This recipe is taken from the inn's own cookbook, Sharing our Best.

On August 27, 1739, a deed was granted by John, Thomas, and Richard Penn, sons of William Penn, to James Anderson, for 35 acres of land --- the birth of Anderson's Ferry and the Accomac Inn. Constructed in 1775, the inn at Anderson's Ferry began its long history of entertaining many distinguished guests. Indeed, the late eighteenth century saw the leaders of Colonial America --- Samuel Adams, General Horatio Gates, Philip Livingston --- pause at the inn on their way to and from meetings of the Continental Congress at York. In the many years that followed, the Accomac Inn flourished as a popular stopover for travelers and guests. Today, the inn remains true to the traditions of its historic past. Gourmet cuisine is served in the Lafayette Room, the Gold Room, and the Queen Anne Room.

Bouillabaisse

1/3 cup olive oil
1 1/4 cups sliced red onions
3/4 cup celery
1/8 teaspoon minced garlic
2 cups fresh tomatoes, peeled, seeded and diced
1 1/2 tablespoons chopped fresh parsley
Pinch of oregano
1/3 teaspoon salt
Pinch of freshly ground pepper
1 1/2 tablespoons tomato paste
1 cup dry white wine
1/3 cup fish stock or clam juice
Pinch of saffron
8 mussels, washed and debearded
8 cherrystone clams, washed
4 snow crab claws, cooked
4 petite lobster tails
1/2 pound medium shrimp, peeled and deveined
1/2 pound sea bass fillet, boneless, and cut into 1-inch squares
1/4 pound sea scallops
Lemon slices and chopped fresh parsley for garnish

In a heavy pot, heat the olive oil. Add the onions, celery, and garlic; simmer for 2 minutes. Add tomatoes, tomato paste, parsley, and all remaining seasonings except the white wine, fish stock, and saffron. Cook the sauce over low heat for 20 minutes. Add the wine and cook for an additional 10 minutes. In a separate pot bring the fish stock and saffron to a boil and add the clams and mussels. Cover and simmer for 5 minutes. Remove the clams and mussels. Discard any shells that have not opened. Add the lobster tails, shrimp, sea bass, and scallops and the tomato paste and cook slowly for 10 minutes. Add the snow crab, clams, and mussels, and cook for 5 minutes. Do not stir while the seafood is cooking to prevent breaking up the fish. Serve in ceramic or glass soup bowls or copper au gratins. Garnish with chopped parsley and lemon juice slices. Serves 4.

Accomac Inn

P.O. Box 127
Wrightsville, Pennsylvania 17368
(717) 252-1521

Seafood Gumbo

The Doherty is a fine hotel in every sense of the word. It offers delicious food and drink. Four generations of Doherty family ownership are the keynotes to the success of this hotel. Three nearby ski resorts offer excellent downhill or cross country skiing.

3 tablespoons shortening
3 tablespoons flour
1 large onion, chopped
1/2 green bell pepper
3 garlic cloves, minced
1 stalk celery (or more)
Salt
2 teaspoons Tabasco sauce
Seafood seasoning to taste
Cayenne pepper (optional)
1 6-ounce crab meat
1 can crab meat
1 12-ounce can Rotel tomatoes
2 pounds boiled shrimp, fresh or frozen, peeled and deveined
1 can okra
1 teaspoon parsley flakes
Shrimp *file*, for seasoning

Heat the shortening in a skillet; sprinkle the flour over the shortening, stirring constantly. Cook over medium high heat until the mixture is brown. Add the onion, bell pepper, garlic, and celery. Cook until the onion is translucent. Transfer from skillet into a 4-quart pot. Slowly add 2 quarts of water. Stir. Add salt and other seasonings, and red pepper only if needed. Add the crabmeat and tomatoes and cook for 1 hour. Add the shrimp and okra and cook until heated. (Important: do not overcook the shrimp). Serve with rice. Pass the shrimp *file*, for seasoning. Serves 6.

Doherty Hotel

604 McSewan
Clare, Michigan 48617
(517) 386-3441

Time seems to have stood still at the Chatham Bars Inn. To this day, it continues to offer its guests the traditions, spirit, and grandeur of a less hurried Cape Cod. It is a Cape Cod landmark, and one of the last of America's grand oceanfront inns. Built in 1914 as a hunting lodge for a wealthy Bostonian family, it has since become famous for gracious service, the very finest cuisine, and unequaled natural beauty. The main dining room, with its touch of formality, serves some of the most acclaimed fare in all of New England.

Oyster and Guiness Soup

6 ounces oysters and their juices
1 ounce bacon, diced
1 onion, diced
1 carrot, diced
2 stalks celery, diced
1 cup white wine
6 ounces Guiness Stout
1/2 cup fish stock
Juice of 1/2 lemon
2 cups heavy cream
Pinch of finely chopped fresh thyme
Pinch of finely chopped fresh parsley
Pinch of freshly grated nutmeg
Pinch of saffron
1 egg
Pinch of salt
Pinch of Cayenne pepper

Cook the bacon until golden brown. Add the onions, carrots, and celery and cook until tender. Add the white wine, Guiness, stock, lemon juice, and the juice from the oysters. Bring to a boil and let simmer for approximately 20 minutes. Add 1 1/2 cups of the heavy cream and continue to cook for approximately 10 minutes more. Add the oysters and herbs along with the saffron, and let the soup simmer.

Whisk the eggs and the remaining heavy cream in a mixing bowl. Pour a small amount of the hot soup into the cream and egg mixture, then pour it back into the soup, stirring constantly. Slowly bring the soup to a boil while constantly stirring, until it is thickened and has a nice shine.

Remove the soup from the heat, season with salt and cayenne pepper, and serve immediately. Serves 4.

Chatham Bars Inn

Shore Road
Chatham, Massachusetts 02633
(508) 945-0096

Lobster Stew

1/2 cup butter
1 teaspoon paprika
Pinch of nutmeg
1 pound cooked lobster meat
1 quart milk
1 quart light cream
Salt and freshly ground pepper to taste
2 tablespoons Worcestershire sauce
2 tablespoons dry sherry (more if desired)

Melt the butter in a heavy pot; add the paprika, nutmeg, and lobster. Cook slowly for 10 minutes. Heat the milk and cream (do not boil) and add to the lobster. Season to taste with salt, pepper, and Worcestershire. Add sherry to taste just before serving. Serves 8 to 10.

Black Point Inn

510 Black Point Road
Prouts Neck, Maine 04074
(207) 883-4126

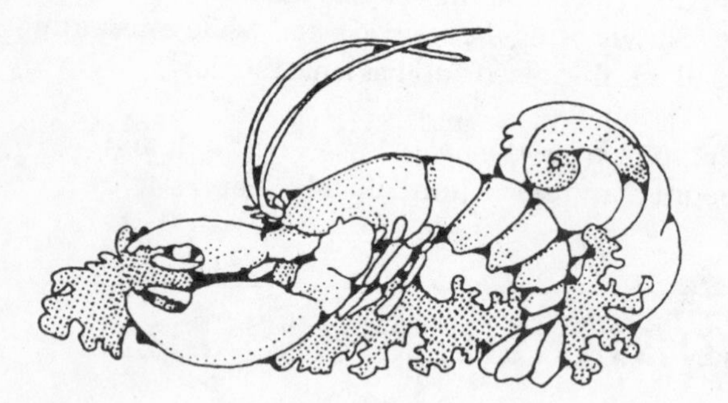

The dining room of this great summer hotel on the New England coast is charming and beautiful with its woodwork of water-stained pine and very old decorative murals of England. Picture windows overlook the gardens and the sea. The food is as appealing as the view—sumptuous buffets at poolside, delectable seafood and New England dishes. First settled about 1630, Prout's Neck was deserted by the colonists 60 years later after trouble with the French and Indians. In 1702, colonists started a new trading post. Then in 1713, Indians ambushed and killed 19 people by Massacre Pond—at a spot just across the road from the present-day Prout's Neck golf course.

The Castine Inn has practiced the art of hospitality ever since it was built in 1898. Guests arriving by car today are greeted as warmly as those who once disembarked from boats at the town wharf (some still do) or stepped out of carriages at the nearest station. The inn is a turn-of-the-century summer hotel situated on a hillside in the center of this beautiful seaside village. From many of the guest rooms, the dining room, and the veranda, there is a view of the gardens and the harbor beyond.

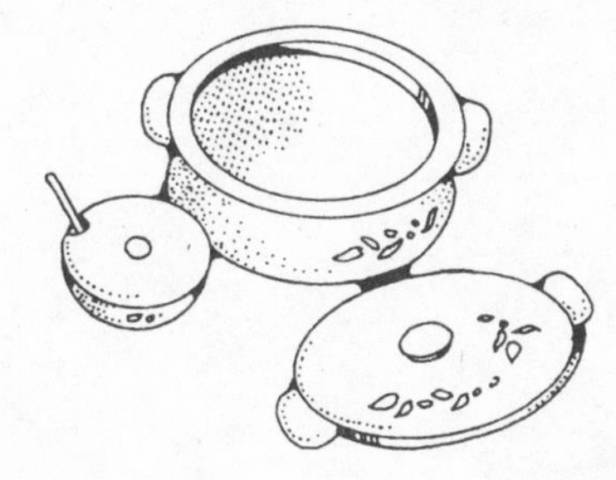

Mussel and Corn Chowder

1 cup white wine
6 pounds mussels, scrubbed and debearded
1/2 pound salt pork, diced
2 onions, finely chopped
3 ears corn or 1 10-ounce can corn kernels
1 quart heavy cream
3 green onions, chopped, for garnish

Pour the wine into a saucepan, add the mussels and steam until the shells open, about 4 minutes. Transfer the mussels and the liquid to a bowl and let cool. Meanwhile, in the same saucepan, saute the salt pork until crisp. Remove from the pan and pour out all but 4 tablespoons of fat. Add the onion and stew gently for 10 minutes. Take the mussels out of the shells and check again for cleanliness. Strain the liquid through a double thickness of rinsed cheesecloth into the saucepan. Add the cream, salt pork, and mussel meats. Shave the corn off the cob or, if using canned corn, drain and rinse it. Add the corn to the pot and simmer very gently for 1 hour. Taste for salt and pepper and serve garnished with the chopped green onion. Serves 8.

The Castine Inn

P.O. Box 41
Castine, Maine 04421
(207) 326-4365

Maine Crab Chowder

1/2 pound salt pork or bacon
2 large onions
3 stalks celery
1/2 carrot
1 tablespoon dried tarragon
1 tablespoon lobster, crab, or shrimp paste
2 pounds fresh Maine crabmeat
3 pounds potatoes, peeled and diced
Tabasco sauce
Salt and freshly ground pepper to taste
1 pint heavy cream

With the fine blade of a meat grinder, grind the pork, onions, celery, and carrot into a stock pot. Add the tarragon and lobster paste. Simmer over medium heat until tender but not brown. In another pan, cover the potatoes with cold water and slowly boil until they are slightly underdone. Add the potatoes and their water to the vegetable mixture. Bring to a slow boil. Add the crabmeat and bring to a boil, then remove from the heat. Just before serving, bring to the boiling point and add the cream. Add salt, pepper, and Tabasco to taste. Serves 8 to 10.

The Oxford House Inn

105 Main Street
Fryeburg, Maine 04037
(207) 935-3442

John and Phyllis Morris are the innkeepers at this lovely Maine inn with charming and comfortable accommodations. The spacious turn-of-the-century yellow house boasts a large porch and big bay windows, creating an instant welcome to guests. The three serve wonderful foods with many creative and unusual dishes.

Surrounded by eight acres of wooded and landscaped grounds, this delightful inn has gazed out over the dry creek valley of Sonoma County since 1881. John A. Paxton, a wealthy San Francisco businessman, built the majestic three-story mansion as a summer home. Now the house stands in the heart of California's wine country. John and Carol Muir are the innkeepers, providing their guests with a tranquil ambience and elegant country lifestyle. The inn is filled with magnificent antique furniture and Persian carpets.

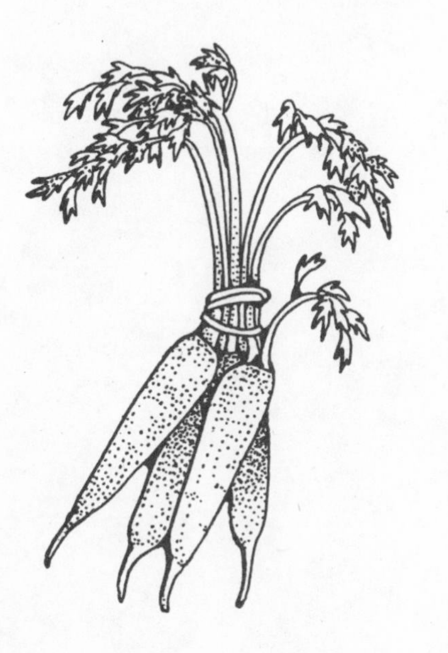

Carrot Soup

2 cups chopped carrots
1/2 cup chopped onions
1 tablespoon chopped fresh basil
1 tomato, peeled, seeded, and chopped
Butter or oil
1 Idaho potato, peeled and chopped
4 cups chicken stock or broth
Salt and freshly ground pepper to taste
Creme fraiche, for garnish

Cook the carrots, onions, basil, and tomato in some butter or oil for a few minutes. Add potatoes and broth, and simmer until the carrots and potatoes are soft. Puree in a blender in batches until smooth. Season with salt and pepper to taste. Garnish with *creme fraiche*. Serves 6.

Madrona Manor

1001 Westside Road
Healdsburg, California 95448
(707) 433-4231

Carrot and Coriander Soup

1 large onion, sliced thin
2 tablespoons unsalted butter
1 clove garlic, minced
1 teaspoon ground coriander
10 carrots (about 1 1/3 pounds), sliced
1 boiling potato (about 1/4 pound), peeled and sliced
5 cups chicken stock or canned chicken broth
1 1/4 cups fresh orange juice
1/2 teaspoon salt
1/2 teaspoon white pepper
2/3 cup heavy cream
1/4 cup minced fresh coriander (cilantro), for garnish

In a kettle, cook the onion in the butter over moderately low heat, stirring, until it is softened; add the garlic, and cook the mixture, stirring, for 2 minutes. Add the ground coriander and cook the mixture, stirring, for 2 minutes. Add the carrots and the potato and cook the mixture, stirring, for 2 minutes. Add the stock, the orange juice, the salt, and the pepper, bring the liquid to a boil, and simmer the mixture for 20 to 30 minutes, or until the carrots are tender. Puree the soup in batches in a blender, transfer it to a saucepan, and stir in the cream. Heat the soup, stirring, until it is hot and add salt and white pepper to taste. Ladle the soup into heated bowls and sprinkle it with the fresh coriander. Makes about 9 cups.

One of the most romantic country inns in America, Black River Inn was built in 1835. It rests on a shaded bank of the Black River in the village of Ludlow. Upon arrival, prepare to enter an earlier century when staircases were made of hand-carved oak and fireplaces of polished marble. *(Continued on following page.)*

Black River Inn

100 Main Street
Ludlow, Vermont 05149
(802) 228-5585

(Continued from previous page.) Some of the best downhill and cross-country skiing in New England is within minutes of the Inn. Also nearby are ice-skating, sledding, hiking and sleigh rides. Awake to the aroma of home-baked breads and muffins. Each evening guests enjoy a creative five-course gourmet dinner.

Velvet Pea and Zucchini Soup

3/4 pounds zucchini, chopped
1/3 cup finely chopped onion
1/3 cup finely chopped white part of green onion
2 tablespoons vegetable oil
1/8 teaspoon dried thyme, crumbled
1 1/2 cups canned chicken broth
1 cup water
2 cups shelled fresh peas (about 2 pounds unshelled)
or 1 10-ounce package frozen peas, thawed
Sour cream, for garnish, if desired

In a large heavy saucepan cook the zucchini, the onion, and the green onion in the oil over moderate heat, stirring, for 3 minutes. Add the thyme, broth and water, bring the liquid to a boil, and simmer the mixture, covered, for six minutes, or until the vegetables are tender. Transfer about 1/3 cup of the peas with a slotted spoon to a small bowl, reserving them for garnish. In a blender, puree the mixture in batches, and season the soup with salt and pepper. Serve the soup at room temperature in bowls, and garnish each serving with a dollop of sour cream and some of the reserved peas. Serves 6.

Black River Inn

100 Main Strret
Ludlow, Vermont
(802) 228-5585

Spinach Soup

1 cup diced onion
3 tablespoons butter
2 cups sliced mushrooms
2 tablespoons flour
2 tablespoons chicken bouillon granules
Bunch of Spinach, washed, stems removed and roughly chopped
2 1/2 cups water
2 1/2 cups milk
Salt and pepper to taste

Saute onion in butter, then add the mushrooms. Stir, then add the flour, stir, and brown. Add the boullion granules, then the spinach, water, milk, and seasonings. Simmer, stirring occasionally until the spinach is wilted, just a few minutes. Serves 6.

Savery Creek Ranch

P.O. Box 24
Savery, Wyoming
(307) 383-7840 82332

This is a wonderful ranch-style inn bordering Medicine Bow National Forest. Just a few miles away is the incredible Red Desert, with wild horses, antelope, arrowheads and fossils. Meals here are special. To quote Joyce B. Saer, the owner and innkeeper, "Many years ago, a cowboy bitterly complained to the cook: 'I can't ride all day 'thout 'taters for breakfast.' " With that in mind, breakfast is hearty at Savery Creek. Lunch is a buffet, and can include roast leg of lamb, sherry chicken, and many fruits, vegetables, and green salads.

Brandied Pumpkin Soup

Warren and Doris Sadler are the innkeepers at this romantic inn located in the heart of the Northern Neck of Virginia. Historic Christ Church (1732) is only a short drive away. Other attractions are Stratford Hall (Robert E. Lee's Birthplace), Epping Forest (George Washington's mother's house), and many other historic places. The inn stands at the head of an entrance drive over 1,000 feet long, bordered on either side by a line of hardwoods and cedars. The grounds consist of 54 acres with approximately 12 acres under cultivation. The inn is noted for its graceful and lofty proportions and its spaciousness throughout.

1/4 cup butter
1/2 cup finely chopped onion
1/4 teaspoon ground ginger
1/4 teaspoon ground nutmeg
3 1/2 cups chicken broth
2 1/2 cups canned pumpkin puree
1 cup half and half
2 tablespoons brandy
Salt and white pepper to taste
Croutons, for garnish

Melt the butter, add the onion, and cook until translucent. Blend in the spices and the chicken broth. Bring to a boil. Blend in the pumpkin and half and half. Reduce the heat and cook until the soup is thoroughly heated, stirring occasionally. Blend in the brandy. Season to taste with salt and white pepper. Serve hot with a crouton for garnish. Makes 8 cups.

The Inn at Levelfields

P.O. Box 216
Lancaster, Virginia 22503
(804) 435-6887

Curried Squash Soup

1 onion
1 large leek
1 bunch green onions
1/2 cup unsalted butter
3 teaspoons curry powder
3 zucchini, unpeeled, grated
3 summer squash, unpeeled, grated
Salt and white pepper, to taste
6 cups chicken stock
3 potatoes, peeled and sliced
1 cup heavy cream

Chop the onion, the leek, and the scallions. Reserve a little of the greener parts of the scallions for garnish. In a heavy pot, melt the butter. When the butter foams and is quite fragrant, add the curry powder, and cook, while stirring, for 2 or 3 minutes. Add the onions, leeks, scallions, and squash and season to taste with salt and pepper. Saute this mixture briefly, then turn down the heat, cover, and cook until the squash is soft and the juices have been extracted. Uncover and let the juices reduce by half. Add the chicken stock and potatoes. Cook, uncovered, for 15 minutes, or until the potatoes are just cooked through.

To serve: Hot, country style,—add the heavy cream and serve in warm soup bowls. Pureed (chilled or hot)—let the soup mixture cool, then puree in patches in a food processor or blender. Strain the puree. Stir in heavy cream. Serve iced or heated. Garnish with reserved scallions.
Serves 12

Governor's Inn

86 Main Street
Ludlow, Vermont
(802) 228-8830

Charley and Deedy Marble are innkeepers of this historic village inn. The inn, originally built by Vermont Governor William Wallace Stickney as his private dwelling, stands as a classic example of the fine craftsmanship of the late Victorian period (circa 1890). Now it serves as a haven for enjoying life's pleasures and as a base for exploring Vermont. The recipe that we include was taken from the inn's own cookbook, A Collection of Recipes from the Inn's Kitchen, by Charley and Deedy Marble.

Sandwich Village is Cape Cod's oldest and most scenic village. Amidst its flowering courtyards, gazebo, historic attractions, antique shops and museums, The Dan'l Webster offers 46 modern rooms. It is renowned for its superb cuisine and award-winning wine cellar. The structure is an authentic replication on the site of the original tap room which stood for two centuries prior to a fire in 1971. Here, Daniel Webster made regular visits from 1820 to 1850, and for 100 years before, was the meeting place for local patriots.

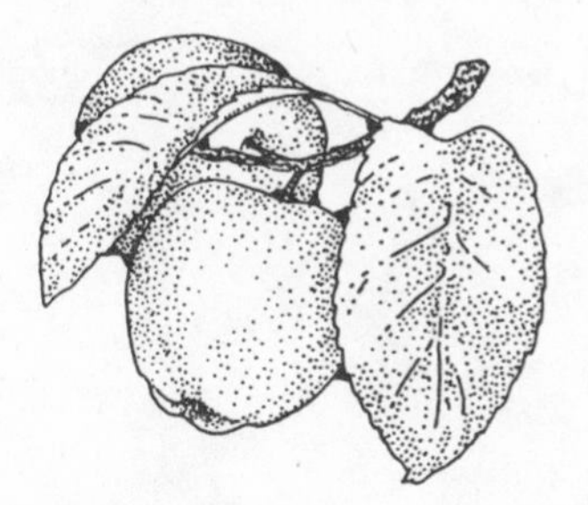

Creamed Butternut and Apple Soup

5 pounds butternut squash, peeled and diced large
1 1/2 pounds apples, cored and quartered (Cortland preferred)
1 inch cinnamon stick
2 quarts chicken stock
1 1/2 cups unsalted butter
1/2 cup pure maple syrup
1/2 teaspoon ground ginger
1/2 teaspoon salt
1/2 teaspoon ground nutmeg
1 pint light cream, heated to hot but not to boiling

Steam the squash, apples, cinnamon, and chicken stock until the squash is soft. Run all through a food mill and return to the pot. Add all other ingredients except the cream and simmer for 15 minutes. Add the hot cream. Strain and serve immediately. Serves 10 to 12.

The Dan'l Webster Inn

149 Main Street
Sandwich Village, Massachusetts 02563
(508) 888-3622

Tomato Cognac Soup

3 pounds canned whole tomatoes, with liquid
1 large onion
6 tablespoons butter
1 tablespoon dried basil
1 pint light cream
1 to 2 tablespoons brown sugar
5 tablespoons Cognac
Salt and freshly ground pepper to taste
Chopped fresh parsley or chives or hot croutons, for garnish

Chop the onion and saute in butter for 20 minutes, until soft but not brown. Squash the tomatoes, then add them and their liquid to the onion. Add the basil, and stir. Bring to a boil, reduce the heat, and simmer, covered, for 30 minutes. Set aside and let cool slightly. Puree in a food processor and reheat.

In a small saucepan, heat the cream with the sugar, whisking often. Pour into the tomatoes. Heat the soup but do not boil.

Add the Cognac and salt and pepper. Garnish with chopped parsley or chives, or fresh hot croutons.

This turn-of-the-century summer retreat for writer Frank Simonds was later converted into an inn by a Swiss couple. Today, the inn's decor and cuisine reflect this harmonious blend of New England and European alpine traditions. The comfortably furnished guest rooms are all named after writers.

Snowvillage Inn

P.O. Box 176
Snowville, New Hampshire 03849
(603) 447-2818

A touch of the past has come alive in Blowing Rock. This grandiose old home, named Ragged Garden when it was built at the turn of the century, has a majestic setting. The cuisine is classic, with a slight emphasis on Northern Italian. Chef/owner Joseph Villani has a distinguished culinary background.

Minestrone

1/4 cup butter or margarine
1/4 cup olive oil
1 large onion, chopped
1 bunch fresh parsley, minced
4 or 5 cloves garlic
3 cups chicken broth
2 cups water
3/4 cup northern or pinto beans
2 teaspoons tomato paste
1 cup fresh green beans
3 stalks celery, chopped coarsely
3 carrots, diced
1/3 head cabbage, chopped
2 zucchini, diced
Salt and freshly ground pepper to taste
1 cup small elbow pasta
6 or 7 fresh basil leaves
1/2 teaspoon freshly grated Parmesan cheese, for garnish

In a large pot, melt the butter and oil together over medium low heat. Add the onion and parsley, cook 5 minutes, and add the garlic. Simmer until the onion is translucent, then add the broth, water, dry beans, and tomato paste. Boil gently for 1 hour and 10 minutes. Add the remaining ingredients, except the cheese, and continue cooking for 1 1/2 hours. Garnish with the Parmesan cheese. Serves 8 to 10.

Ragged Garden Inn

Sunset Drive, P.O. Box 1927
Blowing Rock, North Carolina 28605
(704) 295-9703

French Onion Soup

Here is another delicious treat from Indiana's Patchwork Quilt Country Inn.

20 slices French bread or rolls cut 1/2 inch thick
Melted butter
1 clove garlic
1/2 cup butter
1/4 cup vegetable oil
3 cups thinly sliced onions
1 tablespoon salt
4 quarts chicken broth
3 tablespoons beef stock
Grated Swiss cheese
Grated Parmesan cheese

Place the bread slices in one layer on a baking sheet and bake at 325 degrees for 10 minutes. Coat with melted butter on both sides and rub with the garlic clove. Bake on the other side for 10 minutes. Set aside. Melt the 1/2 cup butter and the oils in a heavy saucepan over medium heat. Stir in the onions and salt and cook uncovered over low heat, stirring occasionally, for 30 minutes or until the onions are a rich golden brown. Add the chicken broth and beef stock; simmer, partially covered, for another 30 to 40 minutes. Skim off fat when necessary. Taste for seasoning. Ladle the soup into bowls, top with croutons, and sprinkle grated Swiss and Parmesan cheese on top. Place under the broiler and broil until the cheese is melted. Serves 20.

Patchwork Quilt Country Inn

11748 County Road 2
Middlebury, Indiana 46540
(219) 825-2417

In 1799, the Holland Land Company offered lots ten miles apart in what is now Clarence, New York, to "any proper man who would build and operate a tavern upon it." The first to accept this offer was a young silversmith named Asa Ransom. Mr. Ransom first built a combination log cabin home and tavern. Then, in 1801, he built a sawmill near the creek that bears his name, and in 1803 he built a grist mill. The dining rooms were added in 1975; great care was taken to retain the charm of the nineteenth century.

Ambassador Soup

4 cups chicken stock
1 tablespoon chicken fat
1 1/2 cups chopped onions
3/4 cup chopped celery
3/4 cup chopped carrots
Salt and freshly ground pepper, to taste
1/2 cup flour
2 cups shredded lettuce
1/3 cup rice
1 cup peas
1 cup milk

Heat the chicken stock in a saucepan. Using a 3-quart sauce pot, heat the chicken fat and saute the celery, carrots and onions. Season lightly with salt and pepper. Cook until the onion begins to get translucent. Reduce the heat and add the flour; stir constantly and cook for 5 to 8 minutes. Then add half of the chicken stock and mix well to dissolve the flour. Add the remaining stock, shredded lettuce, rice, and peas. Bring to a boil and simmer until the rice is tender. Then slowly add the milk, mixing well. Adjust the seasoning by adding salt and pepper to taste. Makes 8 cups.

Note: A combination of half oil and half butter may be substituted for the chicken fat.

Asa Ransom House

10529 Main Street
Clarence Hollow, New York 14031
(716) 759-2315

Roasted Red Bell Pepper Soup

3 ounces butter
1 head garlic
1 onion, diced
10 roasted red bell peppers, peeled, seeded, and cored
3 quarts chicken stock
3 potatoes, peeled and diced
1 cup light cream
Salt and freshly ground pepper to taste

In a 2-gallon pot, quickly saute the garlic and onion in the butter, until the onion is lightly browned. Add the red pepper, potatoes, and chicken stock and bring to a boil. Then reduce to a simmer. Cook until the potatoes are soft, then puree the mixture in batches in a food processor or blender. Add the cream, salt, and pepper to taste. Reheat but do not boil.

Ventana Big Sur

Highway 1
Big Sur, California 93920
(800) 628-1500

From the majesty of its spectacular setting to the quiet solitude it offers each guest, this exceptional inn truly offers the experience of a lifetime. Located south of Carmel on the magnificent Big Sur Coast, Ventana offers the ultimate in luxurious accommodations, peaceful relaxation, and four-star dining.

Here is a delightful eighteenth century-style building of unique charm, completely decorated in the old manner. The visitor is carried back to the times of the Randolphs, the Masons, the Fairfaxes, the Jeffersons, and the Washingtons. Antique furniture and cooking utensils are displayed in an authentic and useful manner. In the scenic main dining room, you will see handhewn beams of huge proportions, old sconces, early samplers, corner cupboards, and much, much more. Excellent meals are served country-style.

Cream of Peanut Soup

2 stalks celery, chopped
1 small onion, chopped
1/4 cup butter
2 tablespoons flour
2 cups chicken broth
1 cup milk
1 cup light cream
1 cup smooth peanut butter
Salt and freshly ground pepper, to taste
Paprika, to taste

Brown the celery and onions in the butter. Add the flour and chicken broth and bring to a boil. Add the milk and cream. Strain. Add the peanut butter and simmer for 5 minutes. Season to taste. Serves 6.

Evans Farm Inn

1696 Chain Bridge Road
McLean, Virginia 22101
(703) 356-8000

Cream of Mushroom Soup

1/4 cup butter
1 pound mushrooms, sliced
1 onion, chopped
2 cloves garlic, minced
3 cups rich chicken stock
1 cup white wine
1/3 cup dry sherry
2 teaspoons basil
2 teaspoons thyme
1 tablespoon cornstarch dissolved in 1/2 cup water
2 cups heavy cream
Salt and white pepper
1/3 pound mushrooms, sliced and sauteed in butter
1/2 cup chopped toasted hazelnuts (optional), for garnish

Saute the 1 pound mushrooms, the onions, and garlic in the butter until the onions begin to soften. Add the chicken stock, wine, sherry, thyme, and basil. Simmer for 10 minutes. Add the cornstarch mixture and cook until thickened. Puree until smooth. Add the cream, sauteed mushrooms, and salt and pepper to taste. Garnish with the hazelnuts if desired. Makes 6 cups.

Manor Farm Inn

26069 Big Valley Road
Poulsbo, Washington
(206) 779-4628

This well-known inn has been featured in many national magazines, including Architectural Digest, Sunset, House and Garden, Esquire, Gourmet, *and* Bon Appetit. *Thanks to its off-the-beaten-path location in Poulsbo it remains as fresh and inviting as the day it opened in 1982. Guests must take a scenic half-hour ferry ride from Seattle across Puget Sound, and then drive twenty minutes up Washington's Kitsap Peninsula. Innkeepers Robin and Jill Hughes offer visitors acres of lush farmland, trout-stocked lakes, and plenty of fine cooking. White walls and light woods provide a serene backdrop for the chef's five-course dinners and sumptous breakfasts. The menu changes daily, emphasizing the Northwest's justly famous seafood and produce.*

Tucked away in a valley, The Heritage blends into the rural country-side so well that you might miss it. It's rustic, with great roaring fireplaces in beautiful rooms rich with the aroma of fresh-hewn wood. The bar has been known to make lifelong friends of complete strangers. The Heritage also offers skiing and ice skating- as well as hot toddies, quiet candlelight dinners, and dancing into the night.

Heritage Inn

Cream of Watercress Soup

1 quart chicken stock with bay leaf
1 large potato, peeled and diced
1 onion, diced
2 bunches watercress, chopped
1 pint heavy cream
3 tablespoons butter
Salt and freshly ground pepper to taste
Freshly grated nutmeg, for garnish

Saute the onions and watercress in the butter in a soup pot. Add the chicken stock and diced potato. Cook until the potatoes are soft. Puree in batches in a blender or food processor and then return to the pot. Add the cream, salt, and pepper and heat until hot but not boiling, stirring to blend well. Garnish with the nutmeg. Serves 6 to 8.

Heritage Inn

Heritage Road
Southbury, Connecticut 06488
(203) 264-8200

Cream of Winter Vegetable Soup

1 cup chopped leeks, white part only
1/4 cup butter
4 to 5 quarts cleaned and chopped winter vegetables (onion, celery root, parsnips, carrots, celery, turnips, Brussels sprouts)
3 cups chicken stock
1/2 to 1 cup heavy cream
Salt and white pepper to taste
Nutmeg

Saute the leeks in butter until soft. Add any combination of the above vegetables to the leeks and stir and cook to coat with the butter (add more butter if needed). Pour in the chicken stock, bring to a boil, reduce heat, and simmer until the vegetables are tender. Remove from the heat and cool slightly. Puree in a food processor or blender in batches until the mixture is smooth. Return to the pot and add cream and seasonings to taste. Reheat when ready to serve but do not boil. Serves 6 to 8.

Huckleberry Springs

P.O. Box 400
Monte Rio, California 95462
(707) 865-2683

Located on 56 acres above the Russian River, Huckleberry Springs offers a quiet and private escape to the Sonoma Coast and Wine Country. Designed to offer its guests comfort and relaxation after the day's adventures, the inn boasts a hillside spa, a swimming pool and gourmet dining in the solarium under the redwoods. The kitchen specializes in varied cuisine all capitalizing on the fresh seasonal produce, seafoods and fine wines of Sonoma. Four cottages offer private baths, skylights, and woodstoves.

This delicious soup is just one of the delicacies available at The Sedgwick Inn, located in New York's beautiful Taconic Valley.

Queen Victoria Soup

2 teaspoons butter
1 small onion, chopped
3 stalks celery, finely chopped
1/2 pound mushrooms, diced
1/2 cup diced cooked chicken
1/2 cup diced cooked ham
1 tablespoon quick-cooking tapioca
2 cups light cream
Salt and white pepper to taste

Heat the butter in a large saucepan and cook the onion until golden but not brown. Add the celery and mushrooms and cook over low heat for 10 minutes, stirring frequently. Add the chicken stock, chicken, ham, and tapioca and cook for 20 minutes, until lightly thickened. Before serving, add the cream and salt and pepper and reheat but do not boil. Serves 4.

The Sedgwick Inn

P.O. Box 250
Berlin, New York 12022
(518) 658-23334

Wisconsin Cream of Cheddar Soup

2/3 cup butter or margarine
1 cup finely chopped celery
1/3 cup flour
1/4 teaspoon salt
1/4 teaspoon freshly ground pepper
1 1/2 cups chicken stock or broth
2 cups light cream
2 cups milk
2 8-ounce cups finely shredded sharp Cheddar cheese
8 slices bacon, cooked crisp and crumbled
1/2 cup finely chopped green onion

In a large saucepan melt the butter over medium heat. Stir in celery. Cook and stir 8 to 10 minutes or until the celery is just tender. Stir in the flour, salt, and pepper. Add the chicken broth. Cook and stir until the mixture is thickened and bubbly. Cook and stir 1 to 2 minutes more. Add the cream and milk alternately to the broth mixture. Heat through. Stir in the cheese. Cook and stir until the cheese is melted. Just before serving, garnish with the bacon and green onions. Serves 8 to 10.

The Victorian Villa

601 North Broadway Street
Union City, Michigan 49094
(517) 741-7383

The Victorian Villa is a nineteenth century inn offering travelers elegant overnight lodging that recaptures the romantic ambience of a century ago. The ornate Italianate mansion was completed in 1876 and occupies a coveted listing on Michigan's Register of Historic Sites. The inn has received numerous honors and recognitions since its grand opening in 1982. Ronald J. and Susan Gibson are owners/innkeepers. The recipe that follows was taken from the inn's cookbook, Cherished Holiday Memories.

For over 100 years, the historic charm and New England hospitality of the York Harbor Inn have welcomed those seeking distinctive lodging and dining. This famous inn, with oceanside ambience and relaxing country charm, has entered its second century of operation. Nestled in the heart of York Harbor, its roomy, oceanfront dining room offers exceptional cuisine.

Brie Cheese Soup

1/4 cup butter
1/4 cup flour
6 cups chicken stock, preferably homemade
12 ounces Brie cheese, at room temperature, with rind removed
6 tablespoons white wine
1/4 cup julienne-cut carrots
1/4 cup julienne-cut celery
1/4 cup thinly sliced mushrooms
1/4 cup heavy cream
Salt and freshly ground pepper to taste
Chopped fresh chives or green onions, for garnish

Melt the butter in a heavy saucepan over low heat. Add the flour and mix well; cook until the mixture just starts to turn golden. Add the stock and whisk vigorously. Bring to a boil and reduce to a simmer. Skim the butter and flour and other impurities that rise to the surface and continue to simmer until the sauce is reduced by one-third and has the consistency of heavy cream. Strain the sauce through a fine sieve.

Cut the Brie into small chunks. Return the sauce to the saucepan and add the Brie. Cook slowly, stirring occasionally, until the cheese has melted. Add the wine and vegetables and simmer lightly until the vegetables are al dente. Heat the cream in a small pan and add it to the soup. Season the soup with salt and pepper. Serve immediately, garnished with chives or green onions. Makes 1 1/2 quarts.

Note: The flavor of this soup can vary depending on the degree of ripeness of the cheese. Ripening can be encouraged by allowing the Brie to sit at room temperature for 3 to 9 hours, depending on personal preference.

York Harbor Inn

P.O. Box 573
York Harbor, Maine 03911
(207) 363-5119

Columbus Potato Soup

Another tempting recipe from the Rau family kitchen at their Texas inn, Raumonda.

4 slices bacon, diced
6 leeks, thinly sliced
1/4 cup chopped onion
2 tablespoons flour
4 cups chicken broth
3 large potatoes, peeled and diced
2 egg yolks, beaten
1 cup sour cream
1 tablespoon chopped fresh parsley
2 tablespoons chopped fresh chervil or tarragon

Saute the bacon for 5 minutes, add the leeks and onions and cook for 5 minutes. Stir in the flour and then add broth. Add the potatoes and simmer for 1 hour. Combine the egg yolks and sour cream. Stir into the soup and add the parsley and chervil. Serves 4 to 6.

Raumonda

P.O. Box 112
Columbus, Texas 78934
(409) 732-5135

Wild Rice Soup

This is a Northwoods country lodge on the Canadian border. The Kerfoot family has been host of the friendly and informal Gunflint Lodge for over sixty years. The lodge is set in the Laurentian Highlands' scenic bluffs, lakes, and valleys; the land is heavily forested with pine, birch, aspen and cedar. This is the country of the Voyageurs and Native Americans ad it remains much the same today as it has been for generations—fairly remote wilderness country, beautiful and unspoiled. The meals at Gunflint are planned for the hefty appetites of active skiers.

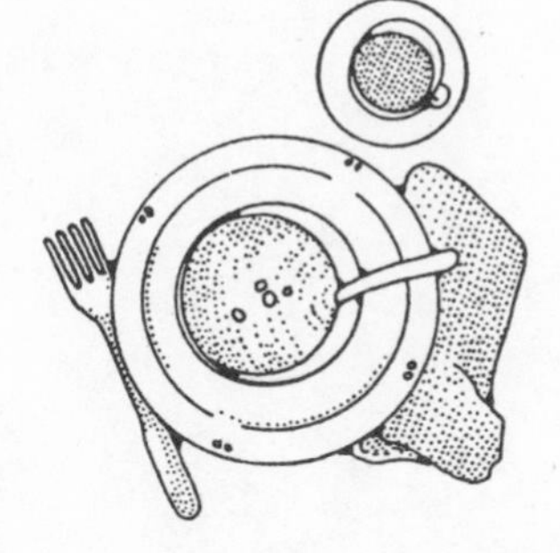

1 tablespoon minced onion
2 tablespoons margarine
3 tablespoons flour
3 cups chicken broth
1 cup cooked wild rice
1 teaspoon salt
2 tablespoons white wine
3/4 cup heavy cream
1/4 teaspoon curry powder
Chopped fresh parsley, for garnish

Brown the onion in the margarine until it is translucent. Blend in the flour and broth, stirring constantly until thickened. Stir in the rice and salt and simmer for about 5 minutes. Blend in the wine and cream, add the curry powder, and simmer until the soup reaches serving temperature. Garnish each serving with chopped parsley. Serves 4 to 6.

Gunflint Lodge

HC64, Box 750
Grand Marais, Minnesota 55604
(218) 388-2294

Lentil Soup

8 cups dried lentils, rinsed and picked over
2 or 3 large red onions, chopped
4 carrots, cut in quarters and sliced
1/2 bulb garlic, chopped
3 tablespoons salt, or to taste
2 tablespoons curry powder, or to taste
Freshly ground pepper to taste

In a soup pot, cover the lentils with water and bring to a boil. Turn the heat down to low and add the onions, carrots, and garlic. Cook until almost tender, then add the seasonings, to taste. Thin with additional water if necessary. Serves 8 to 10.

Pah Tempe Hot Springs Resort

825 North 800 East, 35-4
Hurricane, Utah 84737
(801) 635-2879

Pah Tempe is an ancient Piaute healing center. The springs are near Zion National Park, the Grand Canyon, and Brian Head Ski Center. The Inn has seven cliffside hot pools, a hotel, cabins, and camping facilities. Natural foods and fresh fruits and juices are served. The chuck wagon dinners are superb.

Here is a delightful inn in a peaceful, picturesque town of fewer than 1000 residents. New Harmony was the site of two nineteenth-century Utopian settlements, and many buildings from those days remain open to the public. The New Harmony Inn was built in 1974 but invites the visitor to explore legacies from the past while enjoying comforts of the present. There are 90 guest rooms, many with working fireplaces. Its restaurant, the Red Geranium, is one of Indiana's most popular, with an exceptional menu boasting regional as well as continental favorites.

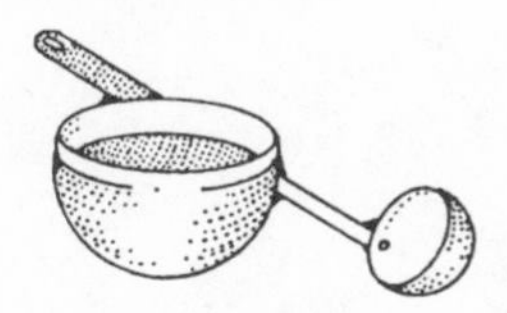

Black Bean Soup

2 cups black turtle beans, rinsed and picked over
1 cup coarsely chopped onion
1 cup coarsely chopped celery, with leaves
1 medium carrot, chopped
1 bay leaf
Pinch of thyme
1 tablespoon Worcestershire sauce
2 1/2 quarts water
3 smoked ham hocks or 1 pound cooked bacon or sausage
1 cup chicken stock or 2 bouillon cubes
Salt and freshly ground pepper to taste
1/4 cup Dry Sack sherry

Place the beans in a soup pot. Add all the other ingredients except the salt, pepper, and sherry. Simmer for at least three hours or until a bean will crush easily. Remove the ham hocks, if used, and the bay leaf. Puree the beans using a food mill or sieve. Return to the heat and add salt and pepper to taste, and the sherry. If the soup is too thin, add a small amount of roux made of equal parts of butter and flour cooked together. Stir over the heat until the soup is rich and creamy. If the soup is too thick, add water or chicken stock. Serves 12.

The New Harmony Inn

P.O. Box 581
New Harmony, Indiana 47631
(813) 682-4491

Green Split Pea Soup

5 cups green split peas
1/2 cup chopped carrots
1/2 cup chopped onion
1/2 cup chopped celery
1 cup chopped ham
5 quarts water
1 bay leaf
1 1/2 teaspoons celery salt
1 1/2 teaspoons salt
1 1/2 teaspoons white pepper
1 1/2 teaspoons onion salt

Place the first six ingredients in a soup pot. Add the seasonings and cook over low heat, stirring frequently, for 3 1/2 hours or until the peas are dissolved. Add more water if the soup is too thick. Makes 1 1/2 to 2 gallons.

Bolo Country Inn

207 Pine Avenue North
Menomonie, Wisconsin 54751
(715) 235-5596

The Bolo Country Inn is a pleasant base for exploring the many diversions of Dunn County. In all seasons, in all types of weather, one enjoys discovering the charm of this special area. The Inn seems to whisper a welcome to all who enter its door. Dining here will leave you with wonderful memories of great food, friendly people, and good times. It will also start you planning your next visit.

Barley Beer-Burger Soup

1 onion, diced
1 pound ground beef
1 cup pearl barley, cooked and drained
3 carrots, diced
1 bunch broccoli, flowerets only
1 cup water
1 bottle beer
Salt and white pepper to taste
Garlic powder

Saute the onion with the ground beef; drain off the fat. In a stock pot, put the barley, onions, ground beef, carrots, broccoli, water and beer. Cook until the vegetables are tender but still crisp. Season to taste with salt, pepper, and garlic powder. Serves 4.

North Garden Inn

1014 North Garden
Bellingham, Washington 98225
(206) 671-7828

The North Garden Inn is a Queen Anne Victorian house on the National Register of Historic Places, superbly suited to attend to the traveler's needs. Many of the beautifully appointed rooms have splendid views of Bellingham Bay. A Steinway grand piano graces the front hall. Innkeepers Barbara and Frank DeFreytas pride themselves on offering warm personal service to the many who make this their home away from home. Fine dining is offered in the formal dining room.

Mulligatawny Soup

This hearty soup recipe comes directly from the kitchen of Chef Richard Alabaugh at West Virginia's historic Blennerhassett Hotel.

1 large chicken, cut into pieces
1/4 pound veal trimmings, cut up
6 cups water
3 tablespoons butter
4 large onions, chopped
2 garlic cloves, minced
2 heaping teaspoons curry powder
5 tablespoons cornstarch
Juice of one lemon
Salt and freshly ground pepper to taste
1 cooking apple, peeled and sliced
3 cups boiled rice

Simmer the chicken and veal in the water for approximately 1 hour. Remove the chicken and skim fat from the stock. Melt the butter in a large skillet. Saute the onions and garlic until translucent. Mix the curry powder and cornstarch with 1/4 cup of the stock to form a paste. Add to the stock and blend thoroughly. Stir in the onions and garlic. Cook for 30 minutes. Remove from the heat and chill.

Before serving, cut the chicken into small pieces, discarding bones and skin. Return the chicken to the soup. Add the lemon juice and salt and pepper to taste. Add the apples and the rice. Simmer for 20 minutes. Serves 8.

The Blennerhassett Hotel

P.O. Box 51
Parkersburg, West Virginia 26102
(304) 422-3131

Once used as a hospital, today this same structure is the well-known Winchester Inn, a Victorian country inn offering lodging and full service dining to the public. Completely renovated by the Gibbs family in 1983, the structure is on the National Register of Historic Places. It honors the past yet adapts itself to the present, an exquisite blend of comfort and tradition. The elegant dining room overlooks tiered gardens and patio seating. Chef Charles Barker takes great pride in offering an unique, eclectic menu.

Sopa de Ajo

6 cloves garlic
3 tablespoons olive oil
6 slices bread, cubed
1 pound tomatoes, peeled, seeded, and chopped
1 bay leaf
3 to 4 cups chicken stock
1 teaspoon paprika
Salt and freshly ground pepper to taste

Peel the garlic. Heat the oil in a deep pan and saute the garlic until it is lightly browned. (The longer you cook the garlic, the more mellow it will become.) Remove the garlic and set aside. Saute the bread cubes in the same oil until crisp. Add the tomatoes, bay leaf, and browned garlic. Add the chicken stock, a small amount at a time, until it reaches the desired consistency. Season with paprika, salt, and pepper. Serve hot. Serves 4.

The Winchester Country Inn

25 South Second Street
Ashland, Oregon 97520
(503) 488-1113

Winterfest Fruit Soup

1 8-ounce package dried mixed fruit
1 cup dried apricots
1/2 cup raisins
5 1/2 cups water, divided
3 cinnamon sticks
1/4 cup quick-cooking tapioca
1 orange, sliced thin
3/4 cup sugar
1/3 cup currant jelly

In a 3-quart pan combine the mixed fruit, apricots, raisins, 3 cups of water, and cinnamon sticks. Cover and simmer until the fruit is plump. Add the tapioca, stir in, cover and cook until the sauce is thickened and the fruit is tender. Add 2 1/2 cups water and the remaining ingredients. Cook until well blended and tapioca is tender, and remove the cinnamon sticks. Serve warm. Serves 6 to 8.

Note: This soup is especially appropriate for a brunch menu.

The Washington House Inn

Corner of Washington and Center
W62 N573 Washington Avenue
Cedarburg, Wisconsin 53012
(414) 375-3550

The Washington House Inn is an experience in romance, elegance, and comfort. The romance of Country Victorian comes alive as you enter the inn. A lovely collection of antique Victorian furniture, marble trimmed fireplace, and freshly cut flowers offer a warm reception. The recipes that follow here are taken from the Inn's wonderful cookbook, The Country Bakery Book.

At the Thomas Sheperd Inn, guests are treated to a full hearty breakfast with true West Virginia hospitality. The inn was built circa 1868 and is part of historically preserved Shepardstown, a community listed in the National Register of Historic Places, and the state's oldest settlement.

Apple Soup

3 pounds tart apples
3 cups apple juice
3 cups water
2 teaspoons grated lemon rind
5 teaspoons fresh lemon juice
1 cup sugar
1 teaspoon ground cinnamon
1/2 teaspoon ground nutmeg
1/2 cup sour cream blended with 1/4 cup milk (optional)
Lemon slices, for garnish

Place all ingredients but the sour cream and milk in a saucepan. Cover and simmer about 20 minutes, until the apples are soft. Puree in a food processor or blender at low speed. Serve hot or cold with a bit of the sour cream mixture drizzled on top, and garnish with a thin slice of lemon. Serves about 12.

Note: For Russian Apple Soup, prepare as above, using 2 cups of water and 1 cup red Bordeaux wine for cooking the apples. Before pureeing, add 1/4 cup red or black currant jelly and stir until melted. Puree and serve hot or cold, with or without the cream topping.

Thomas Shepherd Inn

P.O. Box 1162
Shepherdstown, West Virginia 25443
(304) 876-3715

Cucumber Bisque

Here's a refreshing cucumber soup from The Hidden Inn of Orange, Virginia, in Virginia's wine country.

6 large cucumbers, peeled and seeded
2 yellow onions
2 teaspoons chicken base
1 cup hot water
4 cups half and half
6 tablespoons sour cream
1/2 teaspoon white pepper
1 1/2 teaspoons chopped fresh or dried dill, for garnish

Chop the cucumbers and onion in a food processor. Dissolve the chicken base in the hot water and add to the cucumber mixture. Add the half and half, sour cream, pepper, and dill. Mix well. Chill thoroughly. Serve chilled, sprinkled with dill. Serves 6.

The Hidden Inn

249 Caroline Street
Orange, Virginia 22960
(703)672-3625

For turn-of-the-century charm by the sea, The Old Yacht Club Inn is unique in Santa Barbara. Located just half a block from the beach, the inn was built in 1912 as a private home and opened as an inn in 1980. It is furnished with European antiques and Oriental rugs, creating the"homey" atmosphere of another era. One of the three innkeepers/owners, Nancy Donaldson, is renowned for her culinary artistry—such delicacies as chocolate cheesecake, superb omelettes, wonderful soups, and exquisite sauces and dressings.

Carrot Vichyssoise

4 large carrots, cut into 4 pieces
1 onion, cut into 4 pieces
2 potatoes, peeled and cut into 4 pieces
4 cups chicken broth
1 teaspoon salt
2 cups heavy cream
1/2 teaspoon white pepper
1/8 teaspoon cayenne pepper
Fresh mint leaves, for garnish

Place the carrots, onion, and potatoes in a food processor and process on and off until the vegetables are finely diced. Put the vegetables in a large heavy (Dutch oven) pan and pour in the chicken broth and salt. Bring to a boil and cook over medium heat for 25 minutes. Drain the vegetables and pour the broth into a large bowl. Return the vegetables to the processor and puree until smooth. Add the vegetables to the broth. Whisk in the cream and stir well to mix. Add the peppers. Taste to adjust seasoning. Chill well. Serve with minced fresh mint leaves sprinkled on top. Serves 6 to 8.

The Old Yacht Club Inn

431 Corona Del Mar
Santa Barbara, California 93103
(805) 962-1277

Pumpkin Vichyssoise

This intriguing pumpkin soup is just one of the delights to be found at The Holly Inn.

Butter
1 medium pumpkin, peeled, seeded, and cubed
1 bunch leeks, trimmed and sliced
2 chef's potatoes, peeled and sliced
2 cups chicken stock
2 quarts heavy cream
Nutmeg, for garnish

Saute the leeks in a saucepan with a small amount of butter. Add the pumpkin, potatoes, and stock to cover. Boil until the vegetables are very tender. Let cool and puree in batches in a food processor or blender. Pass through a strainer or sieve. Add the cream and blend well. Chill. Pour into bowls and sprinkle with nutmeg. Serves about 20.

Holly Inn

P.O. Box 2300
Pinehurst, North Carolina 28374
(919) 295-2300

Built in 1900, lovingly tended and restored, The Longwood Inn is comfortable, peaceful, and airy, with an eclectic clean-lined decor. Wide porches with wings and chairs wrap around three sides of the house; there is a large shaded yard with benches, picnic tables, as well as flower and vegetable gardens. The vegetables, naturally, find their way into the kitchen, and the flowers are used as table decorations in the relaxing dining room.

Gazpacho Soup

4 large ripe tomatoes
2 1/2 cucumbers
1 large green pepper
2 bunches green onions
1 to 2 cloves garlic
Salt
1/4 cup red wine vinegar
1/3 cup olive oil
3 cups tomato juice
1 to 1 1/2 cups beef broth or water
Hot pepper sauce
Worcestershire Sauce, to taste
Freshly ground pepper
Plain croutons, for garnish

Peel, seed, and cut the tomatoes and two of the cucumbers into 1/4-inch dice. Wash and trim the pepper and scallions; cut into 1/4-inch dice. Mash the garlic with 1 teaspoon of salt. Beat in the vinegar and oil. Combine with the chopped vegetables, then stir into the tomato juice. Add the broth or water to the desired consistency. Season to taste with hot pepper sauce, Worcestershire sauce, salt, and pepper. Chill. Cut the remaining cucumber half into thin slices. Serve the gazpacho in chilled bowls and top with cucumbers and croutons. Serves 4 to 6.

The Longwood Inn

217 Longwood Road
Bedford, Virginia 24523
(703) 586-2282

Cold Watermelon Soup

3 pounds watermelon meat, seeded
2 tablespoons sugar
4 ounces mineral water
8 ounces sweet white wine (riesling or liebfraumlich)
1/2 teaspoon fresh lemon juice
1 cantaloupe, peeled, seeded, and finely diced, for garnish
1 slice honeydew melon, peeled, seeded, and finely diced, for garnish

Place the watermelon in a food processor or blender. Blend it on low speed for 3 minutes, or until the melon has reached a pureed consistency, but is not foamy. Pour the puree into a mixing bowl. Add the sugar, mineral water, and wine, and blend. Stir in the lemon juice. Chill the soup until it is cold. Serve in soup bowls, garnished with the diced cantaloupe and honeydew. Serves 4.

The Bishop's Lodge

P.O. Box 2367
Santa Fe, New Mexico 87504
(505) 983-6377

The Bishop's Lodge is a full-service resort in the foothills of New Mexico's Sangre de Cristo Mountains. Its various buildings have a rich history, some going back to the early sixteeenth century. The architecture is largely Spanish territorial in style, and the resort retains the flavor of Old Spain. Sumptuous food is served in the appealing dining room.

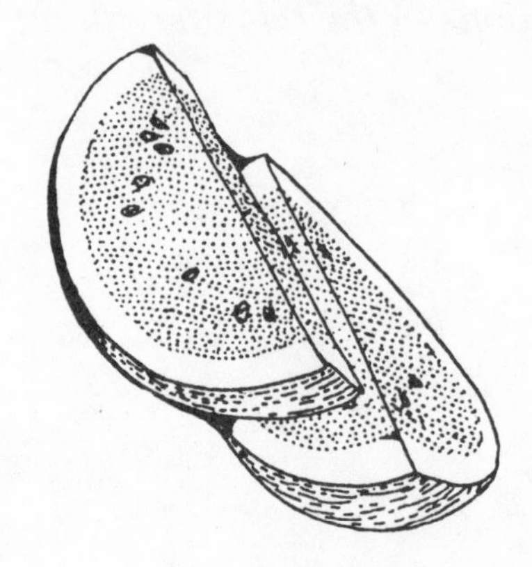

A Victorian style-inn, built in 1898 and restored in 1975, The Delforge Place retains its period character.

Fresh Peach Soup

5 large ripe peaches
1/4 cup sugar
1 cup plain yogurt
1/4 cup fresh orange juice
1/4 cup fresh lemon juice
2 tablespoons peach liqueur

Puree peaches with the sugar in a food processor or blender. Blend in the yogurt. Add the orange and lemon juices. Add the liqueur and mix until smooth. Pour into a bowl, cover, and refrigerate until chilled. Serves 4 to 6.

The Delforge Place

710 Ettie Street
Fredericksburg, Texas 78624
(512) 997-6212

Cantaloupe Mint Soup

1/2 cantaloupe, peeled, seeded, and cut in chunks
20 fresh mint leaves
1 1/2 tablespoons honey
1/8 teaspoon ground ginger
1 cup plain yogurt
1/4 cup fruity white wine
Fresh mint sprigs, for garnish

Place the cantaloupe in a blender or a food processor fitted with the steel blade. Add the mint leaves and process until the canteloupe is pureed. Remove to a serving bowl. Add the honey, ginger, yogurt, and wine; stir well to mix. Cover and chill for 2 hours or more. Pour into small bowls and garnish with mint sprigs. Serves 2.

William Klinger Inn

P.O. Box 29
Hermann, Missouri 65041
(314) 486-5930

This Victorian townhouse, built in 1878 by local miller William Klinger for his family, has been painstakingly restored and carefully renovated for use as a luxurious inn. Tastefully decorated and appointed, the inn now welcomes discriminating travelers and guests. Meals are served in the splendor of an octagonal dining room.

Breakfasts served at this wonderful inn are called "sumptuous culinary creations" and guests are seated at a communal table. Making new friends seems to be a high priority. Another special time is gathering in the early evening to share refreshments before dinner. Barnard-Good House is a totally restored inn located in the National Historic Landmark city of Cape May. Here one steps back in time, happily leaving television, telephones, and air conditioning behind.

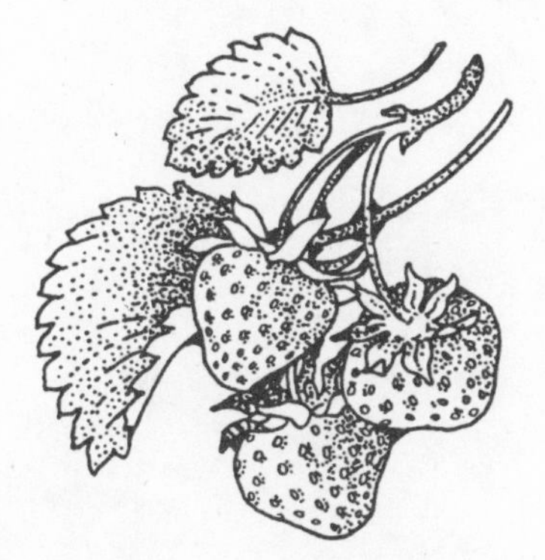

Strawberry Soup

2 1/2 pints very ripe strawberries, hulled
Juice of 1 lemon
2 tablespoons clover honey
Juice of one orange
1 tablespoon creme de cassis
2 tablespoons chopped fresh mint
Fresh mint leaves for garnish

Divide the berries in half, sorting by appearance. Cut the prettier berries in half or into quarters. Toss with the lemon juice and 1 tablespoon of the honey (or more, to taste). Refrigerate. Place the remaining berries in a food processor or mixer and crush to a coarse puree. Beat in the orange juice, creme de cassis, and 1 tablespoon honey (or more, to taste). Set aside until ready to serve.

This soup can be made ahead and refrigerated. Just before serving, stir the mint into the crushed berries. Ladle into shallow champagne glasses, add the cut berries, and garnish with the mint leaves. Serves 6.

Barnard-Good House

238 Perry Street
Cape May, New Jersey 08204
(609) 884-5381

4
Vegetables

The centerpiece of northeastern coastal Maine, the Lincoln House Country Inn is a restored colonial house on 95 acres bordering beautiful Cobscook Bay. Bald eagles, osprey, and seals demand attention along the choice hiking trails. Unusual hospitality, outstanding food and drink, and the unique Woodshed Pub are among the many features. Family owned and operated since 1976, Lincoln House is on the National Register of Historic Places.

Green Beans with Basil

3 tablespoons butter
1/2 cup chopped onion
1/4 cup chopped celery
1 clove garlic, minced
1/2 teaspoon dried rosemary
1/2 teaspoon dried basil, or 2 teaspoons chopped fresh
1 pound green beans

Melt the butter. Add the remaining ingredients except the beans and cook until onions and celery are translucent.

Cook the beans in a separate pan until crunchy. Drain. Toss in the basil sauce and serve. Serves 5 to 6.

Lincoln House Country Inn

Dennysville, Maine 04628
(207) 726-3953

Badlands Style Green Beans

8 slices bacon, diced
1/2 cup chopped onion
2 16-ounce cans green beans, with juice
1/3 cup vinegar
1/4 cup butter
2 tablespoons sugar
1/4 teaspoon salt
1/8 teaspoon pepper

Fry the bacon and onion until the bacon is crisp and add to the green beans (grease and all). Add the remaining ingredients. Heat all together.

Cedar Pass Lodge

P.O. Box 5
Interior, South Dakota 57750
(605) 433-5460

Badlands National Park and Cedar Pass Lodge are easy to reach and yet isolated enough to offer a unique getaway experience. Driving through the park one observes bison, pronghorn antelope, mule, deer, prairie dogs, and coyotes in their natural habitat. A full menu is served in the highly rated Buffalo Dining Room. The Lodge is operated by the Oglala Sioux Tribe under a contract with the National Park Service, and offers comfortable accommodations.

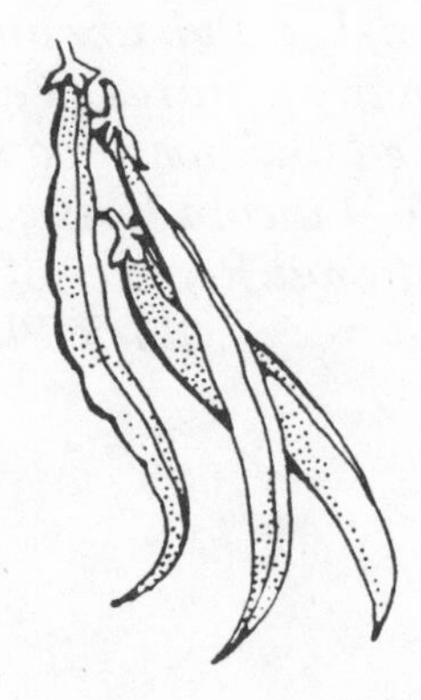

Even people "who don't like brussels sprouts" will love this recipe from Michigan's Victorian Villa.

Brussels Sprouts with Parmesan and Almonds

3 pints Brussels sprouts, trimmed, or two 16-ounce packages frozen Brussels sprouts
1/3 cup coarsely shredded Parmesan cheese
1/4 cup toasted slivered almonds
Butter or margarine
Salt and freshly ground pepper to taste

Cut any large Brussels sprouts in half lengthwise. Place the Brussels sprouts in a steamer basket over, but not touching, boiling water. Reduce the heat, cover, and steam for 15 to 20 minutes, or until just tender. Place the Brussels sprouts in a serving bowl and sprinkle with the cheese and almonds. Dot with butter and season to taste with salt and pepper. Serves 8.

The Victorian Villa

601 North Broadway Street
Union City, Michigan 49094
(517) 741-7383

Baked Tomatoes

4 28-ounce cans whole peeled tomatoes, drained
4 large onions, sliced
1/2 cup butter
1 cup bread crumbs (stale or toasted)
Salt to taste
Cayenne pepper to taste

Saute the onion in the butter until translucent but not brown. Add the bread crumbs and mix well. Line a casserole with half the drained tomatoes and sprinkle with salt and red pepper. Go a little overboard with the pepper; this dish should be fairly hot.

Over this, layer half the onions and bread crumbs. Add another layer of tomatoes, salt, and pepper. Top with the rest of the onion-bread crumb mixture. Bake for 30 minutes at 350 degrees. Serves 8 to 10.

Inn at Asphodel Village

Route 2, Box 89
Jackson, Louisiana 70748
(504) 654-6868

This lovely inn was originally a merchant's house. The back wing was built about 1785 and the larger portion in the 1840s. The Asphodel complex of overnight accomodations, restaurants, and shops is located six miles south of the town of Jackson. Visitors flock here for Shrimp Fettucine, Crab Corn Soup, and many other delicacies.

Along a winding country road about twenty miles west of Boston proudly stands this famous inn. The oldest inn in America, it has an atmosphere of age and tranquility. The inn originally was called the Red Horse Tavern. The name was changed, however, after Henry Wadsworth Longfellow's Tales of a Wayside Inn *were published. Longfellow based the tales on his knowledge of the Red Horse. Henry Ford bought the property in the 1920s and completely restored it. A water-powered gristmill he reproduced is used today to grind meal for breads served at the inn. Its beautiful colonial dining room offers fine cuisine with many regional dishes. You will find here true friendliness and New England hospitality.*

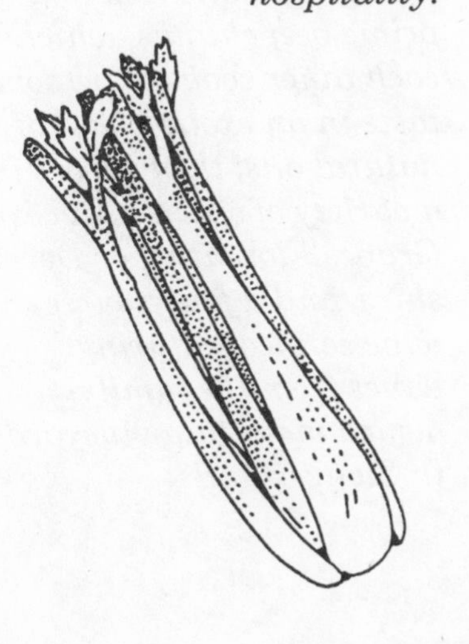

Braised Celery

12 ounces celery hearts
3 tablespoons butter or margarine
2 tablespoons flour
2 cups chicken stock (hot)
1/4 teaspoon celery seeds
Salt and freshly ground pepper to taste

Cut the celery on a slight diagonal, about 1/4 inch thick. Melt butter in a 2-quart saucepan. Add the sliced celery and cook slowly for 10 minutes, stirring with a wooden spoon occasionally to prevent burning and to insure even cooking. Sprinkle flour over the cooking celery and stir to blend the flour and butter. Add the hot chicken stock and stir until the ingredients have blended together for 3 to 5 minutes; stir in the celery seeds. Cover and cook slowly for about 20 to 25 minutes, or until the celery is tender. Stir occasionally while cooking. Season with salt and pepper to taste. Serves 4 to 6.

Longfellow's Wayside Inn

Sudbury, Massachsetts 01776
(508) 443-8846

Red Cabbage

1 cup distilled white vinegar
1 tablespoon sugar
1 teaspoon salt
1 head red cabbage, cut into pieces
3 tablespoons water
2 apples, peeled, cored, and sliced
1 onion, sliced
1 large or 2 small bay leaves, 1/4 teaspoon allspice
a few peppercorns, all tied in cheesecloth
1 tablespoon bacon fat
1 teaspoon cornstarch

Mix the vinegar, sugar, and salt. Add to the cabbage and water. Add the apples, onion, and spice bag. Stir and cook for 15 minutes. Add the bacon fat and cook for 15 minutes longer. Mix the cornstarch with a little of the juice and return to thicken. Stir often. Serves 4 to 6.

Lowell Inn

102 North Second Street
Stillwater, Minnesota 55082
(612) 439-1100

This great inn stands on the site of the stately Swayer House, erected in 1848, some ten years before Minnesota achieved statehood. The Sawyer House of that long-ago day brought the civilized East to the frontier. But as more and more of the East's modernity came to the West, the Sawyer House became an anachronism and fell to the wrecker's ball in 1924. A new Williamsburg-style hotel, the Lowell Inn, rose in its place. Today it recreates the aura of a long ago and gracious era, with fine antiques, linens, tableware, and glassware. The food service is simple but exquisite. The menu consists of Escargot Bourguignonne (imported Burgundy snails sauteed in a secret seasoning), Fondue Bourguignonne (selected prime beef chunks, which each diner cooks to personal taste in an exotic blend of natural oils, then savors in a variety of special sauces), Grapes Florentine or Devonshire, and a four-course wine service featuring wines from the family-owned mountain vineyards in Switzerland.

The name "down to earth" applied to this inn has two meanings. First, the structure itself is low, ground-hugging and earth-integrated, situated on 86 acres of peaceful woods and rolling hills. The second meaning has to do with the hospitality offered to guests. The inn features cozy, quiet rooms and spacious leisure areas. Breakfast is a memorable experience, with cuisine ranging from country to continental. Guests are invited to stroll through the woods and through the pastures inhabited by cattle, horses, and geese. Fishermen may try their luck in two large stocked ponds.

Cabbage Casserole

1/2 head cabbage, chopped
1 small onion, chopped
1/2 green bell pepper, chopped
3 tablespoons butter or margarine
3 tablespoons flour
1 cup milk
1/2 cup shredded Cheddar cheese
Cornbread crumbs

Cook the cabbage, onion, and green pepper in lightly salted water until tender. Drain. Melt the butter in a saucepan. Stir in the flour and cook for 1 minute, stirring constantly. Slowly add the milk, stir until thickened. Add the cheese; blend until melted. Layer the drained cabbage mixture and cheese sauce in a greased casserole. Make several layers, ending with sauce. Bake at 325 degrees F. for about 30 minutes, or until bubbly. Top with crumbs and return to oven until lightly browned. Serves 4.

Note: Corn bread stuffing mix may be used for the crumbs, or sprinkle plain corn bread crumbs with poultry seasoning.

Down to Earth Lifestyles

Route 22
Parkville, Missouri 64152
(816) 891-1018

Curried Squash and Apples with Couscous

Here's a delicious curried squash recipe from Susan and Richard Strafursky's Savannah Inn.

1 small butternut squash, peeled, seeded, and cut into large chunks
1 large apple, cored and sliced
1/2 small onion, sliced
2 tablespoons raisins
1/2 teaspoon curry powder
1 tablespoon honey
2 tablespoons water

Couscous
1/3 cup water
2 tablespoons margarine
1/3 cup couscous
1/2 teaspoon curry powder

To prepare the squash and apple: layer the squash, apple, and onion in a greased shallow baking dish. Sprinkle on top the raisins, curry powder, honey, soy sauce, and water. cover and bake at 375 degrees for 45 minutes. (or microwave on full power for 15 minutes, turning after 8 minutes.)

While the squash and apples are baking, prepare the couscous. Bring the water to a boil in a small saucepan. Melt the margarine in the water. Stir in the couscous and curry powder. Remove from the heat and cover.

When the squash and apples are done, spread the couscous over the casserole and broil briefly to lightly brown the topping. Serves 4.

Note: This recipe works well as a main dish, serving 2.

Savannah Inn

330 Savannah Road
Lewes, Delaware 19958
(302) 645-5592

Ratatouille

1 large onion, minced
1 clove garlic, crushed
1/2 cup plus 2 teaspoons olive oil
6 tomatoes, peeled, seeded, and chopped
3 zucchini, sliced
1 small eggplant, cubed
3 green bell peppers, julienne-cut
1 teaspoon dried basil, or two teaspoons fresh
Salt and freshly ground pepper to taste

Saute the onion with the garlic in olive oil until golden. Saute the eggplant in a separate skillet in 1/2 cup olive oil until golden.

Combine the two mixtures, add the tomatoes, peppers, zucchini, basil, and salt and pepper to taste. Simmer for 30 minutes, uncovered. Serve warm or chilled.

Note: An attractive way to serve chilled ratatouille is in hollowed-out tomatoes. Garnish with finely diced cucumber.

This great inn's proud history goes back more than a century. Originally it was the summer home of the Hamptons of South Carolina. Many of the most famous names in Southern history came to visit the illustrious Confederate General Wade Hampton and to enjoy hunting, fishing, relaxing, and gracious hospitality on the 1200 acre estate. Today, High Hampton retains the tradition and gracious hospitality of its earlier years. The architecture is rustic and blends with the natural beauty of the mountains and valley. The menu features cuisine with selected original recipes.

High Hampton Inn

Cashiers, North Carolina 28717
(704) 743-2411

Oven Fried Potatoes

Here's a tempting potato recipe hearty enough to satisfy the appetite after a long day skiing.

3 baking potatoes
1/4 cup oil
1 tablespoon grated Parmesan cheese
1/4 teaspoon garlic powder
1/4 teaspoon paprika
1/4 teaspoon pepper
1/4 teaspoon salt

Cut the potatoes into wedges, leaving the skins on. Place the wedges in a single layer in a 9 x 13-inch pan. Combine remaining ingredients and brush over the potato wedges. Bake at 375 degrees for 45 minutes, basting occasionally.

Trail's End

Smith Road
Wilmington, Vermont 05363
(802) 464-2727

Chateau Potatoes

2 pound bag frozen hash browns, thawed
1 11-ounce can cream of chicken soup
1 cup sour cream
2 cups grated Cheddar cheese
4 green onions, sliced
1/4 cup butter, melted
Salt and freshly ground pepper to taste
Crushed corn cereal

In a large bowl, combine the soup, sour cream, 1 cup of cheese, onions, and butter. Add potatoes. Season with salt and pepper. Place in a 9 x 13-inch casserole and top with a mixture of the remaining cheese and the corn cereal. Bake at 350 degrees for 45 minutes. Serves 12 to 15.

This delightful inn rises on a bluff overlooking beautiful Lake Arrowhead in the San Bernadino mountains, with a spectacular view of both lake and mountains. In winter, snow and crackling fires add to the beauty and charm. Innkeepers Jody and Oscar Wilson make a stay here pleasant and memorable. Nearby Lake Arrowhead Village offers attractive shops and restaurants.

Chateau du Lac

P.O. Box 1098
Lake Arrowhead, California 92352
(714) 337-6488

Santa Cruz Rancher Potatoes

Here is a delicious western style potato recipe from New Mexico's Bishop s Lodge.

3 baking potatoes
1/3 teaspoon Margarita salt
4 slices bacon, diced
1 red bell pepper, julienne-cut
1/2 teaspoon whole comino seeds
 (or 1/2 teaspoon ground cumin)
1/4 cup grated Monterey Jack cheese
2 green onions, thinly sliced for garnish

In a small saucepan, place the potatoes and salt. Cover with water and boil the potatoes until they are just done. Drain and let cool. Cut the potatoes into cubes (approximately 16 cubes per potato). Saute the bacon in a large saucepan over medium heat. Add the bell pepper, comino seeds, and boiled potato cubes. Saute until the potatoes are golden brown. Place the potatoes in a small baking dish. Sprinkle the cheese over the top. Heat the potatoes at 375 degrees for 5 minutes or until the cheese is melted. Sprinkle the green onions over the top. Serves 4.

The Bishops Lodge

P.O. Box 2367
Santa Fe, New Mexico 87504
(505) 983-6377

Grandview Lodge, built as a home about 100 years ago, has been in operation for over 50 years. Located in the mountains of North Carolina, it is open to guests year-round. Quiet, scenic, and restful, the lodge is located on two and one-half acres of rolling land with its own apple orchards, grape arbors, and rhubarb patch. The family-style meals are planned and prepared using a variety of locally grown fresh fruits and vegetables. Breads, biscuits, and muffins are home baked. The hosts are Stan and Linda Arnold.

Sweet Potato Casserole

3 cups mashed potatoes
1/2 teaspoon vanilla extract
1/2 cup margarine or butter, melted
1 cup sugar, or less
2 eggs, beaten
1/2 cup milk

Topping
1 cup brown sugar
1/2 cup flour
1/2 cup butter, cut in small pieces
1 cup chopped pecans

In a large mixing bowl, beat together the first 6 ingredients, then pour into one lightly greased 9 x 13-inch or 2 9 x 9-inch baking pans. In a food processor fitted with the steel blade, combine the ingredients for the topping until crumbly; or use a pastry blender to cut the butter into the brown sugar and flour until crumbly. Mix in the pecans. Sprinkle the topping mixture over the sweet potatoes. At this point, the dish can be refrigerated, covered. Bake, uncovered, at 350 degrees for 45 to 50 minutes, until browned and bubbly. Serves 4 to 6.

Grandview Lodge

809 Valley View Circle
Waynesville, North Carolina 28786
(704) 456-5212

Baked Yams

1/2 cup brown sugar
1/2 cup white sugar
1/2 cup butter
1/2 cup water
1 teaspoon allspice
1/2 teaspoon nutmeg
1/4 teaspoon ground ginger
1/4 teaspoon salt
5 eggs
3 pounds yams or sweet potatoes, cooked and mashed
Grated rind and juice of 1 orange
Grated rind and juice of 1 lemon

Cook the sugars and butter with the water until the butter is melted and the sugar dissolved. Add the spices and eggs to the yams and mix well. Add the sugar mixture and mix well. When the mixture is cool, add the orange and lemon rinds and juices. Turn into a baking dish and bake at 350 degrees until a crust forms, about 30 minutes. Serves 6 to 8.

Note: At holiday time, bake the yam mixture in orange shells and use to garnish the turkey platter.

Excelsior House

211 West Austin
Jefferson, Texas 75657
(214) 665-2513

This splendid inn has been in continuous operation since the 1850s. It was restored in 1961 by the Jessie Allen Wise Garden Club, which continues to own and operate it. The brick and timber structure was built by Captain William Perry. It has 14 rooms, each furnished in period furniture and featuring museum-quality antiques. The Presidential Suite features a pair of lavishly appointed rooms, each named for former guests, Presidents Ulysses S. Grant and Rutherford B. Hayes. The huge ballroom and magnificent dining room are crowned by two large French Sevres chandeliers. Delicious food is served in the dining room, by reservation only.

For two centuries the Fearrington farm has been part of the landscape between Chapel Hill and Pittsboro. At the center of the village is the Fearrington House, committed to the five C's of hospitality: Character, Courtesy, Calm, Charm and Cuisine. The inn's restaurant has been celebrated in practically every magazine of note. Sophisticated southern cuisine is the order of the day.

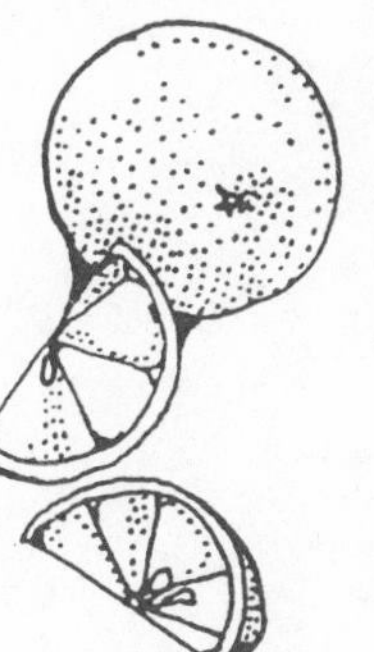

Orange Saffron Rice

A few threads saffron
2 1/2 cups chicken stock
2 tablespoons butter
1 small onion, finely chopped
1 1/2 cups long grain rice
1/3 cup orange juice
Grated rind from 1 orange
2 green onions, thinly sliced
2 tablespoons minced parsley

Soak the saffron in a small amount of water for 5 minutes or add to the chicken stock. Heat the butter in a skillet over moderate heat, add the onion, and cook until translucent. Add the rice and cook for 3 minutes or until it looks transparent. Bring the chicken stock to a boil, and add the rice onion mixture. Reduce the heat, cover and simmer for about 18 minutes. Add orange juice, orange rind, and green onions. Serves 6 to 8.

Fearrington House

2000 Fearrington Village Center
Pittsboro, North Carolina 28717
(919) 542-2121

Risotto alla Pana

This rice dish is just a sampling of Joseph Vinnani's delightful classic cuisine. The Ragged Garden menu features an emphasis on Northern Italy.

3 tablespoons butter
1 onion, finely chopped
1 cup uncooked rice, rinsed
4 to 5 cups chicken stock, heated
1/2 cup heavy cream
4 or 5 teaspoons grated Parmesan cheese

Melt the butter in a heavy pot over low heat; add the onion and cook until soft and translucent. Add the rice and mix well (the rice should be coated with the butter mixture). Then add 1 cup stock and stir until the rice absorbs all the liquid. Continue adding stock, one cup at a time, until the rice is cooked. Stir in the cream and cheese and serve in soup bowls. Serves 4.

Ragged Garden Inn

Sunset Drive, P.O. Box 1927
Blowing Rock, North Carolina 28605
(704) 295-9703

This rice and pecan dish is one of the many recipes for which Texas' Crystal River Inn has become justly famous.

Rice and Pecans

1 1/2 cups rice
3 3/4 cups water
1 1/2 teaspoons salt
2 tablespoons butter or margarine (for toasting pecans)
1 cup pecan halves, toasted
1/4 cup minced parsley
1/4 cup onions, diced and sauteed
1/4 cup celery, diced and sauteed

Cook the rice in salted water using your favorite method. When the rice is fluffy and water is absorbed, stir in the toasted pecan halves, parsley, and sauteed onions and celery using a fork to keep rice fluffy.

Note: To toast the pecans, melt butter or margarine in a skillet over medium heat. Stir the pecans until they are crisp and beginning to brown. Watch and stir to avoid burning. Serves 4 to 6.

Crystal River Inn

326 West Hopkin
San Marcos, Texas 78666
(512) 396-3739

Risi e Bisi con Mele

2 cups brown rice, rinsed
2 1/2 cups water
Salt
1 small onion, chopped
1/2 cup butter
2 baking apples, peeled, cored, and cubed
1/4 cup corn oil
1/4 cup soy sauce
1/2 cup toasted pignoli nuts

In a large saucepan, place the rice and water. Add salt to taste. Bring to a boil and cook rice to the desired tenderness, about 40 minutes. Drain. In a frying pan, saute the onion in the butter until golden. Add the apples and the peas; set aside. In a wok, place 1/4 cup corn oil, or enough to cover the bottom of the pan. Heat until smoking, then quickly add the drained rice. Stir frequently. Add the soy sauce and mix well. Gently blend in the apples, peas, and pignoli nuts. Serve immediately. Serves 6.

Albergo Allegria

Route 296
Windham, New York 12496
(518) 734-5560

Albergo Allegria offers a taste of Europe in the Catskills. Here one enters the grace and beauty of another century with a touch of Gothic Victorian. The food at Albergo Allegria has an Italian flair and satisfies the heartiest appetite. All dishes are homemade and prepared to order by Chef Edward.

The owners of the Great Southern Hotel have a pet squirrel that lives in the trees on their front lawn. This tame squirrel drinks cream from small plastic containers and responds to the sound of a whistle. No wonder the inn is known as a "hotel of home-like atmosphere." Southern cuisine is served in the Victorian Tea Room.

Spinach Cheese Grits

4 cups of water
1/2 teaspoon salt
1 cup quick grits
1/2 teaspoon granulated garlic, or more
1 10-ounce package of frozen chopped spinach, thawed and squeezed dry
2 cups grated Cheddar cheese
4 eggs

Boil the water and add the salt and garlic. Stir in the quick grits. Cook for about 2 minutes. Remove from heat. Stir in one cup of the grated Cheddar cheese. Stir in the spinach. Beat the eggs slightly and stir into the mixture. Pour into a greased baking dish and bake at 350 degrees for 30 to 45 minutes or until puffy and firm in the center. Top with the remaining grated cheese and allow to melt in the warm oven for a few minutes. This dish can be served with any meal from brunch to dinner. Serves 8.

The Great Southern Hotel

127 West Cedar
Brinkley, Arkansas 72021
(501) 734-4955

Williamsburg Carrot Pudding

3 eggs, separated
4 tablespoons sugar
1 1/2 tablespoons cornstarch
1 cup milk
3 cups (2 pounds) sliced, cooked, and mashed carrots
3 tablespoons butter
1 teaspoon salt
1 cup fine bread crumbs
1 cup cream
1/2 teaspoon freshly grated nutmeg
1/4 cup cream sherry

Beat the egg yolks and the sugar until light, and set aside. Mix the cornstarch with a small amount of the milk. Heat the remaining milk, add the cornstarch mixture, and stir until smooth and slightly thickened. Stir a small amount of the hot cornstarch mixture into the egg yolks and sugar. Stir to mix well, then return to the hot milk and cornstarch, cooking and stirring over medium heat until smooth and thick.

Add the carrots, butter, salt, and bread crumbs; blend evenly. Stir in the cream and add the nutmeg and sherry, mixing well. Beat the egg whites until they hold firm peaks; fold into the carrot mixture.

Pour into a greased 2-quart casserole. Place the casserole in a pan of hot water and bake at 300 degrees for 30 minutes. Increase the heat to 350 degrees and bake an additional 45 minutes or until a knife inserted in the center comes out clean. Serves 10 to 12.

Inn at Levelfields

P.O. Box 216
Lancaster, Virginia 22503
(804) 435-6887

This carrot pudding recipe is just one of many that have given the cuisine at Warren and Doris Sadler's historic Inn at Levelfield's a wide-spread reputation for fine dining.

Architecture and antiques are two commodities which one might not expect to find in a small resort hotel, but the Church Hill Inn offers an elegant sampling of each. Most guest rooms exit directly to one of five cozy parlors, each with its own fireplace and some with sitting porches. The inn is designed in the English country style.

Artichoke Souffle

8 to 10 slices bread, cubed
2 cups quartered artichoke hearts
2 cups grated mozzarella cheese
1/2 cup grated Parmesan cheese
1 tomato, sliced (optional)
4 eggs
2/3 cup milk
3 tablespoons mayonnaise
1/2 teaspoon basil
1/2 teaspoon oregano
1 tablespoon chopped parsley

Layer half the bread cubes in a greased 9 x 13-inch pan. Top with artichokes, cheeses, tomato, and the rest of the bread cubes. Whisk the remaining ingredients. Pour over the layers. Cover and chill overnight. Bake at 325 degrees for 40 to 50 minutes. Serves 9 to 12.

Church Hill Inn

425 Gateway Drive
Sister Bay, Wisconsin 54234
(800) 422-4906

Hot 'N' Spicy Red Beans and Rice

These taste-tempting beans should be served over cooked rice. Leftovers are unlikely, but if you have any, they freeze beautifully.

1 lb. dried red beans
1 lb. spicy pork sausage
3 medium onions, chopped
1 1/2 tsp. salt
1 1/2 tsp. pepper
1 tbsp. rosemary
1 tbsp. thyme
1 tbsp. tarragon
1 tbsp. oregano

Rinse the beans and soak in water for approximately 30 minutes. Drain, then cook in just enough water to cover for about 30 minutes over a low fire or in a crockpot. Add the remaining ingredients, cover and simmer for five to six hours or until beans are tender. Stir occasionally during the cooking time, especially at the beginning to break up sausage meat.

Cedar Grove

P.O. Box B
Vicksburg, Mississippi 39181
(601) 636-1605

One of the South's largest and loveliest historic mansions, Cedar Grove is exquisitely furnished with many original antiques, including gaslit chandeliers, gold leaf mirrors, and Italian marble mantels. The mansion was built by John A. Klein as a wedding present for his bride. They returned from their European honeymoon with many architectural amenities today enjoyed by visitors from around the world. Guests stay in luxurious guest rooms or suites, all with private baths. The grounds are enhanced by magnificent formal gardens and gazebos. The formal dining room, still in use today, was the setting for many special occasions. Confederate President Jefferson Davis danced in the magnificent ballroom, and a Union cannonball remains lodged in the parlor wall.

This delectable pepperoni dish comes from Chef Edward's kitchen at Albergo Allegria in New York.

Pepperoni con Mozzarella

6 bell peppers, green, yellow or red
8 ounces mozzarella, homemade preferably
Salt and freshly ground pepper to taste
3 tablespoons chopped fresh basil
4 cloves garlic, crushed
Olive oil

Place the peppers under a hot broiler. When the skin swells and is partially charred on one side, turn another side toward the flame. When all the skin is blistered and slightly charred, remove the peppers; peel them while still hot.

Cut the peeled peppers lengthwise into strips 1 1/2 to 2 inches wide, removing all seeds and the pulpy inner core. Pat the strips dry with a cloth or paper towel.

Choose a serving dish that will hold the peppers in four layers. Arrange a layer of peppers on the bottom. Place a layer of sliced mozzarella over the peppers. Add a pinch of salt, a liberal grinding of pepper, a pinch of basil, and a clove of garlic. Repeat until all the peppers and cheese are used up. Add enough olive oil to cover the top layer.

Put the dish in the refrigerator for at least four hours, then bring to room temperature before serving. If you prepare several days ahead of time, remove the garlic after 24 hours. Serves 6.

Albergo Allegria

Route 296
Windham, New York 12496
(518) 734-5560

Green Pepper and Mushroom Relish

1 cup salad oil
2 cups cider vinegar
1/4 cup sugar
2 Spanish onions, sliced
1 dozen green peppers, seeded and sliced lengthwise
1 1/2 pounds fresh mushrooms wiped clean and sliced
Salt and freshly ground pepper, to taste
Garlic salt to taste
Pinch of oregano

Heat the oil, vinegar, and sugar. Add the onions and peppers. Simmer only until al dente (10 to 15 minutes). Add the mushrooms and seasonings. Simmer for about 10 minutes. Serve warm or cold. Serves 6 to 8.

The Bird and Bottle Inn

Route 9
Garrison, New York 10524
(914) 424-3000

Pleasures of the palate are well-tended at the Bird and Bottle. From 1761, when it was known as Warren's Tavern, the inn has had a colorful and romantic history. During the Revolutionary War, weary travelers tarried over tankards of ale or grog or partook of Warren's fare. Troops of General Washington's army added to the gaiety. The inn's motto reads: "Where those who favor us with their custom shall experience every convenience and attention which they command." Today, the inn's bedrooms are furnished in Early American antiques and feature canopy or four-poster beds, private baths, and wood-burning fireplaces.

Peanut Stuffing

3/4 cup minced onion
1 1/2 cups chopped celery, stalks and leaves
3/4 cup butter or margarine
8 cups soft bread cubes
2 teaspoons salt
1 1/2 teaspoon crushed sage leaves
1 teaspoon thyme leaves
1/2 teaspoon pepper
2 cups coarsely chopped peanuts

In a large skillet, cook and stir the onion and celery in the butter until tender. Stir in about one-third of the bread cubes. Place in a deep bowl. Add the remaining ingredients and toss. Then place in a greased 9-inch baking dish and bake for 30 minutes at 350 degrees. Makes 9 cups.

Note: This stuffing is recommended for turkey, chicken, or pork. The quantity is sufficient for a 12-pound turkey.

At Wayside Inn, a twenty-one-room country inn founded in 1797 in the beautiful Shenandoah Valley of Virginia, fine food and lodging have been time honored traditions for three centuries. In its early days it was a way station where teams of horses waited to harness up to stagecoaches traveling the Shenandoah Valley Turnpike. The inn was refurbished in the 1960s, retaining its eighteenth-century atmosphere and the charm of an older era in a setting of natural beauty, unmarred by time. On Saturday nights, a guitarist strolls from table to table during dinner. On show nights at the nearby Wayside Theater, dinner is served early so guests can be in their seats by curtain time.

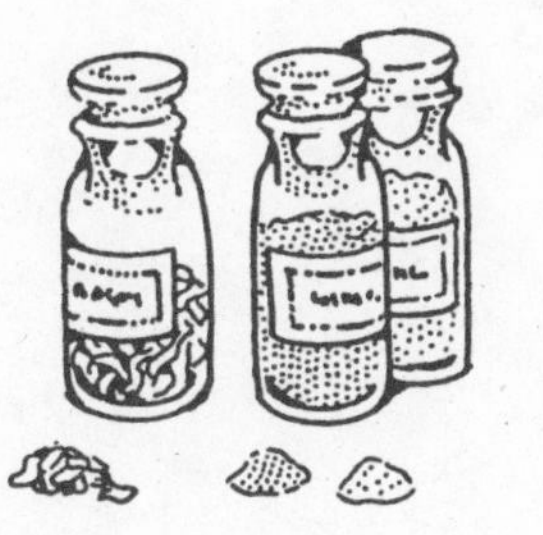

Wayside Inn

7783 Main Street
Middletown, Virginia 22645
(703) 869-1797

Boston Baked Beans

You may have heard of Boston Baked Beans, but you probably haven't tasted the real thing until you've tried this recipe from Maine's Black Point Inn.

2 pounds white pea beans
2 quarts water
1/2 pound fat salt pork
2 teaspoons salt
1 cup molasses
1 teaspoon dry mustard
2 teaspoons brown sugar

Wash and pick beans. Cover with the water and bring to a boil. Boil for a few minutes; turn off the heat and let stand for 1 hour. Without draining, cook the beans slowly until the skins burst. Drain, saving the cooking water. Cover the salt pork with boiling water. Let stand a couple of minutes and drain. Gash the pork every half-inch or so, without cutting through the rind. Put the beans into a large pot (earthen if available). Push the pork into the beans; leaving the rind exposed on top. Mix together the salt, molasses, mustard, and brown sugar. Add 1 cup of the reserved water to this mixture and bring to the boiling point, then pour over the beans. Cover the pot and bake for 6 to 8 hours at 250 degrees F. Add water as needed to keep beans moist. Uncover the beans for the last hour so the rind will be crisp and brown. The beans are traditionally served with brown bread. Serves 10.

Note: If desired, 1 cup chopped onions may be added to the beans before baking.

Black Point Inn

510 Black Point Road
Prouts Neck, Maine 04074
(207) 883-4126

This delicious rice pilaf recipe is one of the specialties of Connecticut's historic Old Lyme Inn.

Harvest Pilaf

8 cups chicken stock or bouillon
1 cup wild rice
1 cup dried currants
4 tablespoons thyme
4 tablespoons marjoram
5 tablespoons salt, or to taste, depending on saltiness of stock or bouillon
4 teaspoons black pepper
1 cup brown rice
1 cup white rice
1 cup toasted pecans, crushed
1 cup toasted pignoli nuts
1 cup bulgur

Bring the chicken stock or bouillon to a boil. Add the wild rice, currants, herbs, and salt and pepper. Return to a boil; after 5 to 8 minutes, add the brown rice, white rice, and nuts. Bring to a boil again; simmer over low heat until the rice is tender and the liquid has nearly all been absorbed, about 20 minutes.

Add the bulgur, stirring in until the grain expands- not more than 3 to 5 minutes --- and until the various grains are well blended. Serves 12.

Old Lyme Inn
P.O. Box 787
Old Lyme, Connecticut 06371
(203) 434-2600

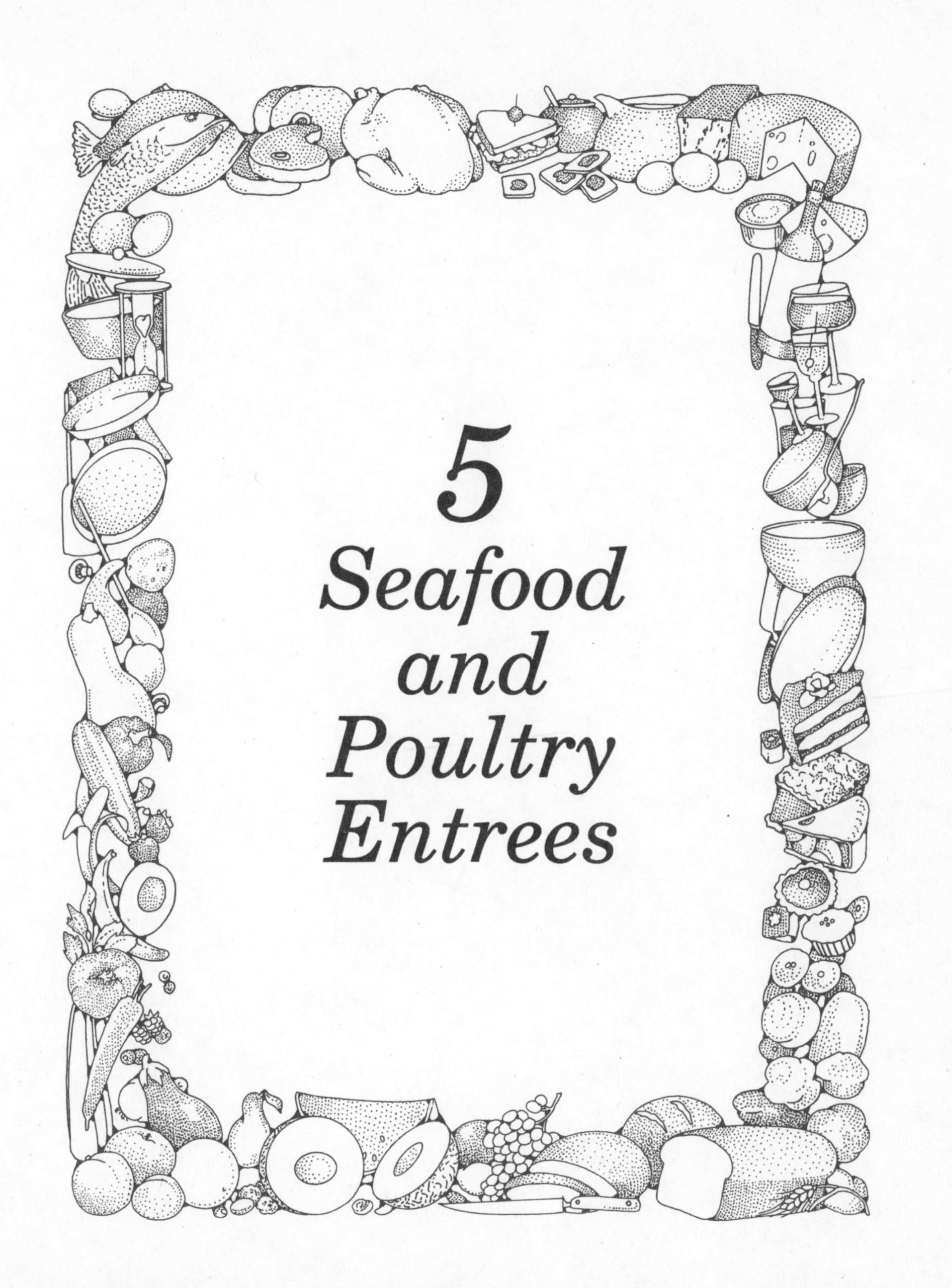

5 Seafood and Poultry Entrees

This turn-of-the-century summer retreat for writer Frank Simonds was later converted into an inn by a Swiss couple. Today, the inn's decor and cuisine reflect a harmonious blend of New England and European Alpine traditions. The comfortably furnished rooms are named after writers. The chalet dining room offers truly breathtaking views of the White Mountains' Presidential Range. The innkeepers are Frank, Trudy, and Peter Cutrone. Snowvillage Inn, known for its excellent food, hosts Steven Raichlin's Cooking School several times a year.

Chicken Marsala

4 lean bacon slices
2 large skinless boneless chicken breasts
4 slices smoked Gouda cheese
1/2 10-ounce package frozen chopped spinach, thawed and drained well
Salt and freshly ground pepper to taste
1/2 cup flour
1/2 cup Marsala wine
1/2 cup heavy cream
1 teaspoon minced fresh parsley

Fry the bacon over medium heat until almost crisp. Drain and cool on paper toweling. Leave the bacon fat in the pan and set aside.

Halve and trim the chicken breasts (remove the tenders if there are any and use for another recipe). Carefully cut a pocket in each breast and stuff with a layer of one strip bacon, 1/4 of the spinach, and one slice of cheese. Close the pocket with one or two toothpicks. Sprinkle the breasts with salt and pepper and lightly coat with flour.

Reheat the pan with the bacon fat over high heat and lightly brown the breasts on both sides. Remove to a warm platter. Add the Marsala and cream, whisking up all the brown particles in the pan. Bring to a boil. Return the chicken breasts to the pan, reduce the heat, and simmer, covered, for 10 minutes.

Remove the breasts and take out the toothpicks. Place on a warm platter. Meantime, reduce the sauce to a creamy-thick consistency and adjust the flavor with salt and pepper.

Pour the sauce over the chicken, sprinkle with minced parsley, and serve at once. Serves 4.

Snowvillage Inn

Snowville, New Hampshire 03849
(603) 447-2818

Tulip Tree Chicken Curry

4 slices bacon
1/2 cup sliced celery
1 onion, chopped
1 clove garlic, minced
2 tablespoons flour
1 cup milk
1 cup water
3/4 cup applesauce
3 or 4 teaspoons curry powder
2 chicken bouillon cubes
3 cups cubed cooked chicken
2 1/2 cups cooked rice
Raisins, for garnish
Chutney, for garnish

Cook the bacon until crisp, drain, and reserve the fat. Crumble the bacon and set aside. Cook the celery, onion, and garlic in the bacon fat. Blend in the flour. Stir in the milk, water, applesauce, curry powder, and bouillon cubes. Cook and stir until thickened and bubbly. Stir in the chicken and bacon. Serve over cooked rice with raisins and chutney. Serves 4.

Tulip Tree Inn

Chittenden Dam Road
Chittenden, Vermont 05737
(802) 483-6213

Here is a true country inn. There's a romantic countryside atmosphere. and elegant country cuisine. The visitors can amble down a country road, picnic by a stream and escape to enjoy the solitude. Here is a chance to rekindle one's zest for life, an opportunity to escape from the everyday, and an occasion to relax.

This New England inn is housed in several charming buildings, the original being a Victorian mansion built in 1875. The inn serves American and continental specialties prepared by experts. Guests dine in the inn's Tavern and Holyoke rooms. They may choose from more than 100 wines from around the world. The kitchen has no doors, so guests may come in to watch their food being prepared or to see the collection of handsome copper cookware.

Chicken Diable

4 broiler chicken halves
4 tablespoons butter
4 cloves garlic, chopped
1 teaspoon freshly ground pepper
4 teaspoons Dijon mustard
Dash of Worcestershire sauce
Salt to taste
Fresh bread crumbs

Make a mixture of the butter and the remaining ingredients, except the bread crumbs. Coat the broiler halves with the mixture. Sprinkle lightly with fresh bread crumbs and bake at 450 degrees for 15 minutes. Remove and paint with more mixture. Return to the oven and bake until done, approximately 30 minutes more. Serves 4.

Yankee Peddlar Inn

1866 Northampton Street
Holyoke, Massachusetts 01040
(413) 532-9494

Breast of Chicken Saute Hongroise

6 large chicken breast halves
Butter or margarine
1/2 tablespoon chopped shallots
1 tablespoon Hungarian paprika
1 cup Supreme Sauce (recipe below)
1 1/2 cups light cream
2 ounces cooked lean ham, cut into strips
3 ounces dry white wine

Saute the chicken breasts in the butter or margarine until they are brown and tender. Place the breasts on a platter and keep warm. In the same pan saute the shallots and add the wine. Add the paprika, Supreme Sauce, and cream. Cook for a few minutes. Sprinkle the ham strips over the breasts. Strain the sauce through a fine sieve and pour over the breasts. Serves 6.

Supreme Sauce
4 teaspoons melted butter
4 teaspoons flour
1 cup chicken stock, boiling
Salt and freshly ground pepper to taste

Whip together the melted butter and flour. Cook slowly, stirring constantly, for 4 to 5 minutes. Do not burn. Slowly add the boiling chicken stock, whisking constantly. Season with salt and pepper. Makes 1 cup.

The Colonial Inn

48 Monument Square
Concord, Massachusetts 01742
(508) 369-9200

This is truly an authentic New England-style inn with a wonderful dining room capturing the atmosphere of a tavern from colonial days. It is decorated with authentic memorabilia of early trades and merchants. The Yankee-style cooking is genuine with authentic flavors to sparkle the appetite. Overlooking the Concord Village Green, the inn offers 60 guest rooms with all the comforts. Its tradition of gracious hospitality dates back to 1716 when Captain James Minot, a soldier and physician, built the oldest part of the inn. Since then various owners have rebuilt and added to the inn.

The Griswold Inn has catered to travelers and neighbors for two centuries. In 1775, Sala Griswold purchased the land and began construction on the inn, opening for business in 1776 and promising "first class accommodations" to travelers. It has offered that ever since. The inn has been under the direction of only five families. Today, it is owned by William G. Winterer, a former New York investment banker.

Since 1776

Griswold Inn

Mrs. Griswold's Breast of Chicken

4 plump chicken breasts
Clarified butter
16 small canned artichoke hearts
2 cups sliced mushrooms
1/2 cup chopped shallots
Few slivers garlic
1 cup dry white wine
1 tablespoon arrowroot or flour mixed with a small amount of water

Bone the chicken breasts, being careful not to remove the skin, and cut into bite-size pieces. Saute these pieces in clarified butter, skin side down, turning carefully until brown on all sides. Place on a heated platter. In the same pan, saute the artichoke hearts until brown. Remove them to the heated platter. Then in the same pan saute the mushrooms, shallots, and garlic. When the mushrooms are tender and the shallots transparent, transfer the chicken and artichokes to the pan. Add the wine; simmer until the chicken is tender. Strain off the juices and thicken with arrowroot or flour and pour over the chicken mixture. It is served at Griswold Inn with brown rice or bulgar wheat pilaf. Serves 4.

Griswold Inn

36 Main Street
Essex, Connecticut 06426
(203) 767-1776

Chicken Breast Parmesan

4 cups bread crumbs
1/2 cup chopped fresh parsley
1 1/2 cups grated Parmesan cheese
4 teaspoons salt
2 teaspoons pepper
20 chicken breasts, skinned and boned
1 cup melted butter

Combine the bread crumbs, parsley, cheese, salt, and pepper. Dip the chicken in the melted butter, then roll in the bread crumb mixture. Bake at 350 degrees for 20 to 30 minutes or until the chicken is done. Serves 10 to 20.

The Inn On The Square

3 West Montgomery
Oakland, Illinois 61943
(217) 349-2289

The Inn on the Square offers a potpourri of the "village experience." It specializes in warm hospitality, fine food, and a friendly atmosphere. Blending the old with the new, the inn offers delightful overnight accommodations, and a wonderful library for relaxation. The tea room serves simple but elegant luncheons, with private dinner parties a specialty in the evening. The University of Illinois, Eastern Illinois University, Lincoln Log Cabin State Park, and an Amish settlement are all nearby.

Located on 60 acres of woods and pastures in the heart of Ohio's Amish country, the contemporary Inn at Honey Run is a weekend retreat, a conference center, a birdwatcher's paradise, and a place to indulge in heartland cuisine. Fresh vegetables, steamed to perfection; pies and breads made by our Amish bakers; simple food made as Grandmother made it, but with concern for health. Nutritional analysis is available for all inn recipes.

Boneless Breast of Country Chicken

4 skinless, boneless chicken breast halves
3/4 teaspoon salt
1/2 teaspoon marjoram leaves
1/4 teaspoon pepper
1 cup half-and-half
1 egg
3/4 cup bread crumbs
1/2 cup butter or margarine

Pound the chicken to a 1/2-inch thickness. Layer the chicken, salt, marjoram and pepper in a shallow baking dish. Pour the half-and-half over the chicken. Cover tightly with plastic wrap and marinate in the refrigerator overnight. To serve, beat the egg with 2 tablespoons of the half-and-half from the chicken. Dip the chicken into the egg mixture and then into the bread crumbs. In a skillet, melt the butter; add the chicken pieces and saute for 5 minutes on each side. Transfer the chicken to a serving platter. Serves 4.

Inn at Honey Run

6920 County Road 203
Millersburg, Ohio 44654
(216) 674-0011

Chicken Breast en Feuilletee

1/2 cup diced onion
2 1/2 tablespoons clarified butter
Salt and freshly ground pepper to taste
Pinch of nutmeg
3 tablespoons flour
1 cup warm chicken stock
2 tablespoons heavy cream
4 boned chicken breast halves, 4 ounces each
Butter
Prepared or homemade puff pastry, or packaged frozen pastry shells that have been rolled out
4 slices cooked ham
4 slices provolone or Swiss cheese
1 egg, beaten
Veloute Sauce

Saute the diced onions in the clarified butter until they are limp and translucent; do not brown. Season with salt, pepper, and nutmeg. Add the flour and blend thoroughly. Add the chicken stock and cream. Cook, stirring constantly, until the sauce thickens. Cool in the refrigerator.
Saute the chicken breasts in a little butter until they are almost done; do not overcook. Trim.
Roll out the puff pastry to a 1/4 inch thickness and cut into four 4-inch squares. Place a chicken breast on one half of each pastry square. Top with a little of the onion sauce, then add a slice of ham and a slice of cheese, trimmed to fit. Brush the edges of the pastry with egg glaze. Fold the empty half of the pastry square over the filling. Press the edges together to make a tight seal. At this point, the pastry envelopes can be frozen for later use. Thaw at least one hour before using. Bake at 350 degrees for about 25 minutes. Serve immediately with Veloute Sauce. Serves 4.

Pine Needles

P.O. Box 88
Southern Pines, North Carolina 28387
(919) 692-7111

Pine Needles is a small, intimate resort inn for those who desire a private getaway offering the ultimate in accommodations, recreation, and dining. The rustic clubhouse overlooks one of the most popular golf courses in the Pinehurst area, known as the Golf Capital of the World. Casual elegance, with warmth, charm, and gracious hospitality, has been the legacy of the Bell family since they bought Pine Needles in 1953. Chef Elbartus Van Lienden shares his culinary artistry here.

Lemon Chicken

2 pounds chicken parts
Salt
1 cup fresh lemon juice
2 teaspoons marjoram leaves
1 teaspoon thyme
1 teaspoon onion salt

Rub the chicken with salt, then place in a baking dish skin side down. Mix the remaining ingredients together and pour over the chicken. Bake at 400 degrees for 45 minutes and then turn over, skin side up, and bake for another 20 minutes, basting the chicken every 10 minutes until brown and crispy. Serves 2 or 3.

The Irma

1192 Sheridan Avenue
P.O. Drawer A
Cody, Wyoming 82414

The Irma Hotel was built by Colonel William F. "Buffalo Bill" Cody in 1902 and named for his daughter, Irma. The hotel is the grand old lady of downtown Cody, and reflects Buffalo Bill's own style, the essence of western hospitality. The restaurant serves both the tourist traveling to Yellowstone Park and the local clientele and offers a menu to fill the needs of both. Entrees include old-fashioned specials such as meatloaf and braised sirloin tips and newer items like teriyaki chicken and seafood-stuffed tomatoes.

Chicken Saute Sec

2 8-ounce boneless, skinless chicken breasts
1/2 cup sliced mushrooms
4 medium shallots, diced fine
1 clove garlic, diced fine
1/2 red onion, diced fine
1 tablespoon olive oil
1 tablespoon chopped fresh oregano
1 tablespoon chopped fresh basil
1/2 cup white wine
1 teaspoon unsalted butter
1/2 cup chicken broth
1/4 cup heavy cream

Saute the chicken, mushrooms, shallots, garlic, and onion in the olive oil for about 5 minutes, turning the chicken frequently. Add the herbs, white wine, butter, and chicken broth to the pan. Reduce by one quarter; add the cream and reduce by half. Serve immediately. Serves 2.

Outlook Inn

Orcas Island
Eastsound, Washington 98245
(206) 376-2581

Located on the sea, on the loveliest of all the San Juan Islands, this inn looks as if it had been transplanted from the Maine coast. It has its own private beach, a pond, and flower gardens. It was first built as a cabin, then expanded into the local general store, barber shop, and post office in 1888, with a jail in the rear. Since that time, there have been several remodelings and additions. Today, the finest food on the island is served to guests and the public by an award-winning chef, Antony Vincenza Carbone.

Here is one of the finest guest ranches in the West, nestled in one of the most spectacular and least explored regions of America: The Sawtooth and White Cloud mountain ranges of central Idaho. Established in 1930, its carpenters hand-crafted the lodge from the same lodgepole pine felled by the basin's pioneers for their early homes. Encircling the ranch are hundreds of miles of trails meandering through the Sawtooth Wilderness; the mountains smell of pine and in late spring are splashed with millions of alpine flowers.

Mediterranean Chicken

1/2 cup plus 1 tablespoon Feta cheese
1/4 cup minced green onion
Freshly ground pepper to taste
4 6-to-8-ounces chicken breast halves, boneless but skin left on
3 tablespoons clarified butter
2 small shallots, minced
1/4 teaspoon chopped fresh parsley or basil
3 small cloves garlic, minced
1 teaspoon dried oregano
1 cup sliced mushrooms
1 tablespoon flour
1/3 cup white wine
1/2 cup chicken stock
1/2 cup diced tomatoes

Mix the 1/2 cup Feta cheese with the green onion and pepper to taste. Flatten the chicken breasts and lightly pound. Divide the Feta filling equally between the four breasts. Place the filling in the middle of each breast and carefully fold the chicken around the filling. Place on a small shallow baking dish. Bake skin side up at 375 degrees for 35 to 40 minutes.

Heat a small skillet over medium heat and add the clarified butter. Add the shallots, parsley, garlic, oregano, and mushrooms. Saute briefly. Add the flour and gently blend. Stirring constantly, slowly add white wine. Once the mixture is blended and slightly thickened, add the chicken stock, continuing to stir until completely blended. Add the tomatoes and 1 tablespoon Feta cheese and let simmer for 10 minutes. Adjust seasonings if needed and serve over the baked chicken breasts. Serves 4.

Note: Minced red bell pepper, green bell pepper, olives, or spinach may be added to the breast stuffing.

The Idaho Rocky Mountain Ranch

HC64, Box 9934
Stanley, Idaho 83278
(208) 774-3544

Country Chicken

1/4 cup (or more) olive oil
4 large red bell peppers, cored, seeded, and quartered
2 2 1/2-pound chickens, quartered
Coarse salt and freshly ground pepper to taste
1 1/2 pounds sweet Italian sausage, pierced
1 1/2 cups dry Marsala wine
1/4 pound mushrooms, sliced
2 cups chicken stock

Heat the oil in a large heavy skillet over medium high heat. Add the red peppers and cook until slightly browned, stirring frequently, about 5 minutes. Remove the peppers, using a slotted spoon.

Pat the chicken dry. Sprinkle with salt and pepper. Add the chicken to the same skillet (in batches if necessary) and brown lightly on all sides over medium high heat (about 10 minutes), adding more oil to the skillet if necessary. Remove the chicken from the skillet. Add the sausage and brown well on all sides, for about 15 minutes. Remove from the skillet and cut into 8 pieces. Pour off the fat from the skillet but do not wash it.

Add the Marsala to the skillet, scraping up the browned bits, and bring to a boil. Reduce heat and simmer for about 2 minutes.

Arrange the chicken skin side up in a single layer in a baking dish. Top with the peppers, sausage and sliced mushrooms. Pour the chicken stock and Marsala over the chicken. Cover tightly. Bake at 350 degrees until the chicken is tender, basting every 15 minutes, for about 1 hour.

Transfer the chicken, peppers, sausage, and mushrooms to a platter. Cover and keep warm. Degrease the pan juices. Pour into a medium saucepan. Boil until the liquid is reduced by a third, about 15 minutes. Spoon the liquid over the chicken. Serves 8.

DeHaven Valley Farm

39247 North Highway 1
Westport, California 95488
(707) 961-1660

De Haven Valley Farm is located in northern Mendocino County, on 20 acres of land featuring meadows, hills, and streams, across the road from the Pacific Ocean. The Victorian farmhouse, built in 1875, has been beautifully restored, and two cottages with fireplaces offer spacious seclusion. Guests enjoy exploring tidepools, visiting a variety of farm animals, and soaking in the hot tub. The farm is also ideally located for side trips to the gigantic redwoods, 25 miles to the north, and the artist's colony of Mendocino, 25 miles south.

Chuck and Shigeko Irwin, a retired Air Force lieutenant colonel and his wife, found their Shangri-La in the far northwest corner of Wyoming. The inn is a tri-level ski chalet named after James Hilton's novel, Lost Horizon. *The cuisine is a blend of Chinese and Japanese. Reservations for a fabulous ten-course dinner must be made at least two weeks in advance. The dinner takes three hours to complete, which means there is only one seating per evening. Guests savor not only the food but a view of the Grand Teton Mountains.*

Chicken and Walnuts

4 1/2 cups cubed boneless, skinless chicken breasts (3/4-inch cubes)
1 tablespoon cornstarch
1/2 teaspoon garlic powder
1/2 teaspoon salt
1/2 teaspoon black pepper
1 tablespoon white wine
1/2 cup soy sauce
3/4 cup brown sugar
1/2 cup walnut halves and pieces
1/3 cup vegetable oil

Mix all ingredients except the oil in a large bowl and let sit for at least 20 minutes. Pour the oil into a wok and heat to 375 degrees. Place the chicken mixture in the wok and stir-fry until the chicken is firm in texture. Serve immediately. Stir-fried or steamed asparagus is an effective accompaniment. Serves 6.

Lost Horizon

Alta, Wyoming
(307) 353-8226

Chicken and Mushroom Fettuccine

1/2 pound mushrooms, sliced
1 onion, chopped
1 clove garlic, minced
1/2 cup butter
1/2 pound egg fettuccine
1/2 pound spinach fettuccine
2 cups half-and-half
Salt and freshly ground pepper to taste
4 chicken breasts, poached and cooled
3/4 cup tomato puree
Grated Parmesan cheese

Saute the mushrooms, onion, and garlic in the butter until soft. Cook the pasta until al dente and drain. Add the half-and-half and seasoning to the pasta. Cut the chicken into bite-size pieces. Add the chicken, vegetables, and tomato puree to the pasta, mixing well. Place in a buttered 9 by 13 inch baking dish and bake at 350 degrees for 30 minutes. Serve with Parmesan cheese. Serves 6.

Hidden Inn

249 Caroline Street
Orange, Virginia 22960
(703) 672-3625

Hidden Inn is located in the heart of historic Orange, Virginia, in Virginia's wine country. A Victorian inn with wraparound verandas, it was built in the 1890s and is surrounded by six wooded acres. Gourmet food is served in the main dining room. The inn is open to the public for lunch. Dinner is served to house guests only in the formal dining room, or, weather permitting, outdoors on the verandas.

In a magnificent area of New Mexico is La Junta Guest Ranch. A setting of pure enchantment welcomes visitors. The food is as great as the view from the dining room.

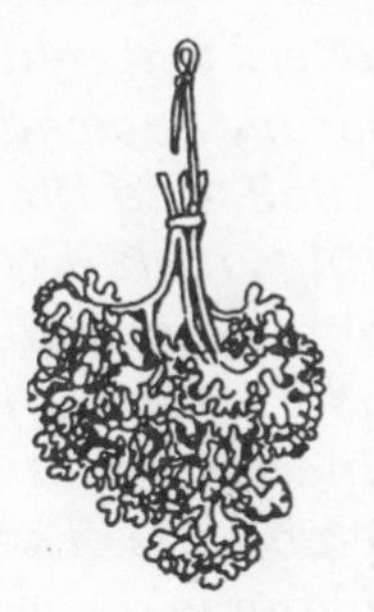

Chicken Spaghetti Sauce

8 chicken breasts, cooked and meat diced
1 large onion, chopped
1 small green bell pepper, chopped
3 stalks celery, chopped
1/2 cup minced garlic
Olive oil
1 pound longhorn cheese, grated
2 8-ounce cans sliced water chestnuts
2 13 3/4-ounce cans chicken broth
1 pound mushrooms, sliced
2 cans Rotel tomatoes
Salt and freshly ground pepper to taste
Cayenne pepper
Worcestershire sauce

In a large skillet, saute the onion, green pepper, and celery in a small amount of olive oil until the onion is translucent. Add the garlic and saute briefly. Mix in the remaining ingredients, except the seasonings. Season to taste with salt and pepper, cayenne, and Worcestershire. Place in a large casserole. Cover and bake for 1 hour at 325 degrees Serve with pasta. Serves 8 to 10.

La Junta Guest Ranch

P.O. Box 139
Alto, New Mexico 88312
(505) 336-4361

New Mexico Enchilada Pie

1/2 pound ground turkey or chicken
9 corn tortillas
1 small yellow onion, chopped
3/4 pound Colby, Monterey Jack, or Longhorn cheese, grated
15 ounces Enchilada Sauce (recipe below)
Salsa

Place the ground turkey or chicken in a small skillet. Cook until no longer raw. Cut the corn tortillas crosswise in thirds. Place a layer of tortilla strips on the bottom of an ungreased 8 by 8-inch baking pan. Place a layer of cooked ground meat, onion, and cheese on the tortilla strips. Top each layer with Enchilada Sauce. Sprinkle grated cheese on top of the last layer. Drizzle Enchilada Sauce over the cheese. Place the pie in a cold oven. Bake at 350 degrees for 30 minutes. Turn off the oven and let the pie sit in the oven for 5 minutes. Cut in squares. Serve with a side dish of salsa. Serves 4.

Enchilada Sauce
1 15-ounce can tomato juice
1/4 teaspoon garlic powder
1/8 teaspoon salt
1/8 teaspoon ground cumin
Chili powder

Combine the above ingredients, adding chili powder to taste. Let boil gently for 5 minutes. Refrigerate until needed. Makes about 2 cups.

Bear Mountain Guest Ranch

P.O. Box 1163
Silver City, New Mexico 88062
(505) 538-2538

Bear Mountain Guest Ranch offers not only attractive and comfortable lodging but also an opportunity to be part of a "mountain nature campus" of 169 acres. The ranch headquarters is a relatively contemporary hacienda, built in 1959, and the outbuildings include two casitas and a spacious bunkhouse. Air-conditioning is unneccessary in these juniper-clad hills. The home cooking is a special feature, along with the opportunity to linger at the dinner table talking with guests from all over the country. Myra McCormick is the owner/innkeeper.

If you enjoy fine food, quiet elegance, and gentle people, you will love the Red Apple Inn. In an entrancing island settling virtually surrounded by Greer's Ferry Lake. The air is clean, the surrounding hills are wooded, and the accomodations are among the best in the region.

Rock Cornish Game Hens with Grapes

2 Rock Cornish game hens
Salt and freshly ground pepper to taste
3 slices bacon, cut in half
2 tablespoons plus 1 tablespoon butter
2 slices bread, crusts removed and cut in triangles
1/2 cup Cognac
1/2 cup cream
2 green onions, finely chopped
1 8 1/4-ounce can light seedless grapes, drained
1/2 cup Port wine
Dash of cayenne pepper
1 teaspoon fresh lemon juice
Sprigs of watercress, for garnish

Sprinkle the game hens with salt and pepper and arrange in a well-buttered shallow roasting pan. Cover each with 3 half slices of bacon. Roast at 350 degrees F. for 50 minutes, basting several times with the juices in the pan.

Heat the 2 tablespoons of butter in a skillet and saute the bread slices until they are golden on both sides. Drain on paper toweling.

Remove the hens from the oven, cut in half, and arrange each half on a triangle of fried bread on a hot serving platter. Keep warm.

To make a sauce, put the roasting pan over direct heat. To the liquid in the pan add the Cognac and reduce by half. Add the cream and boil until the sauce is reduced to a creamy consistency. In a small saucepan heat the 1 tablespoon of butter. Add the green onions and saute for 2 minutes. Add the grapes and Port wine. Heat and ignite the wine. Stir until the flame burns out. Strain the cream gravy from the roasting pan into the grape sauce and correct the seasoning with salt, cayenne, and lemon juice. Pour the sauce over the hens and garnish, if desired, with watercress. Serves 2 to 4.

Red Apple Inn

Heber Springs, Arkansas

Turkey Waldorf

Flour for dredging
Salt, and freshly ground pepper to taste
1 pound turkey cutlets
3/4 cup clarified butter or vegetable oil
1/2 cup apple jack or apple brandy
1 pint whipping cream
4 Granny Smith apples, peeled, cored, and sliced
1/2 cup walnut halves

Season the flour with salt and pepper. Lightly pound the turkey with a mallet or the side of a meat cleaver. Heat the butter in a saute pan just until it begins to smoke. Saute the turkey quickly until tender but not crisp. Pour off the butter and keep the turkey warm over low heat. Add the apple jack, cream, apples, and walnuts. Simmer until the liquid is reduced enough to coat the back of a spoon. Serves 4.

Oxford House Inn

105 Main Street
Fryeburg, Maine 04037
(207) 935-3442

Phyllis and John Morris are the innkeepers at this lovely Maine inn with charming and comfortable accommodations. The spacious turn-of-the-century yellow house boasts a large porch and big bay windows, creating an instant welcome to guests. Three dining rooms full of inviting tables and other decorative items complement wonderful foods with many creative and unusual dishes.

This inn is one of the oldest houses in the country. Built in 1717, it became a restaurant in 1954 and since then has been serving classic French cuisine in a colorful, authentic atmosphere. The Guest House offers luxurious overnight quarters in a quiet setting. The old house is surrounded by shade trees, gardens, and rolling pastures. An overnight stay includes a delicious breakfast the next morning on the porch.

Roast Duck with Cherries

1 duckling (4 1/2 pounds)
Salt and freshly ground pepper to taste
1 carrot, sliced
1 onion, sliced
Giblets, cut up
2 cups chicken stock or water
1 tablespoon sugar
Vinegar
1 or 2 oranges
Arrowroot or cornstarch
1 or 2 tablespoons Cognac
2 tablespoons butter
Bing cherries, pitted, for garnish

Prepare the duck for roasting by removing all extra fat from the cavity. Rinse with cold water and dry. Season the cavity with salt and pepper. Roast at 350 degrees for approximately 90 minutes. Prick the skin but not the muscle of the duck during roasting to aid in fat removal. While the duck is roasting, prepare some stock. Brown the carrot, onion, and giblets in a little butter or duck fat. Add the chicken stock and allow to simmer until the duck is cooked. Remove the duck from the pan and pour off all grease. Deglaze the pan with the stock. Strain the stock. In another saucepan, moisten the sugar with a small amount of vinegar and heat until the sugar caramelizes. Add the juice of one or two oranges and the strained duck stock; allow to reduce until there are 1/2 to 2 cups of sauce. Correct the seasoning and thicken very slightly with arrowroot or cornstarch. Add the Cognac to taste and swirl the butter into the sauce. Arrange the duck on a hot platter, pour over the sauce, and garnish with bing cherries. Serves 4.

Coventry Forge Inn and Guest House

Coventry Road
Road 7 Pottstown
Coventryville, Pennsylvania 19464
(215) 469-6222

Roast Duckling with Orange Sherry Sauce

1 duckling (4 to 4 1/2 pounds)
2 tablespoons plus 1 cup orange juice
1 tablespoon cornstarch
1 tablespoon sugar
1 tablespoon sherry

Remove the giblets and neck from the cavity of the duckling. Place the bird, breast side up, in a roasting pan just big enough to hold it, with sides at least 2 inches high (to catch the grease). Rub the breast with the 2 tablespoons of orange juice. Place the duckling in a 225 degrees oven and roast for 7 hours. Do not baste the bird or prick the skin while it cooks and do not remove the grease as it collects. Remove the duckling from the oven, pour off the grease, and let cool. Remove from the pan and refrigerate overnight (or freeze). When ready to serve, place the duckling in a 450 degree F. oven and heat until brown and crispy, about 20 minutes.

To make the sauce, dissolve the cornstarch in a small amount of water and set aside. Heat the 1 cup of orange juice, add the sugar, and cook until the sugar dissolves. Add the cornstarch and sherry and cook until clear.

Cut the duckling in quarters and serve with the orange sherry sauce. Serves 4.

Dockside

Harris Island
P.O. Box 205
York, Maine 03909

Dave and Harriette Lusty are celebrating their 35th anniversary as owners and operators of Dockside. The Guest Quarters have accommodations to satisfy everyone. Beginning in the "Maine House," built in the 1880s, there are beautifully restored colonial bedrooms overlooking York Harbor. Dockside is situated on its own peninsula, which provides a panorama of both the ocean and harbor activity. The Dockside dining room is adjacent to the guest quarters with a complete and varied menu featuring Maine lobster and other treats from the sea.

New York Magazine describes the Arlington Inn as "One of those rare places where the look, the food, and the service are in high-level harmony." Paul and Madeline Kruzel are the innkeepers. The structure is a stately Greek Revival mansion, built in 1848 as the private home of Martin Chester Deming, a railroad magnate and Vermont politician. Dining here is an exquisite experience. Winner of The Travel Holiday Dining Award, its outstanding creative American cuisine is served each evening by candlelight, with superb service. Champagne brunch on Sunday is a weekly feature.

Vermont Breast of Pheasant

(with Green Peppercorn, Red Currant Sauce and Cranberry Chutney)

3 2 1/2-to-3-pound pheasants (whole or breast only)
Salt and freshly ground pepper to taste
Flour
Clarified butter
2 cups pheasant stock (use bones from pheasant) or chicken stock
2 cups beef stock
1 tablespoon green peppercorn puree
1/2 cup red currant jelly
1 tablespoon cornstarch, mixed with a small amount of water
Cranberry Chutney (recipe below)

Bone out the pheasant breasts and reserve the remaining parts for another use. Sprinkle the breasts with salt and pepper, then dredge lightly in flour. Heat the clarified butter in a saute pan and brown the breasts on both sides. Continue cooking in a 425 degree oven for 5 to 7 minutes.

To make the sauce, place the pheasant stock, beef stock, peppercorn puree, and red currant jelly in a saucepan. Bring to a boil and reduce by half. Thicken with the cornstarch-water mixture. Season with salt and pepper. To serve, place the pheasant breasts on a platter or on individual plates and spoon over the sauce. Pass additional sauce and the Cranberry Chutney. Serves 6.

Cranberry Chutney
1/4 onion
1 tablespoon chopped fresh ginger root
1 clove garlic
1/2 cup raspberry vinegar
1 lemon, cut in eighths
1 orange, cut in eighths
1 pound cranberries
1 apple, peeled, cored, and diced
1 cup sugar
2 teaspoons cornstarch mixed with a small amount of water

Puree the onion, ginger, and garlic in a food processor or blender. Place in a saucepan with the vinegar and cook for 5 minutes. Puree the lemon and orange and add to the saucepan along with the remaining ingredients. Bring to a boil and cook until the skins of the cranberries have popped, about 10 minutes. Stir in the cornstarch mixture and continue cooking until the sauce thickens. Makes about 2 cups.

The Arlington Inn

Historic Route 7A, P.O. Box 369
Arlington, Vermont
(802) 375-6532

Cold Poached Rainbow Trout with Sauce Verte

Vivian Tellier is the dynamic proprietor of both of these inns, which share a four-acre compound at Bushnell's basin on the outskirts of Rochester. Richardson's Canal House is the oldest surviving Erie Canal Tavern. It was built in 1818 and restored in 1978. The Canal House has been serving gourmet meals for over a decade.

1 quart water
1 bay leaf
1 small onion, sliced
4 parsley sprigs
1/2 lemon, sliced
2 mushrooms, sliced
1/2 cup Riesling white wine
8 rainbow trouts (8 to 10 ounces each), boned
Lime slices, for garnish
Sprigs of parsley, for garnish

Sauce Verte
4 sprigs parsley
6 sprigs watercress
6 sprigs fresh dill
1/4 cup chicken stock
2 cups good-quality mayonnaise

Combine the water, bay leaf, onion, parsley, lemon, mushrooms, and lime in a large saute pan. Heat to simmering. Drop the fish into the poaching water (known as court bouillon). Poach the fish until firm, approximately 8 to 10 minutes, and remove with a skimmer onto a cold plate. Quickly scrape off the skin, leaving the flesh intact. Refrigerate the fish.

To make the sauce, heat the herbs in a saute pan with the chicken stock. Pour the mixture into a food processor and process until well blended. Blend in the mayonnaise.

To serve, place the trout on a cold plate. Ladle 4 tablespoons of Sauce Verte over the upper part of the fish. Garnish with lime slices and parsley. Serves 8.

Oliver Loud's Inn and Richardson Canal House

1474 Marsh Road
Pittsford, New York 14534
(716) 248-2500

A visit to this famous inn is an experience to remember. Guests flock here from near and far to relax, soak up the atmosphere, and partake of the excellent cuisine. The inn sits on a mile-long stretch of water reserved for fly fishing only, and the number of fish that may be taken from the stream is strictly limited. Thus, the Allenberry obtains its rainbows from Idaho. The inn is noted for a variety of trout preparations, including the recipe provided here.

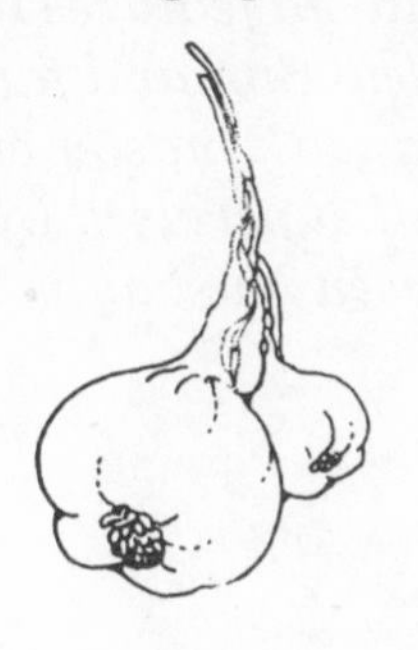

Lewis and Clark's Minted Rainbow Trout

6 dressed trout, about 5 ounces each
Oil
3 cups fresh mint leaves, lightly packed,
 or 3/4 cup crushed dried mint
1 tablespoon salt
3/4 cup salad oil
6 slices bacon

Dry the trout. Brush with oil. Mash the mint with the salt to release the flavor. Add the 3/4 cup oil. If using dried mint, mix it with the salt and oil. Fill the cavities of the trout with the mint mixture, wrap each with one slice of bacon, and secure with toothpicks. Broil over hot coals or under a broiler 4 to 6 inches from the heat for 4 to 5 minutes; turn. Cook for 4 to 5 minutes longer or until the trout flakes when tested with a fork. Serves 6.

Allenberry

P.O. Box 7
Boiling Springs, Pennsylvania 17007
(717) 258-3211

Pan-Fried Catfish with Avocado Tomato Relish

2 eggs
1 cup heavy cream
2 teaspoons salt
1 teaspoon cayenne pepper
1 cup bread crumbs
1 cup cornmeal
4 8-ounce freshwater catfish
4 tablespoons clarified butter
Avocado Tomato Relish (recipe below)

Combine the eggs, heavy cream, salt, and pepper and beat until well blended. Combine the bread crumbs and cornmeal and mix well. Place the fish fillets in the egg mixture and coat well. Place in the cornmeal mixture and coat well. Heat the clarified butter in a large saute pan until just smoking. Place the fish in the pan and turn down the heat. Brown well and turn over. Brown the second side. Transfer the fish to a 450 degree oven and finish cooking for about 5 minutes. Serve on individual plates with a tablespoonful of Avocado Tomato Relish.

Avocado Tomato Relish
2 ripe avocados, peeled and diced
1 large tomato, peeled, seeded and diced
Juice of 2 limes
1 teaspoon chopped garlic
1/4 cup finely chopped onion
1 tablespoon chopped cilantro
1 tablespoon chopped fresh parsley

Combine all ingredients until well blended. Serves 4.

The Old Tavern

Grafton, Vermont

Many call this "New England's Most Elegant Little Inn." And rightfully so. The inn has a heritage that goes back almost as far as our country's; it first opened only 12 years after America's independence and has been impeccably restored. The rich lineage and unspoiled colonial beauty of The Old Tavern are evident everywhere in Grafton. It was a favorite stop on Boston-Montreal stagecoach runs. The Dining Room features traditional New England fare prepared with master culinary skill supervised by Chef Steven Nusbaum-Toll.

The 1661 Inn is located in Old Harbor's historic district and overlooks the Atlantic Ocean. The ocean view dining room features a canopied outdoor deck so that guests enjoy great food either indoors or out. Its partner, Hotel Manisses, was built in 1870, with a complete restoration in 1972. The 18 guest rooms are furnished with turn-of-the-century furniture. The lovely dining room's menu offers unusual selections from freshly shucked seafood to masterfully prepared entrees.

Baked Bluefish

1 8 to 10-pound fresh bluefish, scaled and gutted
1 teaspoon salt
1 teaspoon pepper
2 large carrots, coarsely chopped
1 large onion, coarsely chopped
5 stalks celery, coarsely chopped
1/2 bunch dill, coarsely chopped
1/2 bunch basil, coarsely chopped
1/2 bunch parsley, coarsely chopped
1 cup dry white wine
1/4 cup butter, melted

Season the bluefish inside and out with salt and pepper. Stuff with the chopped vegetables and fresh herbs. Lay the fish on a large baking pan. Place the excess vegetables around the fish. Pour the wine and melted butter over the fish. Bake at 350 degrees F. for 45 minutes or until the fish flakes easily. Serves 10 to 12.

The 1661 Inn and Hotel Manisses

P.O. Box I
Block Island, Rhode Island 02807
(401) 466-2421

Seafood Lasagna

3 tbsp. olive oil
5 garlic cloves, peeled and minced
1 cup chopped shallots or white onions
2 tbsp. dried basil
1 tbsp. dried oregano
Salt and white pepper to taste
4 cups bechamel (white) sauce (below)
1/2 cup freshly grated Parmesan cheese
3 tbsp. dry sherry
1 lb. medium shrimp, cooked, peeled and deveined
1 lb. bay scallops, cooked
2 lbs. fresh spinach, rinsed and stems removed
2 lbs. fresh mushrooms, cleaned and chopped
2 tbsp. butter
1 8 ounce package cream cheese
2 lbs. cooked lump crabmeat, drained
2 lbs. mozzarella cheese, grated
1 1/2 lbs. lasagna noodles

In large skilled over medium heat, heat olive oil. Add garlic and shallots and saute until soft, but not browned, about five minutes. Stir in basil and oregano and season with salt and pepper to taste. Remove from heat. Set aside one cup bechamel sauce. Stir onion-garlic mixture into remaining three cups bechamel. Stir in Parmesan and sherry and heat gently. Fold in cooked shrimp and scallops. Adjust seasoning and set aside. Meanwhile, steam spinach just until tender and bright green. Drain well and pat dry between paper towels. Chop coarsely.In large skillet over medium high heat, saute mushrooms in hot butter until tender and liquid has evaporated. cut cream cheese into small cubes. Shred crabmeat, removing any shells. Set aside. Cook lasagna noodles according to package directions. Drain well. While noodles are cooking, spread very thin layer of reserved bechamel sauce (less than one half cup) in bottom of greased 13 1/2 x 9 x 4 baking pan. Cover with layer of cooked noodles, trimming to fit pan if necessary . Spread half of seafood sauce over noodles then half of chopped spinach, half of cream cheese cubes, a fourth of grated mozzarella, half of sauteed mushrooms and half of shredded crabmeat. Repeat layers, beginning and ending with lasagna noodles. Spread noodles with remaining bechamel sauce and top with remaining mozzarella. Bake, uncovered, at 350 degrees until bubbling and lightly browned and heated through, 45 minutes to one hour. Let stand 10 to 15 minutes before serving. Serves 12 to 16.

Story Inn

P.O. Box 64
Nashville, Indiana 47448
(812) 988-2273

Bechamel Sauce
Melt 1/2 cup (8 tbsp) butter in a large heavy saucepan over medium heat. Stir in 1/2 cup flour and cook and stir about two minutes. Do not brown. Remove from heat and gradually stir in four cups milk until smooth. Return to heat and cook and stir until thickened and smooth. Season to taste with salt and white pepper.

Since the 1850s, the Story General Store has served Brown County travelers. Now this historic landm has been restored into a country in unique as its setting. Nestled at th juction of Brown County State Par the 10 O'clock Treaty Line, and the Hoosier National Forest, one can fi lodging here in the old buggy asser operation on the second floor, or in surrounding cottages. All of the roc are furnished with period antiques The full service gourmet type restaurant features expertly prepar meals that marry seasonal produce and hard-to-find meats, game, fish and seafood.

Here is a delightful restored country estate in Connecticut's quiet corner. It is listed on the National Register of Historic Places and its dining room carries a four star rating.

Grilled Swordfish with Pink Peppercorn Sauce

1 pound center-cut swordfish, skin removed and cut into 4 fillets
3 tablespoons fresh lemon juice
Salt and freshly ground pepper to taste
Rose paprika powder to taste
Olive oil
2 tablespoons butter
2 green onions, chopped
2 teaspoons chopped garlic
1/2 teaspoon lemon pepper
1 teaspoon pink peppercorns
4 tablespoons Riesling white wine

Marinate the fillets in a mixture of the lemon juice, salt and pepper, and paprika for 30 minutes. Drain off any remaining marinade, pat the fish dry, and brush lightly with olive oil. Place on a hot grill. Let the fish take on grill marks on both sides but do not cook through. Set fish aside.

Place the butter in a saute pan and add the green onions, garlic, lemon pepper, and pink peppercorns. Saute briefly, then add the wine and bring to a boil. Place the swordfish in the sauce and let simmer for 3 minutes, basting constantly. Remove the fish and serve each fillet with 1/2 tablespoon of the sauce spooned over the top. Serves 4.

The Inn at Woodstock Hill

94 Plaine Hill Road
South Woodstock, Connecticut 06267
(203) 928-0528

Baked Stuffed Salmon

1 yellow onion, diced
Clarified butter
2 tablespoons Italian seasonings
2 eggs
1 pound Dungeness crab
Chopped fresh parsley
Bread crumbs
4 fillets of salmon (8 to 10 ounces each)

Saute the onions in the butter and Italian seasonings until the onions are translucent. Remove from the heat and let cool. Add the eggs, crabmeat, parsley, and enough bread crumbs to absorb the moisture. Make a slice lengthwise through the middle of each fillet all the way through the flesh to the skin, being careful not to butterfly the meat. Fill each cavity with stuffing. Squeeze lemon over each piece of fish. Bake at 400 degrees F. for 10 to 12 minutes until just done. Serve with Hollandaise Sauce. Serves 4.

Chico Hot Springs Lodge

Drawer D
Pray, Montana 59065
(406) 333-4933

Chico Hot Springs is high country at its best — it is located in south central Montana's Paradise Valley, with the Absaroka mountain range defining the eastern skyline, the Gallatin range the west, and the famous Yellowstone River running between the two. Chico's history centers on its hot pools, whose "restorative" powers have been put to use for over a century. The water in the pools is between 100 and 104 degrees with no chlorine or other chemicals. The food is absolutely wonderful, thanks to Alan Kilmurray, who oversees its preparation.

For two centuries, the Fearrington farm has been part of the landscape between Chapel Hill and Pittsboro. At the center of the village is The Fearrington House, a place dedicated to the five C's of hospitality — Character, Courtesy, Calm, Charm, and Cuisine. Sophisticated southern cooking is the order of the day.

Poached Salmon with Cucumber Dill Mayonnaise

1 4-pound fresh salmon, boned and skinned
4 bay leaves
1 lemon, sliced
6 to 7 sprigs fresh thyme
4 stalks celery, chopped
1 onion, sliced
1/4 teaspoon vegetable oil
1 teaspoon salt
1 teaspoon whole black peppercorns
Cucumber Dill Mayonnaise (recipe below)

Cut the salmon into six individual portions. Fill a large roasting pan with 3 to 4 quarts water, making certain the pan is large enough to hold the salmon. Add the bay leaves, lemon, thyme, celery, onion, oil, salt, and peppercorns. Bring to a boil. Poach the salmon for about 15 minutes over moderate heat sufficient to keep the stock at a simmer. Cool the salmon in the cooking liquid, drain on absorbent towels, and refrigerate. To serve, garnish each portion with a tablespoon of Cucumber Dill Mayonnaise and pass extra sauce in a separate container. Serves 6.

Note: A good rule of thumb to use in poaching the salmon is to cook the fish 5 minutes per inch of thickness. For example, a 3-inch thick salmon would need to be poached for 15 minutes.

Cucumber Dill Mayonnaise
1/2 cup cucumber, peeled, seeded, and finely chopped
Salt to taste
1 cup mayonnaise, preferably homemade
1/2 cup sour cream
3 tablespoons lemon juice
Dash of Tabasco Sauce
4 tablespoons chopped fresh dill

Salt the cucumber and let it drain in a colander for about 30 minutes. Pat dry with absorbent towels. Blend with the rest of the ingredients and chill for several hours before serving. Makes 1 3/4 cups.

Fearrington House

2000 Fearrington Village Center
Pittsboro, North Carolina 28717
(919) 542-2121

Prawns In Beer Batter

20 under-10-count shrimp
2 cups beer
2 tablespoons baking powder
1/2 cup cornstarch
Salt and freshly ground pepper to taste
2 tablespoons paprika
3 cups flour
Orange Horseradish Sauce (recipe below)

Peel and devein the shrimp, leaving on the tails. Place the beer in a bowl. Add the baking powder, cornstarch, salt, pepper, and paprika. Whip until dissolved. Add 2 cups of the flour while whipping until the consistency of pancake batter. Preheat a deep fryer to 350 degrees. Dust the shrimp in flour and then dip in batter. Drop in the deep fryer for about 4 minutes. Serve with Orange Horseradish Sauce. Serves 4.

Orange Horseradish Sauce
1 cup orange marmalade
1/4 cup chutney
1/4 cup honey
1 teaspoon ground ginger
Horseradish

Mix all the ingredients except the horseradish together and add horseradish to taste. Chill well.

Clinton House Inn

Clinton, New York

An authentic country inn and one of the outstanding landmarks of the Mohawk Valley area, Clinton House has been visited by many distinguished people, including several presidents. The structure was built in 1820, an example of the Federal-style of architecture. The food is delicious and the service most gracious.

Built as a private home by a former mayor of Golconda, this gabled mansion on the Ohio River has been a licensed hotel since 1928. Many travelers and boarders have enjoyed the hospitality of various owners since that time. A costly renovation in 1981 has restored the joy and light to the delicately curved pressed glass windows. The restaurant seats 60 in beautifully decorated formal dining rooms. It draws diners from a 100-mile radius, with cuisine best described as ethnic American. From deep-fried chicken to elegant French-inspired entrees, there is a dish for every palate. Golconda is a typical sleepy river town with turn-of-the-century facades reflecting a simpler time.

Country Italian Shrimp with Sausage

1 pound Italian sausage, preferably hot, casing removed
1 green bell pepper, chopped
1 red bell pepper, chopped, or 1/2 cup chopped pimento
1/2 cup sliced onion
4 tablespoons shredded green onion
1/2 pound mushrooms, sliced
2 tablespoons butter
2 tablespoons olive oil
3 pounds (16 to 20 count) shrimp, shelled and deveined
1 tablespoon finely chopped garlic
2 pounds fettuccine, cooked al dente, drained, and tossed with butter
1 cup grated Parmesan cheese
8 ounces mozzarella cheese, shredded

Saute the sausage, peppers, onion, green onion, and mushrooms until the pink is gone from the sausage and the vegetables are crisp tender. Set aside. In the same skillet, melt the butter, heat the olive oil, and add the shrimp and garlic. Saute until the shrimp are just cooked through. In a large bowl, place the fettuccine, cheeses, sausage and vegetable mixture, and shrimp, including the butter and olive oil. Toss until well combined. Serves 6.

The Mansion of Golconda

P.O. Box 339
Golconda, Illinois 62938
(618) 683-4400

Baked Stuffed Shrimp

6 jumbo shrimp, peeled and deveined, with tails left on
1/2 cup finely chopped scallops
Bread Stuffing (recipe below)
Lemon Butter (recipe below)

Split the shrimp through the center and wash thoroughly. Place approximately 1 teaspoon of finely chopped scallops into each shrimp, using a total of 1/2 cup. Top with Bread Stuffing. Place in a pan with a little water to prevent the shrimp from drying. Bake for 20 minutes at 350 degrees F. Sprinkle with Lemon Butter before serving. Serves 2.

Bread Stuffing (for 8 to 10 shrimp)
4 cups coarsely chopped fresh bread crumbs
4 tablespoons freshly grated Romano cheese
1/4 cup sherry wine
2 teaspoons paprika
3 tablespoons finely crushed potato chips
4 tablespoons melted butter

Combine all ingredients and mix well.

Lemon Butter
1/2 cup butter, browned
Juice of 2 lemons
1/2 teaspoon salt
1/2 teaspoon Worcestershire sauce

Combine all ingredients.

Publick House

P.O. Box 187
Sturbridge, Massachusetts 01566
(508) 347-3313

When Colonel Ebenezer Crafts founded this inn in 1771, America was an English colony. The original building was a tavern and a pub. A strong feeling of history permeates the structure. The famous have walked through the front door for more than 200 years. Always present is the magnificent aroma of Yankee cooking. The inn faces the common of the colorful town of Sturbridge, which is also the location of Old Sturbridge Village, a restored farming community.

In a magnificent area of New Mexico is this great guest ranch, La Junta. The cuisine is as great as the view from the dining room.

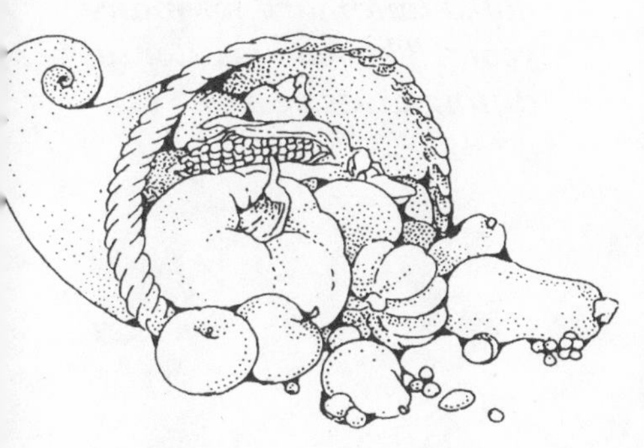

Shrimp Creole

1 cup flour
1 cup oil
2 cups chopped onions
1 cup chopped celery
1 cup chopped green bell pepper
1 cup minced garlic
1 28-ounce can tomatoes
2 6-ounce cans tomato paste
6 13 3/4-ounce cans chicken broth
1/2 cup fresh lemon juice
3 pounds shrimp, peeled and deveined
Salt and freshly ground pepper to taste
Tabasco Sauce
Cayenne pepper
2 tablespoons chopped fresh parsley
2 tablespoons chopped green onion tops

Make a roux by combining the flour and oil in a large saute pan and cooking, stirring constantly, until the mixture turns golden brown. Add the onions, celery, green pepper, and garlic to the pan, then the tomatoes and tomato paste. Cook for 5 minutes. Add the broth and lemon juice. Simmer for 1 hour. Add the shrimp and cook for 10 minutes. Season to taste with salt, pepper, Tabasco, and cayenne. Add the parsley and green onion tops 5 minutes before serving over rice. Serves 10.

La Junta Guest Ranch

P.O. Box 139
Alto, New Mexico 88312
(505) 336-4361

Crepes with Crabmeat Au Gratin

This inn's great claim to fame is that its history is inseparably intertwined with the history of the Colonies. Built in 1710, it has been a noted landmark for many years. The food is colonial dining at its best.

Mornay Sauce
Crepes
2 tablespoons butter
1 pound crabmeat
Grated Parmesan Cheese

Prepare the Crepes and Mornay Sauce. In a small pan, melt the butter and lightly saute the crabmeat. Add enough Mornay Sauce to bind (about one third of the recipe) and toss gently to blend. Remove from the heat. Spoon the mixture into crepes and roll, folding the sides in. Place a thin layer of Mornay Sauce in the bottom of a 13 by 9-inch baking dish, then line with stuffed crepes. Ladle more sauce over the crepes. Sprinkle lightly with grated Parmesan cheese and bake at 375-400 degrees F. until lightly browned. Serves 6 to 8.

Crepes
2 cups flour
5 tablespoons sugar
Pinch of salt
5 eggs
1 cup cream
1 to 1 1/2 cups milk
2 tablespoons butter, melted
Clarified butter or light cooking oil

Sift together the flour, sugar, and salt. Whisk the eggs and cream, then add the dry ingredients, mixing thoroughly. Blend in enough milk to make a smooth, thin pancake batter. Stir in the melted butter. Let the batter rest in the refrigerator before using. *(Continued on following page)*

Colligan's Inn

Stockton, New Jersey

(continued from previous page) To cook the crepes, brush a crepe pan with clarified butter or light cooking oil and place over moderately high heat. When the pan begins to smoke slightly, add a small amount of batter and roll the pan to coat the bottom evenly. Brown the crepes lightly on both sides and turn onto a platter to cool. Continue making crepes until all the batter has been used.

Mornay Sauce

5 cups milk
1 oignion pique (1/2 small onion
 stuck with 2 cloves and 1 bay leaf)
1/2 cup butter
1/2 cup flour
1 1/4 cups grated Gruyere or mild Cheddar cheese
1/2 cup cream
2 egg yolks
Pinch of nutmeg
Salt and white pepper to taste

Fasten the bay leaf to the onion half with 2 cloves and place in a saucepan with the milk. Bring just to a boil, then reduce the heat and simmer for 10 minutes. In a separate saucepan melt the butter and blend in the flour to make a light roux. Stir with a wooden spoon until cooked but not brown (3 or 4 minutes). Add the roux to the hot milk and blend well while bringing slowly to a boil. Reduce the heat and remove the oignion pique. Add the grated cheese and simmer gently until melted and smooth, stirring frequently. In a mixing bowl whip the egg yolks and cream for a liaison, whipping constantly. Then add the hot cheese sauce to the liaison, whipping constantly. Then add the liaison to the cheese sauce and blend well, keeping the temperature below boiling, preferably by using a double boiler. Season to taste with nutmeg, salt, and white pepper.

Colligan's Inn

Stockton, New Jersey

Crabcakes with Cayenne Mayonnaise

1 pound lump crabmeat, picked over
1 red bell pepper, roasted, peeled and diced
1 ear fresh corn, cooked and kernals removed
1/2 bunch cilantro (Chinese parsley), chopped fine
1 clove garlic, minced
6 tablespoons Dijon mustard
6 tablespoons cornmeal
Flour for dredging
Peanut oil for frying
1 cup mayonnaise
1 tablespoon cayenne pepper, or to taste
1 tablespoon Tabasco sauce, or to taste
5 fresh figs, split in half, for garnish
1 package enoki mushrooms
10 long chives, 10 to 12 inches long, for garnish

Combine the crabmeat, red bell pepper, corn, cilantro, garlic, Dijon mustard, and cornmeal in a bowl; gather about 1/3 cup of the mixture into the hands and form a cake about 1 1/2 inches in diameter, pressing tightly to squeeze out the moisture. (These cakes have no egg and little binder, so the pressing is important to hold them together.) Dredge each cake in flour. Put one inch of peanut oil in a large frying pan and heat almost to the smoking point. Add the cakes, a few at a time, and sear quickly on each side. (The whole operation takes little time, one or two minutes per side.) Put aside and keep warm. Makes about 18 cakes; serve 3 per person.

Combine the mayonnaise, cayenne, and the Tabasco, and refrigerate.

To garnish the plate, put the cayenne mayonnaise into a "ketchup style" squirt bottle. Pipe seven straight lines of mayonnaise completely across the plate, from top to bottom, approximately 1/2 inch apart. Turn the plate 90 degrees and pipe 7 more lines across the plate just as before, to form a lattice pattern. Place the fried crabcakes in the middle of the plate on top of the mayonnaise. Place 5 to 6 enoki mushrooms in the center of the crabcakes so they are standing straight up. Place two long chives also in the center of the crabcakes as if they were sprouting. Place two fig halves on either side of the crabcakes.

Nassau Inn

Princeton, New Jersey

Located in the heart of Princeton, this great inn enjoys a long and illustrious legacy as the university town's social hub. Originally built in 1756, the expanded inn now features 218 guest rooms (each appointed with handsome period furnishings); three restaurants; and abundant meeting and conference space. Innkeepers Nelson and Beth Zager subscribe to a unique spirit of management that combines old-fashioned country charm with all the appointments of today's finest hotels. Dining opportunities at the inn include Palmer's, where award-winning cuisine is featured at dinner time under the direction of Exucutive Chef Don Woods; The Greenhouse, overlooking famous Palmer Square, where meals are served in a more casual atmosphere; and the Tap Room, whose menu offers hearty American fare.

Wakulla Springs Lodge is located in the Edward Ball Wakulla Springs State Park near Tallahassee. The Spanish-style lodge, built in 1937, features marble floors, hand-painted ceilings, and period furniture. The lodge has 27 guest rooms as well as a spacious dining room serving three delectable meals daily.

Crab Imperial

1 pound fresh crabmeat, picked over
1/4 teaspoon salt
2 dashes Worcestershire sauce
1/2 teaspoon granulated garlic
2 stalks celery, minced
1/3 cup mayonnaise
1 teaspoon fresh lemon juice
1/4 teaspoon Accent
Butter
Grated Parmesan cheese
Cracker crumbs

Butter a casserole dish. Combine all ingredients, except the cracker crumbs and cheese in a bowl and mix well. Let sit for 1 hour. Place the mixture in the casserole dish. Top with the cracker crumbs and Parmesan cheese. Dot with butter. Bake at 350 degrees for 20 minutes. Serves 4.

Wakulla Springs Lodge

Wakulla Springs, Florida

Mushrooms Stuffed With Crab Imperial

1 pound Maryland backfin crabmeat
2 tablespoons finely diced onions
2 tablespoons finely diced green bell pepper
2 eggs
4 tablespoons butter
1 pound fresh bread crumbs or 1 pound diced bread
Salt, freshly ground pepper, and
Worcestershire sauce to taste
15 large whole mushrooms
4 tablespoons mayonnaise

Mix together the crabmeat, onions, green pepper, 1 of the eggs, butter, and bread crumbs. Add the salt, pepper, and Worcestershire sauce. Stuff the fresh whole mushrooms with crab filling. Mix the other egg with the mayonnaise and pour over top of the stuffed mushrooms. Bake at 350 degrees F. for 20 minutes. Serves 5.

Blue Coat Inn

800 North State Street
Dover, Delaware 19901
(302) 674-1776

Once a private home, the Blue Coat Inn today offers a varied bill of fare in country-style surroundings. The inn takes its name from the uniform worn by Colonel John Haslett's Delaware Regiment of 1776.

6

Meat Entrees

Located on the sea, on the loveliest of all the San Juan Islands, this inn looks as if it had been transplanted from the Maine coast. It has its own private beach, a pond, and flower gardens. It was first built as a cabin, then expanded into the local general store, barber shop, and post office in 1888—with a jail in the rear. Since that time, there have been several remodelings and additions. Today, the finest food on the island is served to the guests and the public by the Outlook Inn's award-winning chef, Antony Vincent Carbone.

Blackened Rib-Eye Steak with Roquefort Sauce

1/2 tablespoon paprika
1/2 tablespoon cayenne pepper
1/2 tablespoon dried basil
1/2 tablespoon dried oregano
1/2 tablespoon brown sugar
1/2 tablespoon black pepper
1/2 tablespoon white pepper
1/2 tablespoon dried sage
2 10-ounce rib-eye steaks
Roquefort Sauce (recipe below)

Combine the seasonings well to make a blackening mixture and coat the steaks with the mixture. Heat a cast-iron skillet to a high temperature. Place the coated steaks in the pan and cook to the desired doneness. Top with the Roquefort Sauce. Serves 2.

Roquefort Sauce
2 tablespoons white wine
3 small shallots, minced
1 cup heavy cream
2 ounces blue cheese, crumbled

In a saucepan, reduce the wine by half. Add the shallots and reduce by one-fourth. Add the cream and cheese and reduce by half.

Outlook Inn

Orcas Island
Eastsound, Washington 98245
(206) 376-2581

Lemon-Pepper Steak

This tempting recipe from the Meadowlark Manor is a fitting centerpiece to a dinner you'll remember.

2 beef rib steaks (about 12 ounces each)
2 teaspoons lemon pepper
2 tablespoons butter or margarine
1 tablespoon vegetable oil
Salt to taste
2 tablespoons chopped green onions and tops
2 teaspoons flour
1/4 teaspoon salt
1/2 cup heavy cream
1 tablespoon brandy

Pat the steaks dry with paper towels. Sprinkle both sides of the steaks with lemon pepper, pressing it into the meat. Cover and let stand for 30 minutes. Heat 1 tablespoon of the butter and the oil in a large skillet. Brown the steaks for 3 to 4 minutes on each side. Remove to a hot platter, sprinkle with salt and keep warm. Pour the fat from the skillet. Add the remaining 1 tablespoon butter to the skillet and saute the green onions for 1 minute; mix in the flour and 1/4 teaspoon salt. Stir in the cream and brandy gradually. Cook and stir until bubbly. Pour over the steaks.

The Meadowlark Manor

241 West 9th Avenue
Red Cloud, Nebraska 68970
(402) 746-3550

Billed as Kittitas County, Washington's, finest country inn, The Moore House was originally built by the Chicago, Milwaukee, St.Paul and Pacific Railroad to house men who had the job of getting trains over some of the most hazardous track in the country. Constructed in 1909 and recently placed on the National Register of Historic Places, it has been lovingly renovated. Hearty food served on Olympian Hiawatha dining car china greets guests as they enter the large and friendly dining room.

Steak au Poivre

6 tablespoons peppercorns
6 tenderloin steaks, 1-inch thick
4 tablespoons butter
2 tablespoons oil
1 cup white wine
2 tablespoons brandy

Crush the peppercorns coarsely and pound firmly into both sides of the steaks with a mallet. In a large skillet melt 2 tablespoons of the butter and the oil over a high flame. When the butter and oil begin to sizzle, put in the steaks and cook to the desired doneness. Remove to a serving platter.

Stir the wine and brandy into the pan juices. Simmer on a low flame for 2 minutes. Add the remaining 2 tablespoons of butter. Pour over the steak and serve immediately. Serves 6.

The Moore House

P.O. Box 861
South Cle Elum, Washington 98943
(509) 674-5939

The Carpetbagger

1 large onion
1 green bell pepper
3 stalks celery
32 oysters, shucked, reserving liquid
5 teaspoons olive oil
Old Bay Seasonings
Shake of lemon pepper
1 teaspoon lemon juice
4 10-ounce, center-cut beef filets
1/4 cup white wine
1 tablespoon flour
1 cup light cream
Crisply fried bacon, crumbled (optional)

Cut the vegetables into thin strips. Put the liquid from the oysters in a pan with the vegetables. Season with Old Bay, lemon pepper, and lemon juice. Saute in the oil until the vegetables are crisp. Add the oysters and saute until they begin to curl. Strain the mixture, reserve four oysters. Stuff each of the filets with seven oysters, adding bacon if desired. Chill. Mince the remaining mixture including the four oysters. Add the wine. Put in a saucepan and bring to a simmer. Mix the flour and cream together until smooth. Add to the sauce. Stir until thick and smooth. Broil the filets to the desired doneness. Pour over the sauce and serve at once.

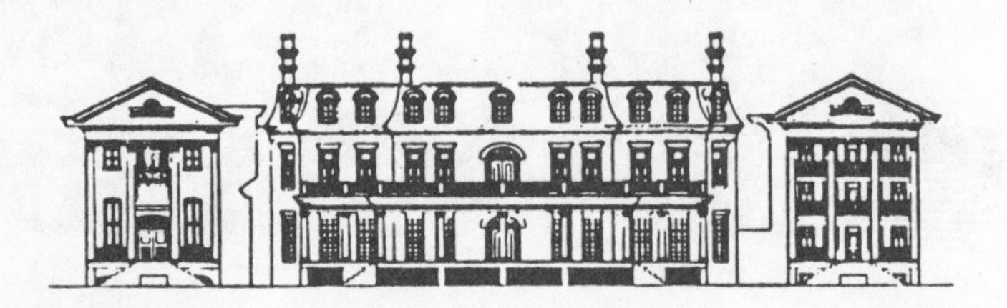

Martha Washington Inn

150 West Main Street
Abingdon, Virginia 24210
(804) 628-3161

The buildings that now constitute Martha Washington Inn have long been the most outstanding historic buildings of this section of the country. The center building, erected in 1830 by General Francis Preston as a residence, has been associated with the social life, the culture, and the educational progress of the area since that time. In 1937, the property was converted into a 100-room inn. The main dining room seats 300. It is especially famous for its superb southern dishes, including Old Virginia country ham, fried chicken, spoon bread, and hot biscuits.

Once used as a hospital, this structure is today the well-known Winchester Inn, a Victorian country inn offering lodging and full service dining to the public. Completely renovated by the Gibbs family in 1983, the structure is on the National Register of Historic Places. It honors the past but adapts itself to the present, an exquisite blend of comfort and tradition. The elegant dining room overlooks tiered gardens and patio seating. Chef Charles Barker takes great pride in offering an eclectic menu.

Teng Dah Filet

3 pounds beef tenderloin, in one piece
Finely chopped lemon rind
Cracked black pepper

Marinade
1/2 cup plus 1 tablespoon water
1/2 cup plus 1 tablespoon soy sauce
Pinch of nutmeg
1/8 teaspoon crushed anise
1/8 teaspoon ground cinnamon
3 teaspoons prepared horseradish
3 teaspoons pepper
2 teaspoons minced garlic
2 tablespoons sugar
1/3 cup fresh lemon juice

With a sharp boning knife, *carefully* remove most of the fat and silverskin from the filet. Since this is the most expensive cut of beef, work slowly to eliminate waste. With a paring knife make small incisions approximately an inch apart down the length of the filet. Stuff a small amount of lemon rind and cracked pepper in each incision.

In a mixing bowl combine the marinade ingredients. Immerse the tenderloins in the marinade for at least 8 hours (72 hours maximum), in a shallow baking dish.

Cut the filet into serving size portions. Broil to the desired doneness, and slice across the grain. Warm the marinade and pour over the sliced tenderloin.

Note: An interesting accompaniment for the Teng Dah is Japanese horseradish (wasabi).

Winchester Country Inn

35 South Second Street
Ashland, Oregon 97520
(503) 488-1113

Waldorf Astoria Stew

2 to 3 pounds round steak, cut into chunks
2 potatoes, cut up
1 to 2 cups sliced carrots
1 cup chopped celery
1 onion, chopped
2 tablespoons tapioca
1 tablespoon sugar
Salt and freshly ground pepper to taste
1 11-ounce can tomato soup
1 soup can water
1 bay leaf

Combine all ingredients in a roasting pan and bake at 250 degrees for 5 hours. (Or cook at a higher temperature for less time.) Serves 6 to 8.

The Logging Camp Ranch

8 Cr 3, Box 27
Bowman, North Dakota 58623
(701) 279-5501

Above the river, in the pines, there is a North Dakota few have experienced. Four generations of Hansons have owned and operated the 10,000-acre Logging Camp Ranch. This is not a dude ranch. It is a real, live, working ranch, much as it was in the 1880s. What it offers is as simple—and as complex—as the nature around it: wilderness, wildlife and wonder. Log cabins with showers and bathrooms are provided for overnight guests, who share bountiful meals with the owners and workers. Seven different unspoiled ecological systems, including North Dakota's only ponderosa pine forest, are part of the land owned by the ranch.

Overlooking the majestic Colorado River, the Riverside Hotel, built in 1903, offers a genteel retreat for those who wish to escape the daily routine. The dining rooms, antique bar, lobby, and 21 rooms are simply decorated and furnished with modest antiques—"grandma style," the owner calls it. The restaurant features country style cuisine but the "genteel" entrees are all prepared to order. One firm rule here is "eat your vegetables," all of which are fresh. Return visits are commonplace.

Biste Entomado

1 pound thinly sliced steak, tenderloin or club
5 tablespoons olive oil
Granulated garlic, to taste
Salt and freshly ground pepper to taste
Pinch of oregano
1 small green bell pepper, sliced into thin strips
1 small onion, sliced into thin strips
1/4 cup tomato sauce
1/4 cup tomato paste

In a skillet, saute the steak strips in 3 tablespoons of olive oil, adding granulated garlic, ground black pepper, salt, and a pinch of oregano. Saute until the steak is slightly brown and still rare or medium rare.

In a separate skillet, saute the bell pepper and onion in 2 tablespoons of the olive oil, adding the tomato sauce and tomato paste when the onions are translucent. Continue to saute for 3 minutes. Place the steak slices on plates and top with the sauteed tomato mixture. Serves 2 or 3.

The Riverside Hotel

509 Grand Avenue
Hot Sulphur Springs, Colorado 80451
(303) 725-3589

Barbecued Flank Steak

1 flank steak, approximately 1 1/2 pounds
1/2 teaspoon salt
1/4 teaspoon coarse ground pepper
1 teaspoon basil
1 teaspoon rosemary
2 cloves garlic, minced
1 onion, chopped
1/2 cup wine vinegar
1 cup salad oil

Combine the first eight ingredients to make a marinade. Place the steak in a shallow pan and pour the marinade over top. Cover and place in the refrigerator for at least 2 hours and preferably 4 to 6 hours. Turn the steak in the marinade occasionally.

Remove the steak from the marinade and grill over high heat approximately ten minutes per side for medium. Strain the onions from the marinade and saute them in a small skillet until tender. Use the onions as a garnish for meat. Slice the steak on the diagonal. Serves 3 or 4.

The Old Miner's Lodge

615 Woodside Avenue
P.O. Box 2639
Park City, Utah 84060-2639
(801) 645-8068

This inn is a renovated 1893 building located in the national historic district of the colorful resort town of Park City. The Lodge was established in 1893 as housing for local miners seeking their fortunes from the ore-rich hills of Park City. Today, the spirited warmth and hospitality of Park City's illustrious past remain.

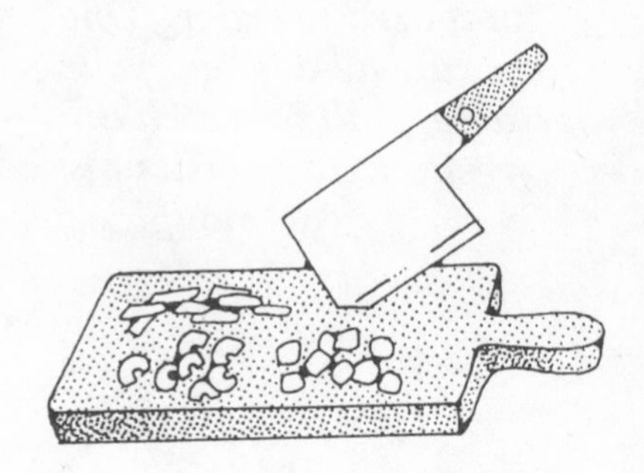

Add an Oriental flair to your next dinner with this exotic entree.

Szechwan Shredded Beef with Broccoli

1 1/2 pounds top round of beef
1/4 cup diced green bell pepper
2 tablespoons dry white wine
1/2 cup oyster sauce
1 tablespoon cornstarch
Pinch of salt
Freshly ground pepper to taste
2 tablespoons vegetable oil
1 tablespoon shredded fresh ginger root
1 tablespoon red pepper flakes
2 1/2 cups broccoli pieces or slices
Sesame seeds

Remove the fat from the meat. Cut it across the grain into slices and then into narrow strips. Place the meat in a bowl with the green bell pepper. Combine the wine, oyster sauce, cornstarch, salt, and pepper in a small bowl. Pour the mixture over the beef and marinate for 10 minutes.

Pour the oil into a wok and add the ginger root. Heat to 375 degrees F. Add the beef mixture and stir-fry until done, adding the red pepper flakes halfway through the cooking process. Serve on a bed of uncooked broccoli and sprinkle with sesame seeds. Serves 6.

Lost Horizon

Route 1, Box 3590
Alta, Wyoming
via Driggs, Idaho Post Office 83422
(307) 353-8226

Picadillo

4 pounds lean beef chuck, cut in 1-inch cubes
1 tablespoon salt
1/4 cup olive oil
2 large onions, finely chopped
6 cloves garlic, minced or pressed
6 to 8 large tomatoes, peeled, seeded and chopped
3 red or green bell peppers, seeded and chopped
3/4 cup small pimento-stuffed olives
3/4 teaspoon ground cloves
1 teaspoon ground cumin
2 tablespoons red wine vinegar
1 1/2 cups raisins
1 cup slivered almonds (optional)

Put the beef in a large Dutch oven. Add the salt and enough water to cover. Bring to a boil, cover, and reduce heat. Simmer until the beef is tender, about 1 1/2 hours. Uncover and simmer until most of the liquid has evaporated, about 1 hour or more. In another pan, heat the oil and saute the onion and garlic until soft and golden. Stir in the tomatoes and cook for five minutes. Add the peppers, olives, cumin, cloves, and vinegar. Cover and simmer for 15 minutes. Uncover and cook until the sauce is thick, about 30 minutes. combine the tomato sauce and beef, stir in the raisins and cook for 10 minutes longer. Mix in the almonds, if desired. Serves about 12.

Mayan Ranch

P. O. Box 577
Bandera, Texas 78003
(512) 796-3312

Internationally famous Mayan Ranch is by far the most popular ranch in the famous Texas Hill Country (also known as LBJ Country). There is a wide variety of activities, culinary and otherwise, from cowboy breakfasts cooked out on the trail to steak fries and barbecues.

The Mexican style food surpasses that of any in the Hill Country—if not in all of Texas. Judy Hicks has her own cookbook, Miss Judy's Wild Western Recipes, from which this recipe was taken.

Texas Style Chili

10 lbs ground beef
2 cups chopped onion (or more to taste)
3 tbsp. garlic powder (or use fresh pressed garlic)
3 tbsp. cumin
2 cups chili powder (dark red)
1 cup paprika
1 #10 can tomatoes, crushed
Salt, pepper to taste

Cook off meat first, then add onion and seasonings. Add crushed tomatoes. If you wish to add beans, do so after cooking. Good toppings are beans, onions and shredded cheese. We toss in a whole jalapeno pepper or two while cooking to "enhance" the flavor. Simmer slowly until done.

Mayan Ranch

P. O. Box 577
Bandera, Texas 78003
(512) 796-3312

Sauerbraten

Here's an old favorite that's still quite popular at Iowa's Ox-Yoke Inn.

4 pounds boneless bottom round of beef
1 cup vinegar
2 cups water
2 bay leaves
3 whole cloves
2 tablespoons flour
2 teaspoons salt
Freshly ground pepper
2 large onions, sliced
Browned flour

Put the meat, vinegar, water, bay leaves, and cloves into an earthen crock and let stand in a cool place for 2 or 3 days. Baste frequently and turn over once a day. Then drain the meat, saving the liquid. Sprinkle the meat with the flour, salt, and pepper and brown in hot fat on all sides. Add the marinade and onions and cover. Cook slowly for 1 1/2 hours or until tender. Remove the meat, strain the liquid, and thicken with browned flour to make a rich, brown gravy. Slice meat and add to the gravy. Serves 12.

Note: To brown flour, place it in a heavy skillet or pan and stir over low heat until the flour becomes brown.

Ox-Yoke Inn

P.O. Box 230
Amana, Iowa 52203
(319) 622-3441

Offering a panoramic view of the Mississippi River, this National Register Home is completely furnished with an impressive collection of period antiques, many of which were furnishings made by John Belter, Charles Baudoine, and P. Mallard. Fine porcelains include Meissen, Dresden, Teplitz, Royal Bonn, and Old Paris. The house features unique architecture, fine millwork and sophisticated brickwork. Gene Weber and Durrell Armstrong are the proprietors; Weber is the chef and has an excellent reputation.

Grillades

4 pounds beef, (round steak or veal rounds), 1/2 inch thick
1/2 cup bacon drippings
1/2 cup flour
1 cup chopped onion
1 cup diced green onions
1/4 cup chopped celery
1 1/2 cups chopped green bell pepper
2 cloves garlic, minced
2 cups peeled, seeded, and diced tomato
1/2 teaspoon tarragon
2/3 teaspoon thyme
1 cup water
1 cup red wine
3 teaspoons salt
1/2 teaspoon pepper
2 bay leaves
1/2 teaspoon Tabasco sauce
2 tablespoons Worcester sauce
3 tablespoons chopped fresh parsley

Remove the fat from the meat, and cut into serving pieces. Pound to 1/4-inch thick. Put in a Dutch oven. Brown the meat well in batches in 4 tablespoons of bacon grease. As it browns, place aside on a platter.

To the Dutch oven, add 4 more tablespoons bacon grease and flour. Stir to make a dark brown roux. Add the onion, green onions, celery, green bell pepper, and garlic and saute until the vegetables are limp. Add the tomatoes, tarragon, and thyme and cook for 3 minutes. Add the water and wine. Stir well for several minutes. Add the meat, salt, pepper, bay leaves, Tabasco, and Worcestershire. Lower the heat and continue cooking. If using veal rounds, simmer, covered, for 1 hour. If beef is used, simmer 2 hours, or until tender. Remove the bay leaves, and stir in the parsley. More liquid may be added if needed. Let sit for several hours or refrigerate overnight. Serve over grits or rice. Serves 8 to 10.

Weymouth Hall

P.O. Box 1091
Natchez, Mississippi 39121
(601) 445-2304

Bourbon Ribs

Here's a tempting ribs recipe from Vicksburg's historic Cedar Grove Inn.

4 pounds beef or pork ribs
1 onion, chopped (about 1/2 cup)
1/2 cup light molasses
1/2 cup catsup
2 teaspoons finely shredded orange rind
1/3 cup orange juice
2 tablespoons cooking oil
1 tablespoon vinegar
1 tablespoon steak sauce
1/2 teaspoon prepared mustard
1/2 teaspoon Worcestershire sauce
1/4 teaspoon garlic powder
1/4 teaspoon salt
1/4 teaspoon pepper
1/4 teaspoon hot pepper sauce
1/8 teaspoon ground cloves
1/4 cup bourbon

Place the ribs in a large Dutch oven or saucepan and add water to cover. Bring to a boil, then reduce the heat and simmer, covered, for 40 to 55 minutes or until the ribs are tender. Remove from the heat and drain thoroughly. While the ribs are cooking, prepare the sauce by combining all of the remaining ingredients in a pan. Bring the mixture to a boil and simmer gently, uncovered, for 15 to 20 minutes. When the ribs are tender and the sauce is prepared, grill the ribs over slow coals on a barbecue for about 45 minutes. Turn every 15 minutes and baste with the sauce. Serves 4.

Cedar Grove

P.O. Box B
Vicksburg, Mississippi 39181
(601) 636-1605

If you like veal, you'll love this recipe from Vermont's Inn at Weston.

Veal Provencale

1 1/2 pounds veal, diced
Flour
1 tablespoon oil
1 tablespoon butter
1/2 cup peeled, seeded, and diced tomatoes
1/2 cup thinly sliced mushrooms
1 garlic clove, diced
1 heaping teaspoon oregano
1 teaspoon basil
Salt and freshly ground pepper to taste
1/2 cup dry white wine
4 tablespoons grated fresh Parmesan cheese

Soak the veal for a day in milk or in lemon juice 1 hour. Dry thoroughly. Coat with flour and brown in the oil and butter until light brown. Do not crowd the veal in the pan or it will not saute properly. Add the tomatoes, mushroom, and garlic. Mix and season with oregano, basil, salt, pepper, and wine. Put into a casserole, sprinkle with Parmesan cheese, and cover. Bake at 325 degrees for 45 minutes.

Inn at Weston

P.O. Box 56
Weston, Vermont 05161
(802) 824-5804

Savory Veal Loaf with Sun-Dried Tomato and Chive Mayonnaise

1 pound ground veal
3/4 cup smoked bacon, diced small (8 to 10 thick slices)
1 large red onion, finely chopped
1 small red bell pepper, finely chopped
1 tablespoon butter
2 slices rye bread
2 slices white bread
4 eggs
2 teaspoons salt
1/2 teaspoon cayenne pepper
3 dashes Tabasco sauce
1/4 cup catsup
1 tablespoons Worcestershire sauce
6 sprigs parsley, finely chopped

Combine the veal and bacon and refrigerate until needed. Saute the onion and pepper in the butter. Put the bread into a food processor and process into medium-fine crumbs. Beat the eggs; add to them the last 6 ingredients. Combine the bread crumb mixture and the meat together. Grease a small baking sheet and form the veal into a loaf. Bake at 375 degrees for approximately 45 minutes. Allow the meat to rest at least 15 minutes before cutting. Serve with Sun-Dried Tomato and Chive Mayonnaise. Serves 8.

Sun-Dried Tomato and Chive Mayonnaise
1 egg yolk
2 tablespoons sun-dried tomatoes, finely diced
Juice of 1/2 lemon
Pinch of salt
dash of pepper
(Continued on following page)

The Barrows House

Dorset, Vermont 05251

The Barrows House grounds are part of a parcel of land that originally belonged to the Dorset Church in 1784. The main inn's front rooms and those above were built in 1804. *(continued on following page)*

Much energy and time have been spent restoring and redecorating this lovely building and the surrounding cottages by Sally and Tim Brown, who bought the property in 1986. Chefs Tim Blackwell and Gary Walker provide the culinary expertise to prepare hearty breakfasts and full gourmet dinners daily.

(Continued from previous page)

1/2 cup olive oil
1 cup vegetable oil
3 tablespoons finely chopped chives
1 tablespoon Dijon mustard

Combine and whip the first five ingredients. Combine the oils. At first add them drop by drop to the egg yolk mixture, whipping all the time. As the mayonnaise comes together and no oil spots are appearing on top of the mixture, add the remaining oil in a slow, steady stream. If a thicker mayonnaise is desired, add more vegetable oil to thicken. Add the chives and mustard; adjust the salt and pepper. Use as a condiment for the warm veal loaf or as a spread for Savory Veal Loaf sandwiches on crusty French bread. Makes 1 1/2 cups.

Barrows House

Dorset, Vermont 05251
(802) 867-4455

Blanquette de Veau a l'Ancienne

(Old-fashioned Veal Stew with Onions and Mushrooms)

2 pounds veal shoulder, cut into 2-inch cubes
Salt and freshly ground pepper
1/2 pound mushrooms, quartered
1/4 pound pearl onions (frozen can be used)
2 tablespoons butter
Juice of 1/2 lemon
Pinch of sugar
1 onion, quartered
1 carrot, cut in half
1 small stalk celery
Bouquet garni (1 bay leaf, pinch of thyme, 5 peppercorns, parsley sprigs, and 1 crushed garlic clove tied in cheesecloth)
4 tablespoons butter
4 tablespoons flour
1 egg yolk
1 tablespoon heavy cream
Chopped parsley, for garnish

Put the meat into a saucepan and cover with water. Add salt. Bring to a boil and skim. Add the quartered onion, the carrot, celery, and bouquet garni. Cook until the meat is fork tender (about 50 minutes). While the meat is cooking, prepare the roux, mushrooms, and pearl onions.

To make a roux for the sauce, melt the butter in a saucepan. Beat in the flour and cook, stirring, over low heat for 5 minutes. Set aside and let cool. (Continued on following page.)

Pasquaney Inn

SR 1, Box 1066
Bridgewater, New Hampshire 03222
(603) 744-9111

The Pasquaney is a 26-room inn located a little over 100 miles from Boston on Newfound Lake. Constructed on a hillside, it dates back to 1840. It offers the comfortable feel of grandmother's house, and fine European cuisine is served.

(Continued from previous page.) Place the mushrooms in a shallow saucepan, cover with water, and add 1 tablespoon butter, salt and pepper to taste, and the lemon juice. Cover and cook over low heat until tender. Set the mushrooms aside in the braising liquid.

Place the onions in a shallow saucepan, barely cover with water, and add 1 tablespoon of butter, salt and pepper to taste, and a pinch of sugar. Cover and cook over medium heat, shaking the pan until the liquid is evaporated and onions begin to glaze. Do not brown.

When the meat is tender, remove it from the cooking liquid, discard the bouquet, onion, and carrot and set the meat aside. Strain the liquid into the roux and cook over medium heat, stirring, until the mixture is thickened, smooth, and cooked through (about 10 minutes). Add the meat to the sauce along with the onions, mushrooms, and some of the mushroom liquid. Correct seasoning. Combine the egg yolk and cream and stir into the stew, *off the heat*. Do not reboil. Serve immediately, garnished with parsley. Accompany with rice pilaf. Serves 4.

Pasquaney Inn

SR 1, Box 1066
Bridgewater, New Hampshire 03222
(603) 744-9111

Veal Steak Cordon Bleu

4 veal cutlets, pounded thin
2 slices cooked ham
2 slices Swiss cheese
1 egg, beaten
Fine bread crumbs
2 to 4 tablespoons margarine
Lemon slices
Parsley

Top two of the veal cutlets with ham and cheese. Trim off the ends if they overlap. Dip remaining cutlets in the beaten egg and place firmly on top of each cheese slice. Dip each "sandwich" in egg and then in bread crumbs—keeping the layers together, coating both sides. Melt the margarine in a skillet. Add the prepared cutlets and cook over medium heat, turning once, for about 5 minutes on each side or until golden brown and tender. Garnish with lemon slices and parsley. Serves 2.

Woodbound Inn

Post Office
Jaffrey, New Hampshire 03452
(603) 532-8341

Here is a snug country inn, emphasizing a friendly welcome and continuing hospitality. The inn caters to guests who enjoy informal resort life in the country at a high elevation. Families are especially welcome. Programs and activities are planned for children, and a baby-sitting service is offered. There are handcraft workshops, square dances, cookouts, beach lunches, and in the winter, cross-country skiing, ice skating, tobogganing, and snowshoeing. Accommodations are provided for ninety-four guests. Woodbound provides real home-cooked meals, hot breads, and pastries. Its foods are bountiful and delicious.

The Inn at Long Last is one of Vermont's very best and offers one of the most distinctive menus in New England. The inn is housed in a gracious, plantation- style home on the Village Green. It is old-fashioned in comfort and young in spirit. The 35 guest rooms are filled with Colonial antiques. The grounds include a heated pool, tennis courts, and a gracious patio.

Grilled Veal Tournedo and Sweetbreads with a Gin Creme Fraiche Sauce

2 4-ounce veal medallions (from the loin)
2 4-ounce veal sweetbreads, poached, pressed, and trimmed
2 shallots, finely diced
1/4 teaspoon dried juniper berries
4 tablespoons butter
2 tablespoons gin
4 tablespoons veal stock
2 tablespoons creme fraiche
Salt and freshly ground pepper to taste

Season the veal medallions and sweetbreads with salt and pepper and coat in oil. Grill over a hot fire until medium rare. Keep warm. To make the sauce, saute the shallots and juniper berry in the butter, add the gin, and reduce until almost dry. Add the veal stock and reduce by half. Whip in the creme fraiche and season to taste. Arrange the veal and sweetbreads on a plate and spoon the sauce over the meat. Serves 2.

The Inn at Long Last

P.O. Box 589
Chester, Vermont 05143
(802) 875-2444

Veal Oporto

12 medium veal scallops
Flour
6 tablespoons butter
3 tablespoons olive oil
2/3 cup Port wine
Salt and freshly ground pepper to taste
1/2 cup heavy cream
Butter
Buttered noodles
Toasted bread crumbs

Pound the scallops thin and flour them lightly. Saute in butter and olive oil, turning to brown evenly. When the scallops are brown and tender, add the wine and cook gently for 2 minutes. Season to taste. Remove the meat to a hot platter and add the cream to the pan. Stir to scrape up all the brown bits and flavor with a little butter. Pour the sauce over the veal. Serve on buttered noodles sprinkled with toasted bread crumbs. Serves 12.

Bradford Inn

Main Street
Bradford, New Hampshire 03221
(603) 938-5309

Here is a historic country inn offering good food, good friends, and good lodging. It was built in 1898 with a wide staircase and spacious halls to welcome visitors to its attractive parlors. All rooms have private baths and there are also family suites. The Bradford Inn serves regional New England cuisine in its large attractive dining room. Connie and Tom Mazol are the innkeepers.

Try this delectable recipe from the Heritage Inn!

Escalope de Veau Portugaise

12 3-ounce scallops of veal, pounded thin
Seasoned flour
Clarified butter and olive oil, half of each

Dredge the veal in the flour and pat dry. Set aside on parchment paper or waxed paper. Heat a large saute pan with clarified butter and olive oil and saute the veal in batches. Remove the scallops to an ovenproof platter as they are cooked. Pour over Sauce Portugaise and serve. Serves 6.

Sauce Portugaise
4 shrimp, peeled, deveined, and diced
8 cloves garlic, minced
8 ounces fresh white mushrooms, quartered
4 tablespoons dry sherry
Juice of 2 lemons
8 ounces cherry tomatoes, cut in half
4 ounces stuffed green olives, diced
1 cup butter
1 bunch parsley, chopped, or half parsley and half basil

In a small saute pan, cook the diced shrimp and garlic in a small amount of oil for 2 to 3 minutes. Add the mushrooms and cook until they brown. Add the sherry, lemon juice, tomatoes, and olives. Next, flake in the butter and parsley. Do not allow to boil.

Heritage Inn

Heritage Road
Southbury, Connecticut 06488
(203) 264-8200

Saltimbocca Alla Romana

8 slices veal, sliced thinly and pounded
Salt and freshly ground pepper to taste
1/2 cup flour
2 tablespoons butter
8 thin slices prosciutto ham
8 thin slices mozzarella cheese

Sprinkle salt and pepper on each slice of veal. Dredge the veal in flour, shaking off excess flour. Heat butter in a saute pan. When it foams, place veal in the pan. Do not crowd. Saute for 1 minute each side. Place the veal in a baking dish, and top with prosciutto and cheese. Place in a broiler, 4 inches under the flame, just until the cheese melts. Serve immediately. Serves 4.

Ragged Garden Inn

Sunset Drive, P.O. Box 1927
Blowing Rock, North Carolina 28605
(704) 295-9703

A touch of the past has come alive in Blowing Rock. This grandiose old home, named Ragged Garden when it was built at the turn of the century, boasts a majestic setting. In three different dining areas, guests dine in the grandeur of days gone by. The cuisine is classic with a slight emphasis on Northern Italian. Chef/Owner Joseph Villani has a distinguished culinary background.

This famous resort was founded by David Walley in 1860. It is nestled against the Sierra Nevadas on the route between San Francisco and Virginia City that was traveled by stagecoaches, pony express riders, and migrant mine workers. David's wife, Harriet, joined him in 1862, and together they built a hotel with 40 guest rooms. The inn has a fine dining and lounge area named The Zephyr after the winds that blow from the Sierras. On Sunday, a champagne brunch delights the guests. The grounds of the resort are dotted with six hot mineral pools ranging in temperature from 96 to 104 degrees F.

Veal Chasseur

4 3-ounce slices Provimi veal, pounded
Flour
8 tablespoons clarified butter
4 mushrooms, sliced
3/4 cup dry sherry
1/2 cup brown sauce
2 tablespoons diced tomato, peeled and seeded
Pinch of tarragon
Pinch of white pepper
Salt to taste
Splash of brandy
2 teaspoons unsalted butter
Sprigs of fresh tarragon, for garnish

Dredge the veal in flour, shaking off any excess. Heat 4 tablespoons of the clarified butter in a saute pan until very hot. Saute the veal to medium rare and remove from the pan. Add the remaining clarified butter to the pan. Add the mushrooms and cook for 1 minute. Add the sherry. Flame the sherry to remove the alcohol. When the flame subsides, add the brown sauce, tomato, tarragon, and white pepper. Reduce until the sauce thickens. Salt to taste. Add the brandy and unsalted butter, and mix thoroughly. Return the veal to the pan to reheat. Layer the veal slices on two dinner plates and pour over the sauce. Garnish with the fresh tarragon.

Walley's

P.O. Box 26
Genoa, Nevada 89411
(702) 782-8155

Lamb Curry

2 cooking apples, peeled, cored, and sliced
2 onions, sliced
1 green bell pepper, chopped
1 garlic clove, crushed
2 tablespoons olive oil
2 tablespoons flour
1 tablespoon curry powder
1/2 teaspoon salt
1/2 teaspoon marjoram
1/2 teaspoon thyme
1 cup consomme
1/2 cup dry red wine
1 lemon, juice and grated rind
1/2 cup raisins (optional)
2 whole cloves
2 cups diced cooked lamb
1/2 cup shredded coconut
1 tablespoon sour cream

Saute the apples, onions, bell pepper, and the garlic in oil until the onions are limp. Sprinkle the flour, curry powder, salt, marjoram, and thyme over top. Mix well, and cook 5 minutes, stirring constantly. Add the consomme, wine, lemon juice and grated rind, raisins, and cloves. Simmer for 20 to 30 minutes. Add the lamb and coconut. Heat for at least 15 minutes. Just before serving, add the sour cream and mix well. Serve over rice. For added glamour, serve side dishes of chopped peanuts, toasted coconut, and chutney. Serves 4.

Red Apple

P.O. Box 192
Eden Isle
Heber Springs, Arkansas 72594
(501) 362-3111

If you enjoy food, quiet elegance, and gentle people, you will love the Red Apple Inn. In an entrancing island setting, the Red Apple is surrounded by 35,000-acre Greers Ferry Lake. The air is clean, the surrounding hills are wooded, and the accommodations are without equal in the entire Southwest. Dining is at treetop level, with a magnificent panoramic view of the dazzling lake. Each table features an Eden Isle rose.

Chico Hot Springs is a place the visitor has to experience to fully appreciate. It is not a fancy place but its quality is unique. Chico is relaxation, Montana-style--the high country at its best. It is located in south central Montana's Paradise Valley with the Absaroka mountain range defining the eastern skyline, the Gallatin range the west and the famous Yellowstone River running between the two. High country at its best. Chico's history centers on its hot pools, whose "restorative" powers have been put to good use for more than a century. The water in the pools is between 100 and 104 degrees F. with no chlorine or other chemicals.

Lamb Wellington

4 to 5 6-ounce lamb loins
4 bunches fresh spinach or 2 10-ounce packages frozen spinach
4 6 x 6-inch squares puff pastry
Rosemary, garlic salt, and freshly ground pepper to taste
1 cup brown sauce or brown gravy
6 tablespoons red wine
1 tablespoon green peppercorns

In a very hot saute pan, sear the lamb loins on all sides to seal in the juices. Blanch the spinach and set on towels to dry. Place the puff pastry squares on a lightly floured cutting board. Lay an even layer of dry spinach about 1/8-inch thick on top of each pastry square and top with a lamb loin seasoned with rosemary, garlic salt, and pepper. Roll as for egg rolls, folding the ends in. Bake at 350 degrees for 12 to 15 minutes for medium rare.

In a small saucepan, reduce the wine by one-third; add it to the brown sauce. Add the peppercorns, simmer, and reduce by one-quarter.

To serve, spoon some sauce onto each of four plates and top with a lamb Wellington sliced into six medallions. Serves 4.

Chico Hot Springs Lodge

Drawer D
Pray, Montana 59065
(406) 333-4933

Roast Lamb with Crushed Black Pepper, Rosemary, and Mint

4 tablespoons crushed black peppercorns
3 tablespoons fresh rosemary leaves
1/2 cup fresh mint leaves
5 garlic cloves, crushed, plus 2 garlic cloves, slivered
1/3 cup Oriental soy sauce
3/4 cup dry red wine
1 boned but untied leg of lamb, about 5 pounds (weighed after boning)
3 tablespoons Dijon mustard

Combine 2 tablespoons of the crushed peppercorns, the rosemary, mint, 5 cloves of garlic, soy sauce, and red wine in a shallow bowl or pan. Marinate the lamb in the mixture for eight hours or so, turning occasionally.

Remove the lamb from the marinade and drain; reserve marinade. Roll the roast, tying it with kitchen twine. Make small slits evenly in the lamb, just large enough for the garlic slivers. Insert the slivers.

Spread the mustard over the lamb and pat 2 tablespoons of the crushed peppercorn into the mustard. Set the roast in a shallow roasting pan just large enough to hold it and pour the reserved marinade carefully around, but not over the roast.

Bake at 325 degrees for 90 minutes, or 18 minutes per pound for medium rare, basting occasionally. Or roast to your liking (approximately another 10 to 15 minutes for well-done meat). Let the roast stand for about 20 minutes before carving. Serve with pan juices. Serves 6 to 8.

DeHaven Valley Farm

39247 North Highway 1
Westport, California 95488
(707) 961-1660

DeHaven Valley Farm is located in northern Mendocino County, on 20 acres of meadows, hills, and streams, across the road from the Pacific Ocean. The Victorian farmhouse, built in 1875, has been beautifully restored, and two cottages offer spacious seclusion. Guests can enjoy exploring tidepools, visiting a variety of farm animals, and soaking in the hot tub. The farm is also ideally located for side trips to visit the gigantic redwoods, 25 miles to the north, and the artist's colony of Mendocino, 25 miles south.

This historic hotel boasts 100 years of hospitality, luxurious accommodations, exceptional service, and understated elegance. Its Harmans Restaurant is world class, featuring European cuisine and impeccable service. Parkersburg enjoys a wonderful setting in the tranquil ambience of the Ohio Valley, and the Blennerhassett offers country inn amenities in an in-town location. This recipe is courtesy of Chef Richard Alabaugh.

Herbed Lamb Stew

1 1/2 pounds boneless lamb or beef stew meat, cut into 3/4-inch cubes
2 tablespoons cooking oil
1 quart water
1/2 teaspoon salt
1/4 teaspoon pepper
1 clove garlic, minced
1 bay leaf
2 teaspoons instant beef bouillon granules
1/2 teaspoon dried thyme
1/2 teaspoon dried oregano
1/2 teaspoon dried marjoram
4 medium carrots, sliced 1/2-inch thick
4 stalks celery, sliced 1 inch thick
2 onions, cut into wedges
1/2 cup sour cream
1/4 cup flour

Heat the oil in a Dutch oven. Add the meat and brown. Add the water, salt, and pepper. Bring to a boil. Reduce the heat, cover and simmer for 30 minutes. Stir in the carrots, celery, and onions. Cover and simmer for about 25 minutes more or until the meat and vegetables are tender. Add the herbs and spices. Combine the sour cream, flour, and 2 tablespoons of water. Stir about 1/2 cup of the hot mixture into the sour cream mixture. Return to remaining hot mixture. Cook, stirring, until thickened and bubbly. Serves 5.

Blennerhassett Hotel

P.O. Box 51
Parkersburg, West Virginia 26102
(304) 422-3131

Pork Chops in Cream

Here's a delicious pork chop recipe from Elizabeth Farrell's Elizabethian Inn.

6 center cut pork chops, 2 inches thick
Bouquet of seasonings including equal amounts
 white pepper, garlic powder, thyme, basil,
 and caraway seeds
4 tablespoons vegetable oil
1 1/2 cups beef stock
3 cups minced mushrooms
4 tablespoons chopped green onions
1 cup light cream
1 tablespoon butter, melted
1 tablespoon flour
3 tablespoons Cognac
3 egg yolks
Salt and freshly ground pepper to taste

Sprinkle the pork chops with the seasoning mixture on both sides. Heat the oil in a heavy skillet until sizzling. Add the chops, sear, and brown on each side. Remove the chops; reserve the juices.

Place the pork chops in a roasting pan and pour over the beef stock. Cover and bake at 325 degrees until fork tender—for up to two hours.

Add the mushrooms and onions to the skillet along with the reserved juices and heat. Add 1/2 cup cream and bring just to a boil.

Blend the melted butter and the flour in a skillet, whisking until smooth. Bring to a boil and simmer for 2 minutes. Stir in the Cognac.

Blend the egg yolks and the remaining 1/2 cup of cream in a small bowl. Combine with the sauce in the skillet. Add salt and pepper to taste. Heat over low heat, stirring constantly, but do not boil. Serve over the pork chops. Serves 6.

Note: The beef stock can be reserved for another use.

Elizabethian Inn

463 Wrigley Drive
Lake Geneva, Wisconsin 53147
(414)248-9131

7 Breakfasts and Brunches

High Meadows Inn is considered Virginia's vineyard inn, just minutes south of Charlottesville and just north of historic Scottsville. The inn occupies a grand house, where guests stay in beautifully appointed rooms, each furnished with individually collected period antiques, original botanicals, and steel engravings. Twenty-two acres of gardens, footpaths, forests, and ponds guarantee privacy and quiet. High Meadows was recently placed on the National Register of Historic Places. This recipe was selected from the inn's own cookbook written by the chef-owner, Peter Sushka, The Best of High Meadows.

Creamy Breakfast Ambrosia

2 cups sliced peaches (or pears, apples, or other fruit)
2 bananas, sliced
10 to 12 strawberries, sliced
2 oranges, peeled and sliced
1 tablespoon fresh lemon juice
1 cup coconut
1 cup miniature marshmallows
1 cup vanilla or lemon yogurt
1 tablespoon sugar (optional)

In a large bowl, combine the fruit and lemon juice. Toss lightly. Stir in the coconut, marshmallows and yogurt—and sugar if desired. Chill for 1/2 to 1 hour and serve in stemmed clear sherbet glasses. Serves 8.

High Meadows Inn

Route 4, Box 6
Scottsville, Virginia 24590
(804) 286-2218

Sour Cream Ambrosia

3 oranges, peeled and sectioned
1/2 pound green seedless grapes
1/2 cantaloupe, peeled and cut in chunks
1/4 pineapple, peeled and cut in chunks
1/2 cup shredded moist coconut
1/4 cup chopped pecans
1 cup sour cream
1 tablespoon honey
1/4 teaspoon vanilla extract
Pomegranate seeds, for garnish

In a medium bowl, mix the fruits, coconut and pecans. Stir together the sour cream, honey, and vanilla and mix well into the fruits. Serve in footed glass dessert dishes, garnished with pomegranate seeds. Serves 6.

Grant Corner Inn

122 Grant Avenue
Santa Fe, New Mexico 87501
(505) 983-6678

Here is an exquisite Colonial manor in beautiful Santa Fe. With an ideal location just two blocks from the historic Plaza, the inn is nestled among intriguing shops and galleries. Built in the early 1900s as a home for a wealthy New Mexico ranching family, the inn boasts charming guest rooms, each appointed with antiques and treasures from around the world. A varied menu provides delicious treats. The following recipe was taken from the inn's own cookbook, Grant Corner Inn Breakfast and Brunch Cookbook, *by Louise Stewart.*

High on the side of the Bighorn Mountains in a whispering pine forest, you will find this rustic lodge built and operated by Ron Spahn, a former Yellowstone Park ranger. It is at the edge of the one million acre Bighorn National Forest. Deer, moose, eagles and turkeys are commonplace and even elusive bear and mountain lions are never far away. Hearty food is served on a deck with a 100-mile view. Western-style supper cookouts followed by evening wildlife safaris are a tradition at the lodge.

Creamy Eggs

8 eggs, beaten
1/4 cup milk
1/4 teaspoon salt
Dash of freshly ground pepper
2 tablespoons butter
1 3-ounce package cream cheese with chives, cubed
Chopped fresh parsley, for garnish

Beat the eggs, milk, salt, and pepper until combined. Melt the butter in a skillet over low heat, and pour in the egg mixture. As the eggs begin to set, drop the cheese cubes on top. Cook until the eggs are no longer runny and the cheese is melted. Garnish with parsley. Serves 4.

Spahn's Bighorn Mountain Lodge

P.O. Box 579
Big Horn, Wyoming 82833
(307) 674-8150

Eggs Chasseur

8 slices bacon, diced
1/2 onion, diced
1 clove garlic, diced
1/2 pound mushrooms, diced
6 tomatoes, peeled, seeded, and diced
2 tablespoons dried tarragon
Salt and freshly ground pepper to taste
4 English muffins, split
8 eggs

Saute the bacon until the fat is rendered. Add the onion and garlic, and saute until translucent. Add the mushrooms and saute for 3 minutes. Add the tomatoes and tarragon and simmer for 10 minutes. Adjust the seasoning.

Toast the halved English muffins and poach the eggs. Spoon the sauce over the toasted muffins and top with poached eggs. Serves 4.

Winchester Country Inn

35 East Second Street
Ashland, Oregon 97520
(503) 488-1113

Once used as a hospital, the well-known Winchester Inn is a Victorian country inn offering lodging and full service dining to the public. Completely renovated by the Gibbs family in 1983, the structure is on the National Register of Historic Places. It honors the past but adapts itself to the present, offering an exquisite blend of comfort and tradition. The elegant dining room overlooks tiered gardens and patio seating. Chef Charles Barker takes great pride in offering an eclectic menu.

Built in the 1760s by the founder of Westminster, the Winchester Country Inn is one of Carroll County's oldest buildings. A professional team including a curator, historian, architect and other artisans has restored its rich beauty while adding present-day comforts. The interior has been refurbished with antiques and period furnishings, including pieces from prominent Carroll County families. Beautiful pine flooring, original moldings, hand blown windowpanes, and period fixtures throughout make the Winchester one of the most authentically antique country inns in America.

Baked Scrambled Eggs

6 eggs, beaten
1/3 cup milk
1 teaspoon salt
1 teaspoon pepper
1/4 pound American cheese, cubed

Combine the ingredients in the order given. Bake in a well-buttered casserole at 350 degrees for 30 minutes or until puffy and a knife inserted in the center comes out clean. Serves 4 to 6 people.

Winchester Country Inn

430 South Bishop
Westminster, Maryland 21157
(301) 876-7373

Eggs Florentine

1/4 cup butter
1 large onion, chopped
4 tablespoons flour
4 cups milk
1/2 teaspoon Tabasco sauce
1/2 teaspoon salt
Pinch of nutmeg
8 ounces sliced mushrooms
2 10-ounce packages frozen chopped spinach, thawed and
drained well
8 eggs, hard-cooked
Hollandaise sauce

Melt the butter in a large skillet; saute the onions until golden. Stir in the flour and cook for a few minutes. Gradually add the milk. Stir and cook until the mixture boils and thickens. Stir in the Tabasco sauce, salt and nutmeg. Add the mushrooms and spinach.

Spoon the spinach mixture into eight individual ramekins. When ready to serve, bake at 350 degrees for about 5 minutes, until bubbly. Top with a sliced hard cooked egg and Hollandaise sauce. Return to the oven and bake at 350 degrees for another 5 minutes. Serves 8.

Romeo Inn

295 Idaho Street
Ashland, Oregon 97520
(503) 488-0884

This delightful inn is romantically set in one of Ashland's quiet residential areas near the Oregon Shakespearean Festival. Built in the early 1930s, the classic Cape Cod structure sits elegantly amid towering Ponderosa pines overlooking the Rogue Valley. Margaret and Bruce Halverson are the innkeepers, and the food they serve is a gourmet's delight.

Here is an historic landmark and one of the most beautiful showplaces in the Southwest. Sagebrush Inn was built of adobe in the Pueblo-Mission style in 1929 to cater to the trade between New York and Arizona. It offers an unsurpassed view of the Sangre de Christo Mountains. With its graceful portals, enchanting patios and authentic architecture, the inn captivates and charms all guests. A newer addition, the Sagebrush Village, offers alternative family lodging. Two huge dining facilities offer award winning New Mexican and Continental cuisine. The town of Taos has become one of the foremost art colonies in the world.

Green Chili Huevos Rancheros

1 pound diced pork
Meat tenderizer
1 cup chopped green chilies
2 quarts water
1 tablespoon garlic powder
1 tablespoon chicken base
2/3 cup flour
1/3 cup melted butter
1 teaspoon Maggi seasoning or salt
Kitchen Bouquet (optional)
Corn tortillas
Butter
Eggs
Grated Cheddar cheese

Saute the pork with a pinch of meat tenderizer. Cook until brown. Add the green chilies (mild, medium, or hot). Cover with the water. Bring to a boil and add the garlic powder and chicken base. Blend the flour and melted butter to make a roux. Add the roux to the pork and let boil for 3 to 4 minutes, stirring occasionally. Add the Maggi seasoning. Let the mixture simmer, stirring occasionally. Add Kitchen Bouquet for color, if desired. Melt a small amount of butter in a pan. Add the tortillas, turning several times until they are soft. Cook the eggs as desired. Top with the chili mixture and grated Cheddar cheese. Serve with the tortillas. Makes 2 quarts of chili.

Note: The chili mixture may also be used in making burritos or enchiladas.

Sagebrush Inn

P.O. Box 1566
Taos, New Mexico 87571
(505) 758-2254

Apple Brie Omelet

The Old Yacht Club in Santa Barbara is especially famous for its omelets. Here is one reason why.

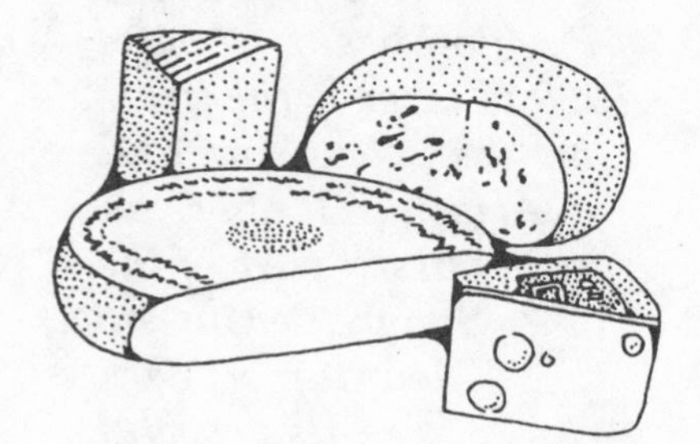

1 tablespoon plus 2 tablespoons butter
2 green Pippin apples, peeled, cored, and sliced
2 tablespoons brown sugar
1/2 teaspoon ground cinnamon
8 eggs
4 tablespoons water
4 ounces Brie cheese (plastic covering removed), sliced
Lemon pepper

Melt the 1 tablespoon of butter in a skillet. Add the apples and saute for 5 to 6 minutes, until softened. Add the sugar and cinnamon, stir, and cook for 5 minutes more.

To prepare the omelet, whisk together the eggs and water for 1 to 2 minutes. Heat a 12-inch pan and melt the 2 tablespoons butter over low heat. Pour the egg mixture into the pan. Allow to harden on the bottom. Using a spatula, push the cooked part to the middle of the pan and allow the liquid to run around the edges and cook through. Continue until the eggs are set but not hard. Be careful not to brown the bottom.

When the eggs are firm, place the apple mixture over the top of one half of the omelet. Place the sliced Brie on top of the apples. Use a spatula to fold the plain half of the omelet over the filling. Cover the pan and cook for 4 to 5 minutes, until the cheese melts. Sprinkle with the lemon pepper. Serves 4 to 6.

The Old Yacht Club Inn

431 Corona del Mar
Santa Barbara, California 93103
(805) 962-1277

"The Chanticleer and the Fox" is one of the stories told in Chaucer's Canterbury Tales. It is a barnyard fable whose origin comes from the heart of Europe. The Chanticleer Inn reflects this same European country feeling in Ashland. This snug and cozy inn is just a short walk from the Oregon Shakespearean Festival with the Rogue River's whitewater rafting and Mount Ashland's ski slopes a short distance away. Delicious food is served in the sunny dining room.

Orange Omelet Souffle with Orange Sauce

3 tablespoons sugar
12 eggs
3 tablespoons flour
1 tablespoon grated orange rind
Orange Sauce (recipe below)

Combine the sugar with the egg whites. Combine the flour and orange rind with the egg yolks and beat well. Refrigerate both mixtures. Right before baking, whip the egg white mixture until stiff. Gently fold the egg white into the yolks. To bake, place a small amount of Orange Sauce in the bottom of six or eight buttered ramekins (depending on size.) Gently mound spoonfuls of the souffle mixture into the ramekins. Bake at 375 degrees for about 10 minutes or until lightly brown and set. Garnish with sliced strawberries, and add Orange Sauce. Serves 6 to 8.

Orange Sauce
3 cups fresh orange juice
1/2 cup butter
Brown sugar

Combine the orange juice and butter in a saucepan. Add brown sugar to taste. Heat until warm.

Chanticleer Inn

120 Gresham Street
Ashland, Oregon 97520
(503) 482-1919

Egg Casserole

10 eggs
1/2 cup melted butter
1 pound Monterey Jack cheese, grated
1 pint cottage cheese
1/2 cup flour
1 teaspoon baking powder
1/2 teaspoon Spike (or salt)
2 4-ounce cans chopped chilies
1 4-ounce can sliced olives
Chopped zucchini, spinach, mushrooms, sauteed in butter
(optional)
Nasturtium blossoms, cherry tomatoes, avocado, or orange
slices, for garnish

Beat the eggs, then beat in the next six ingredients. Add the chilies and olives, and any of the optional ingredients. Grease a 9 by 13-inch baking dish, and pour in the prepared ingredients. Bake at 350 degrees for 35 minutes or until a knife comes out clean. This dish may be prepared the night before and warmed up for breakfast. Cut in squares, garnish, and serve with homemade salsa and cottage bacon slices. Serves 10 to 12.

Here is an intimate country retreat hidden away from the road yet within walking distance of the ocean and the historic Old Town district of Half Moon Bay. Flower boxes, rose gardens and patios make outdoor living an added pleasure. The cuisine is unforgettable, and diners overlook the Pacific Ocean.

Mill Rose Inn

615 Mill Street
Half Moon Bay, California 94019
(415) 726-9794

This hearty Texas-style casserole is one of many treats served up at the famous Excelsior Inn.

Breakfast Casserole

1 pound pork sausage
1/4 cup chopped onion
1/4 cup chopped green bell pepper
1/4 cup chopped celery
1/4 cup chopped green chilies
1 teaspoon salt
1 teaspoon dry mustard
2 cups milk
6 to 8 eggs, lightly beaten
6 slices whole-wheat bread, cubed
1 cup grated Cheddar cheese

Fry the sausage and crumble; drain off all but 3 teaspoons of the fat. Saute the onions, pepper, celery, and chilies in the reserved fat. Mix the sauteed ingredients with the sausage and remaining ingredients in a large bowl. Pour into a greased 9 by 13-inch baking dish and bake at 350 degrees f. for 1 hour. Cut in squares and serve. Serves 9 to 12.

Excelsior House

211 West Austin Street
Jefferson, Texas 75657
(214) 665-2513

Mexican Quiche

15 eggs
1/2 pound Cheddar cheese, grated
1/2 pound Monterey Jack cheese, grated
1 pint cottage cheese
1 7-ounce can green chilies, chopped
1/2 cup flour
1 teaspoon baking powder
Red salsa, for topping
Sour cream, for topping
Chopped green onions, for topping

In a large mixing bowl, combine all ingredients and mix well. Pour into a greased 9 by 13-inch baking dish (or three large casseroles). Bake at 350 degrees F. for 45 minutes or until a knife inserted in the center comes out clean and the mixture is set. Cut in squares and serve. Pass the toppings. Serves 12.

La Posada de Taos

P.O. Box 1118
Taos, New Mexico 87571
(505) 758-8164

Here is a private "hacienda" in the heart of beautiful Taos. There is a special magic about Taos and about this lovely inn. "La Posada" is Spanish for "inn." La Posada de Taos gives its guests modern comforts they require in an atmosphere of friendliness. The hospitality is highly personal, and will bring visitors back time after time.

Andrew Jackson was President of the young Republic when this inn was built. Thirty years later The Beechmont was a silent witness to the Civil War's first major battle on free soil when Federal troops commanded by General Kilpatrick retreated, with Jeb Stuart's Confederate cavalry in hot pursuit. Now, in calmer times, it has been restored to its federal period elegance and offers the visitor a bridge across the centuries. Terry Hormel, a gourmet chef, blesses his guests with delectable multi-course breakfast feasts, served in the formal dining room.

Florentine Tarts

1 onion, minced
1/2 cup butter, melted
1/2 10-ounce package frozen spinach
1/2 teaspoon celery seed
1/2 teaspoon dry mustard
1/2 teaspoon beaumonde seasoning
1/2 teaspoon nutmeg
1 cup diced ham or smoked turkey
2 tablespoons plus 1/2 cup flour
12 eggs
2 tablespoons confectioners' sugar
1 teaspoon baking powder
1 pound cheese, shredded
1 pound large curd cottage cheese

Saute the onion in the butter. Add the spinach, spices, meat, and the 2 tablespoons of flour. Whisk together the eggs, 1/2 cup flour, sugar, and baking powder. Add the cheeses. Add the spinach mixture. Ladle into muffin tins until full. Bake at 350 degrees for 15 minutes. Unmold and serve. Serves 12.

Beechmont Inn

315 Broadway
Hanover, Pennsylvania 17331
(717) 632-3013

Cinnamon Raisin Breakfast Pudding

1 loaf whole-wheat cinnamon-raisin bread, unsliced
Confectioners' sugar
Fresh berries
1/2 cup melted butter
5 whole eggs
3 egg yolks
3/4 cup sugar
3 cups milk
1 cup half and half
1 tablespoon vanilla extract
1 teaspoon cinnamon
1/2 teaspoon nutmeg

Trim the end pieces from the loaf and cut the bread into 8 slices. Arrange in greased baking dishes (one 9 by 13 by 2-inch and one large loaf pan). Beat together the whole eggs and yolks. Whisk in the remaining ingredients. Pour evenly over the bread. Cover with foil and refrigerate overnight. Drizzle with the melted butter and bake, covered, at 350 degrees F. for 45 to 60 minutes or until cooked through. Dust with powdered sugar and top with fresh berries. Serves 8.

The Lovelander

217 West 4th Street
Loveland, Colorado 80537
(303) 669-0798

There is true, old-fashioned hospitality at this famous Colorado inn where Bob and Marilyn Wilgen offer heartfelt welcomes to their guests. The inn is a rambling Victorian built in 1902, when Loveland's thriving sugar beet industry was the force behind a bustling area economy. The Lovelander combines the essence of Victorian style with contempory convenience. An ample Colorado breakfast is served around the handsome Empire dining table, and, in summer, on the porch.

Try this inventive bread pudding recipe from La Posada de Taos.

Double Boiler Bread Pudding

2 tablespoons cold butter
3/4 cup firmly packed brown sugar (dark or light)
6 slices Honey Wheatberry bread, cubed (leave crusts on)
2/3 cup raisins
2 eggs
1 pint half-and-half
1 teaspoon vanilla extract
1/8 teaspoon salt
Heavy cream, whipped, for garnish

Coat a 2-quart top of a double boiler with the butter. Pat brown sugar over the butter. Layer the bread cubes and raisins in the pan. Beat the eggs, half-and-half, vanilla, and salt in a medium bowl. Pour over the raisins and bread cubes. Cover the pan, place over boiling water, and cook until the pudding is set, about 90 minutes. Remove from water and let set for ten minutes. Invert onto a serving platter. Serve immediately, with whipped cream. Serves 4.

Note: This bread pudding is similar to Capirotada, a Native American bread pudding made with Cheddar cheese. This recipe complements egg dishes, however.

La Posada de Taos

P.O. Box 1118
Taos, New Mexico 87571
(505) 758-8164

Cheese and Fruit Delight

This is a recipe that has been a favorite at the Mill Rose Inn for years. Try it!

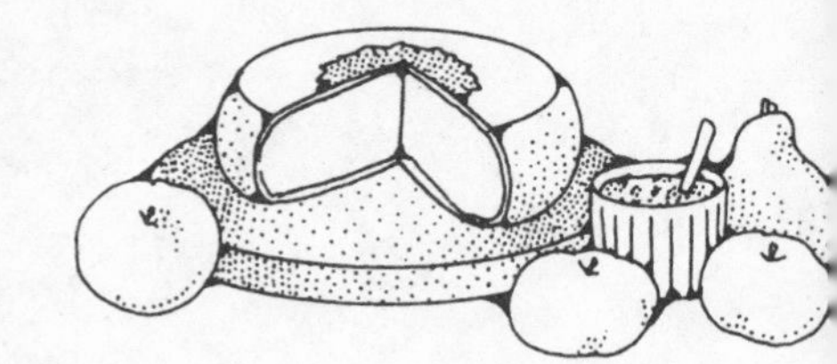

2 cups milk
2 cups flour
12 eggs
1 cup melted butter
1 quart low fat cottage cheese
2 pounds Monterey Jack cheese, grated
Croissant crumbs
Sour cream or creme fraiche
Fruit conserves

Blend together the milk, flour, eggs, melted butter, and cottage cheese. Butter a 9-by-13-inch baking dish. Sprinkle the grated cheese on the bottom. Pour the egg mixture over the cheese and top with croissant crumbs. Bake at 350 degrees for 45 minutes. Cut into squares and top with sour cream and fruit conserves. Serves 12.

Mill Rose Inn

615 Mill Street
Half Moon Bay, California 94019
(415) 726-9794

George and Betty Delforge are justly famous for this recipe. You'll find it something very special!

San Saba Pecan French Toast

4 eggs
2/3 cup orange juice
1/3 cup milk
1/4 cup sugar
1/4 teaspoon ground nutmeg
1/2 teaspoon vanilla extract
1 8-ounce loaf Italian bread, cut in 1-inch slices
1/3 cup butter or margarine, melted
1/2 cup pecan pieces

With a wire whisk beat together the eggs, orange juice, milk, sugar, nutmeg, and vanilla. Place the bread in a single layer in a casserole that just fits the slices. Pour the milk mixture over the bread. Cover and refrigerate overnight, turning once. Pour the melted butter on a jelly roll pan, spreading evenly. Arrange the soaked bread slices on the pan in a single layer. Sprinkle with the pecans. Bake at 400 degrees until golden, 20 to 25 minutes. Serve with maple syrup and butter, if desired. Serves 4.

The Delforge Place

710 Effie Street
Fredericksburg, Texas 78624
(512) 997-6212

Baked French Toast

3 eggs, beaten lightly
2/3 cup milk
3 tablespoons sugar
1 tablespoon Grand Marnier liqueur
8 1-inch-thick slices French or Italian bread
1/4 cup unsalted butter
Orange marmalade, for sauce

In a large flat dish combine the eggs, milk, sugar, and liqueur. Add the bread in one layer and let it soak in the mixture for 2 minutes. Turn and let soak until all the liquid is absorbed. In a large, flat baking dish melt the butter in a 400 degree oven; add the bread in one layer. Bake for 15 minutes. Turn and bake for 10 minutes more or until the underside is golden. Serve with pureed orange marmalade with Grand Marnier added to taste, heated. Serves 4.

The Historic Hotel Higgins

P.O. Box 741
Glenrock, Wyoming 82637
(307) 436-9212

The fascinating Hotel Higgins was built just after the turn of the century, in the glorious days when Wyoming was a roaring Wild West locale. Today, the inn still maintains its historical charm and offers the most sophisticated dining in The Paisley Shawl. None of the elegance and charm have been lost at the Shawl, where guests are delighted with outstanding gourmet food.

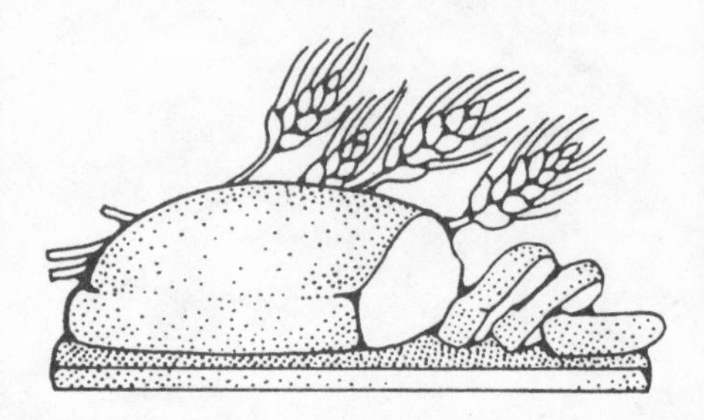

A pair of wealthy gamblers pooled their resources in 1872 and built an elegant, exclusive clubhouse for their friends. They spared no expense, and hired a famous architect to design a grand villa. This beautiful building is now The Mainstay Inn in the heart of historic Cape May. It looks much as it did when the gamblers were there. The recipe that follows is taken from the Inn's own cookbook, Breakfast at Nine, Tea at Four, *by Sue Carroll.*

Mainstay French Toast

1 cup brown sugar
1/2 cup butter
2 tablespoons corn syrup
2 tart apples, peeled and sliced
5 eggs
1 1/2 cups milk
1 teaspoon vanilla
1 loaf French bread, cut in 3/4 inch slices
Apple syrup

Cook the sugar, butter, and syrup until syrupy. Pour into a 9 by 13-inch baking dish. Spread apple slices over the syrup. Place the bread on top of the apple slices. Whisk together the remaining ingredients and pour over the bread. Cover and refrigerate overnight. Bake, uncovered, for 40 minutes at 350 degrees. Cut in squares and serve with a spicy apple syrup. Serves 9.

The Mainstay Inn

635 Columbia House
Cape May, New Jersey 08204
(609) 884-8690

French Toast with Sauteed Fruit and Raspberry Butter

3 eggs
1/4 cup milk
1 1/2 teaspoons ground cinnamon
Dash of nutmeg
Dash of vanilla extract
2 cups mixed fruit (any combination of raspberries, blackberries, halved strawberries, sliced apples, sliced kiwi)
1 tablespoon butter
1 tablespoon sugar
French bread, cut in 3/4-inch slices (enough for 18 slices)
Confectioners' sugar, for garnish
Raspberry Butter (recipe below)

Combine the first five ingredients and beat until smooth. Saute the mixed fruit briefly in the butter. Stir in the sugar and cook until it dissolves. To make the French toast, dip the slices of French bread into the batter and fry on a hot griddle until brown. Sprinkle with confectioners' sugar. Serve with the sauteed fruit, Raspberry Butter, and maple syrup. Serves 6 to 8.

Raspberry Butter
1 cup whipped butter
1/4 cup raspberries

Blend the butter and raspberries in a food processor or blender until fluffy.

The Beal House Inn

247 Main Street
Littleton, New Hampshire 03561
(603) 444-2661

The Beal House Inn is a Main Street landmark in Littleton. The Federal Renaissance building was constructed in 1833 and has been used as an inn for 54 years. It is tastefully decorated with antiques and collectibles. The Carver family serves wonderful food by candlelight and fireside, specializing in hot popovers served with preserves and pure maple syrup.

THE BEAL HOUSE INN - 1833 - LITTLETON - NEW HAMPSHIRE

The four seasons provide nature's backdrop to this gracious and historic Georgian inn. The inn offers the peacefulness of a home away from home, and nearby Lake Sunapee provides year-round recreation.

Oatmeal Pancakes

1 1/2 cups rolled oats
1/2 cup flour
1 teaspoon baking soda
2 eggs
2 cups buttermilk or sour milk
1 teaspoon sugar
1 teaspoon salt
Raisins or chopped fruit (optional)

Combine well all ingredients, except the raisins or fruit and let sit overnight or at least 1/2 hour to thicken. Add optional raisins or fruit and cook pancakes slowly over low heat. Makes about 1 dozen pancakes.

Inn at Coit Mountain

HCR63, Box 3
Newport, New Hampshire 03773
(800) 367-2364

Zucchini and Walnut Sour Cream Pancakes

1 1/3 cups milk
1 cup sour cream
2 eggs
2 tablespoons butter, melted
2 cups pancake mix
1 cup grated zucchini, squeezed dry
1/4 cup chopped walnuts

Combine the milk, sour cream, eggs, and melted butter in a bowl. Mix thoroughly, add the pancake mix, and stir to combine. The mixture should be lumpy. Pour onto a hot, lightly greased pancake griddle or frying pan. Cook until bubbles appear and the underside is golden. Turn only once. Serve with plenty of butter and warm syrup. Makes about 2 dozen pancakes.

The Five Gables Inn

Murray Hill Road
East Boothbay, Maine 01966
(207) 633-2353

Ellen and Paul Morissette are the innkeepers in this wonderful hillside inn, which affords stunning views of Linekin Bay. Built over 100 years ago. it has enjoyed a long tradition of hospitality. All of its many rooms have an ocean view. A wraparound veranda with plenty of comfortable seats, is the perfect spot to view the magnificent bay and distant islands. The dining room offers Paul Morissette's gourmet creations, developed during his 25 years' experience as a chef and restaurant owner in Vermont. He shares a favorite with us here.

Greenvale Manor is in the historic Northern neck of Virginia on a peninsula overlooking the Rappahonnock River and Greenvale Creek. The manor house was built in 1840 and is filled with antiques. On warm days, guests enjoy breakfast on the sunny veranda with its gorgeous water views, and later in the day, and on weekends, a cookout with locally cought steamed crabs is enjoyed by all. Year-round, with crackling fires during the colder months, Greenvale Manor is a special getaway for lovers of all ages.

Ham and Cheese Strata

8 slices firm-textured white bread with crusts, cubed (or French bread)
3 slices thickly cut ham, cubed
1 1/2 cups grated Cheddar cheese
8 eggs
2 cups milk
4 tablespoons butter, melted
1/2 teaspoon dry mustard
Salt and freshly ground pepper to taste

Prepare the night before serving. Butter a 9 by 5 by 3-inch ovenproof glass loaf dish. Layer the dish with the bread, ham, and cheese, beginning with bread and ending with ham. Combine the eggs, milk, melted butter, salt, pepper, and mustard in a blender or food processor. Blend thoroughly on high speed, about 10 seconds. Pour over the bread, ham, and cheese mixture and refrigerate overnight. Bake at 350 degrees until firm--45 to 60 minutes. Cut in squares. Serves 6.

Greenvale Manor

P.O. Box 7
Mollusk, Virginia 22517
(804) 462-5995

Mexican Souffle

You'll impress a few guests of your own with this remarkable recipe from the Church Hill Inn. Start breakfast with some zip by serving this Mexican Souffle.

4 to 6 slices bread, cubed
2 cups grated Swiss cheese
2 cups grated Monterey Jack cheese
3 ounces chilies, drained and chopped
Chopped onion (optional)
Chopped tomato (optional)
6 eggs
2 cups milk
1/2 teaspoon salt
1/2 teaspoon oregano
1/4 teaspoon garlic powder
1 1/2 teaspoons paprika

Layer half the bread cubes in a greased 7 by 11-inch pan. Cover with the cheeses, chilies, and optional onions or tomatoes. Whisk together the eggs, milk, and spices. Top the cheeses with the rest of the bread cubes. Pour the egg mixture over the bread and cheese. Cover and chill overnight. Bake at 350 degrees for 45-50 minutes. Cut in squares. Serves 6.

Church Hill Inn

425 Gateway Drive
Sister Bay, Wisconsin 54234
(800) 422-4906

Since the 1850s, the Story General Store has served Brown County travelers. Now this historic landmark has been restored into a country inn as unique as its setting. Nestled at the junction of Brown County State Park, The 10 O'clock Treaty Line, and the Hoosier National Forest, one can find lodging here in the old buggy assembly operation on the second floor, or in the surrounding cottages. All of the rooms are furnished with period antiques. The full service gourmet type restaurant features expertly prepared meals that marry seasonal produce and hard-to-find meats, game, fish and seafood. You can dine indoors amid memorabilia from a earlier times or outdoors overlooking landscaped gardens.

Banana Walnut Pancakes

1 cup flour
1 cup whole-wheat flour
1/4 cup wheat germ
1 tablespoon baking powder
1 1/2 teaspoons baking soda
Salt (optional)
3 eggs, at room temperature
1/4 cup safflower oil
2 cups buttermilk, at room temperature
6 tablespoons honey
2 ripe bananas, peeled and mashed
1/2 cup finely chopped walnuts
Maple syrup
Vanilla yogurt, cinnamon, and additional bananas

In a large bowl, stir together the flours, wheat germ, baking powder, soda, and salt to taste. In a separate bowl, beat the eggs. Mix in the oil, buttermilk, honey, and bananas, mixing well. Stir in the nuts. Pour the egg mixture into the dry ingredients. Stir just until the dry ingredients are moistened. Brush a hot griddle or skillet lightly with additional oil. Drop the batter, about 1/4 cup per pancake, onto the griddle and spread a little with a spoon to make a flat pancake. Cook over medium heat until lightly brown on the bottom and bubbles form on top. Turn over and brown lightly on the second side for 1 to 2 minutes. Serve with maple syrup or vanilla yogurt flavored with cinnamon and sliced bananas. Makes about 20 pancakes.

Story Inn

P.O. Box 64
Nashville, Indiana 47448
(812) 988-2273

Blueberry Pancakes

2 1/2 cups buttermilk, or milk soured with lemon juice
3 tablespoons oil
3 tablespoons sugar
1/2 teaspoon salt
1/4 teaspoon vanilla extract
2 eggs
1 teaspoon baking soda
1/3 cup yellow cornmeal
2 to 3 cups flour
1 16-ounce can blueberries, or 1 package frozen

Place all ingredients except the cornmeal, flour, and blueberries in a blender. Blend with on/off speed for 2 minutes until combined. Add the cornmeal a little at a time, blending on low speed. Add 1 cup of the flour slowly while continuing to blend and only enough of the remaining 2 cups to make a smooth batter. (For thin pancakes, you will need only about 2 1/3 cups of the flour. For thicker pancakes, use the entire amount.) Let the batter stand in a large pitcher for at least 10 minutes before pouring onto a hot, lightly oiled griddle. Just before pouring onto the griddle, drain and rinse the blueberries under cold water, then drain well again. Fold into the batter. Makes 16 pancakes.

My Blue Heaven

1041 5th Street
Pawnee, Nebraska 68420
(402) 852-3131

Legend has it that the town of Pawnee City is on the exact spot where the largest village of the Pawnee Indians was located. The name "Pawnee" was supposedly derived from the word "pony," and the Pawnee were known as "the tribe of many ponies." Visitors flock to My Blue Heaven for small-town hospitality and all the comforts of home, including bountiful breakfasts.

Bear Mountain Guest Ranch has been located on a "mountain nature campus" since 1959. On the inn grounds are a beautiful two- story hacienda, two casitas, and a spacious bunkhouse. The view from each features juniper-clad hills. Myra McCormick is the owner and manager.

Buttermilk Whole-Wheat Pancakes

1/2 cup whole-wheat flour
1/2 cup white flour
1/2 teaspoon soda
1/4 teaspoon salt
1 egg
2 tablespoons safflower or corn oil
1 cup buttermilk

In a medium bowl, sift together the dry ingredients. Set aside. In a large bowl, beat the egg well. Add the oil and buttermilk. Add the sifted dry ingredients all at once, stirring only enough to dampen. Add more buttermilk, if necessary. The batter should be thin enough to pour.

Heat a griddle or frying pan over high heat and pour on the batter. When the pancakes have bubbles on top and are brown on the bottom, turn over with a spatula. Brown on each side only once. Serve immediately with butter and warm syrup. Makes about 15 pancakes.

Bear Mountain Guest Ranch

P.O. Box 1163
Silver City, New Mexico 88062
(505) 538-2538

Gingerbread Pancakes

2 1/2 cups flour
5 teaspoons baking powder
1 1/2 teaspoons salt
1 teaspoon baking soda
1 teaspoon ground cinnamon
1/2 teaspoon ground ginger
1/4 cup molasses
2 cups milk
2 eggs
6 tablespoons butter, melted
1 cup raisins

Combine all the ingredients except the raisins. Beat with an electric mixer until well blended. Stir in the raisins. Drop on a hot griddle or skillet. Cook until bubbles form on the surface, then turn. Makes about 18 pancakes.

The Greenbriar Inn

315 Wallace
Coeur d'Alene, Idaho 83814
(208) 667-9660

Built in 1908, the Greenbriar is Coeur d'Alene's only nationally registered historic mansion. During most of its history, the structure was used as a boardinghouse. (Some say it was also a bordello at one time.) The third floor, with its gracefully arched windows, was once a dance hall. A four-course gourmet breakfast is served to house guests, and a dining facility has been added for both guests and the public to enjoy.

Innkeepers Al and Karen Hutson have brought the tranquility and beauty of springtime in Coeur d'Alene indoors and added a touch of country living, offering a "down home" aura. The furnishings have been selected for comfort and a homey feeling. Delicious cuisine is served in the delightful dining room.

Apple Pancakes with Hot Cider Syrup

1 1/4 cups flour
2 1/2 teaspoons baking powder
2 tablespoons sugar
3/4 teaspoon salt
1 egg
1 1/4 cups milk
3 tablespoons melted butter
1/4 teaspoon ground cinnamon
1 cup finely chopped apples
Cider Syrup (recipe below)

Mix the flour, baking powder, sugar, and salt until well blended. Add the egg, milk, and butter and stir until dry ingredients are moistened. Fold in the chopped apples. Cook the pancakes on a hot griddle or a heavy skillet until bubbles form on the surface. Turn and cook until done. Serve with butter and hot Cider Syrup. Makes 1 dozen pancakes.

Cider Syrup
1 cup sugar
1 tablespoon biscuit mix
1 teaspoon ground cinnamon
2 cups apple cider
2 tablespoons lemon juice
1/4 cup butter

Mix all the ingredients except the butter in a saucepan. Cook, stirring constantly, until the mixture thickens and boils. Boil for 1 minute. Remove from heat and stir in the butter. Serve hot. Leftover syrup will keep in the refrigerator for a few weeks. Makes about 2 1/2 cups.

Cricket on the Hearth

1521 Lakeside Avenue
Coeur d'Alene, Idaho 83814
(208) 664-6926

German Apple Pancakes

1/3 cup flour
1/4 teaspoon salt
1/3 cup light cream
1/3 cup plus 1 teaspoon sugar
3 eggs
1 egg yolk
1 cup thinly sliced apples
2 tablespoons unsalted butter
1 tablespoon ground cinnamon
3 eggs
1 egg yolk

Whisk the flour, salt, light cream, and 1 teaspoon sugar. Whisk in the eggs and egg yolk. In a 10-inch skillet saute the apples in the butter for 2 minutes. Sprinkle the 1/3 cup sugar and cinnamon over the apples. Pour the egg and flour mixture over the apples. Bake at 400 degrees for 12 to 15 minutes. Cut in wedges and serve. Serves 3 or 4.

Skyline Guest Ranch

P.O. Box 67
Telluride, Colorado 81435
(303) 728-3757

Skyline Guest Ranch is located in the southwestern corner of Colorado. Owners Sherry and Dave Farney proudly say, "We've found a way of life at Skyline that's been awfully good to us. Best of all, we've discovered that the more we share it, the better it gets." Amid the high meadows of Colorado's San Juan Mountains, the ranch is surrounded by 14,000-foot snow-capped peaks. Clear mountain streams fill the sparkling lakes.

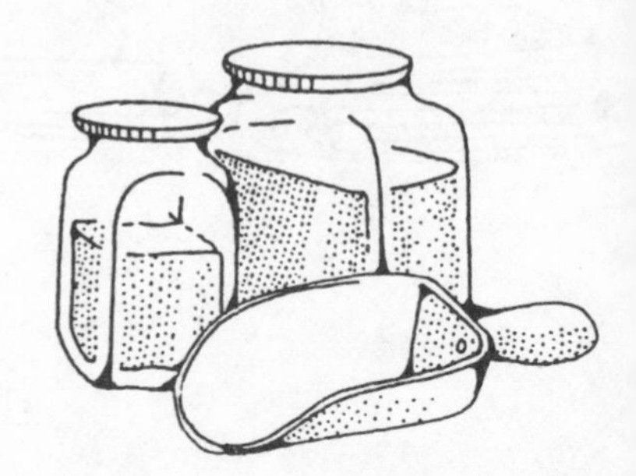

Located in the shiretown of Orange County, Vermont, the Shire Inn offers comfortable and elegant accommodations for guests traveling through Central Vermont and the Upper Connecticut River Valley. Built in 1832 by a successful Chelsea chair manufacturer, the inn has an ample village setting of 17 acres. Dinner at the inn is a memorable event—a culinary drama in six acts. Mary Lee Papa does the cooking, and expertly so.

Puffed Pancakes

6 eggs
1 cup milk
1/4 cup orange juice
1/2 cup sugar
1 cup flour
Pinch of salt
4 tablespoons butter

In a blender or food processor, mix all ingredients except the butter. Blend well. Heat the oven to 425 degrees and melt the butter in a 13 by 9-inch baking dish until it sizzles. (Try not to let the butter brown.) Pour the batter into the sizzling butter. Bake until puffed and brown, about 20 minutes. Serve immediately. Top with strawberry sauce for sundaes, powdered sugar, or sliced fruit. Serves 6.

Shire Inn

P.O. Box 37
Chelsea, Vermont 05038
(802)685-3031

Finnish Pancakes

4 eggs
1 cup flour
2 1/2 cups milk
2 tablespoons honey
4 tablespoons butter
Syrup
Confectioners' sugar
Fresh fruit

Combine the eggs, flour, milk, and honey and blend well. Preheat the butter in a 10-inch cast-iron skillet in a 450 degree oven for 10 minutes. Reduce the heat to 375 degrees, add the batter, and bake for 20 minutes. Cut into wedges. Drizzle with your choice of syrup, sprinkle with confectioners' sugar, and top with your choice of fresh fruit. Serves 4.

Grist Mill Inn

310 East Main Street
Homer, Michigan 49245
(517) 568-4063

This late Victorian home in a sleepy Michigan village is renowned both for its exceptional food and its creative use of the decorative arts. Guests love to browse through the rooms, which are filled with the owner's collection of quilts and other vintage linens. In the heart of Michigan's antique country, the inn is only a few minutes away from Marshall, the Williamsburg of the Midwest, and Allen, self-styled antiques capital of Michigan. Cycling along the many tree-lined country roads and canoeing on the scenic Kalamazoo River are favorite outdoors activities for guests.

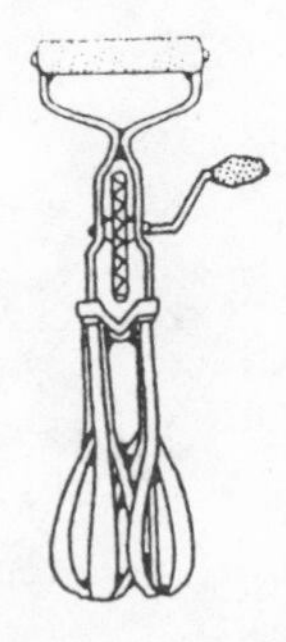

Custer Mansion is a Gothic structure built in 1891 by Newton Tubbs, who came to the Black Hills after gold was discovered in 1876. Tubbs grew potatoes on his land, and sold or exchanged them at the lumber mill for lumber to build his house. Because of this Custer Mansion is also known as "the house that potatoes built." Breakfasts are home cooked, home-baked, and all-you-can-eat, served by friendly hosts Mill and Carole Seamos. In summer, some guests choose to dine on the slate patio under the huge willow trees.

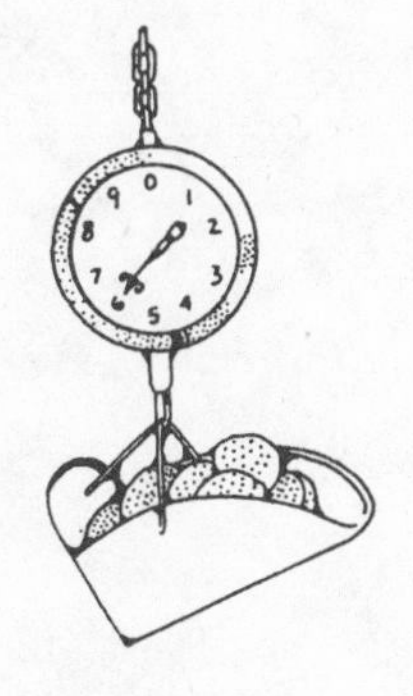

Whole Wheat Buttermilk Waffles

2 eggs, beaten
2 cups buttermilk
1 teaspoon baking soda
2 teaspoons baking powder
1 cup flour
1 cup whole wheat flour
1/2 teaspoon salt
6 tablespoons soft shortening or oil

Combine all ingredients and beat until smooth. Bake in a heated waffle iron according to manufacturer's instructions. Makes 5 or 6 waffles.

Custer Mansion

Custer, South Dakota 57730
(605) 673-3333

Cream Waffles

2 eggs
1 3/4 cups milk
1/2 cup butter, melted
2 cups flour
4 teaspoons baking powder
1/2 teaspoon salt
1 tablespoon sugar

Beat the eggs, add the remaining ingredients, and beat until smooth. Do not stir the batter between bakings. Serve with warm Cinnamon Cream Syrup. Makes about 6 round waffles

Cinnamon Cream Syrup
1 cup sugar
1/2 cup light corn syrup
1/4 cup water
1/2 to 3/4 teaspoon ground cinnamon
1/2 cup evaporated milk

Combine the first four ingredients and bring to boiling over medium heat, stirring constantly. Cook and stir for 1 minute. Cool for 5 minutes and stir in the evaporated milk.

Note: The syrup keeps well in the refrigerator, tightly covered, for weeks. To reheat, warm slowly or it will over-cook and become stringy.

The Homeplace

5901 Sardis Road
Charlotte, North Carolina 28228
(704) 365-1936

At The Homeplace, the warm and friendly atmosphere hasn't changed a bit since 1902. Situated on wooded acreage in southeast Charlotte, this completely restored inn features rooms decorated and furnished with the guest's enjoyment and comfort in mind. The food will be long remembered; Peggy and Frank Dearien are perfect hosts.

Magic Canyon Ranch overlooks magnificent Kachemak Bay, and views from its windows range from green fields to sparkling glaciers. This is a place for quiet seclusion in a natural setting, where photo opportunities abound. Guests are invited to barbecue their own freshly caught fish and gather wild greens. The ranch's accomodations include spacious suites furnished with brass beds and handmade quilts.

Herb Waffles with Seafood Sauce

2 cups flour
1 tablespoon baking powder
1/2 teaspoon salt
2 cups milk
2 eggs, separated
1 tablespoon chopped fresh parsley
1 tablespoon finely chopped onion
1 teaspoon chopped fresh sage
1 teaspoon chopped fresh thyme
6 tablespoons melted butter
Seafood Sauce (recipe below)

Combine the dry ingredients. Beat the milk and egg yolks, fold in the parsley, onion, sage, and thyme, and add to the dry ingredients along with the butter. Beat the egg whites until stiff but not dry and fold into the batter just before cooking. Cook in a waffle iron according to manufacturer's instructions. Serve the waffles with Seafood Sauce. Makes 5 or 6 waffles.

Seafood Sauce
1/4 cup chopped onion
1/4 cup chopped celery
1/4 cup butter
3 tablespoons flour
1 cup chicken broth
1 cup milk
1 pound cooked fresh seafood (shrimp, crab, or salmon)
1 tablespoon fresh lemon juice
Chopped fresh parsley, for garnish

Saute the onion and celery in the butter. Stir in the flour, then the broth and milk. Cook, stirring constantly, for about 10 minutes, or until the sauce is thickened. Add the seafood and lemon juice and reheat, stirring constantly. Garnish with the parsley and serve over the Herb Waffles.

Magic Canyon Ranch

40015 Waterman Road
Homer, Alaska 99603
(907) 235-6077

Fresh Corn Waffles with Cilantro Butter

1 cup flour
1/2 cup yellow cornmeal
2 tablespoons sugar
2 teaspoons baking powder
1/4 teaspoon salt
1 egg
2 tablespoons melted unsalted butter
1/2 cup water
1 cup fresh corn (remove from the cob just before adding)
1 teaspoon vanilla extract
Cilantro butter (recipe below)
Pure maple syrup

In a large bowl, mix together the flour, cornmeal, sugar, baking powder, and salt. In a separate bowl whip together the egg, melted butter, water, corn, and vanilla. Add the egg mixture to the flour mixture, and mix until just combined. Heat a waffle iron, oil, and cook the waffles according to manufacturer's instructions. Serve the waffles with Cilantro Butter and maple syrup. Makes about 4 waffles.

Cilantro Butter
1/2 cup unsalted butter, softened
1/4 cup chopped cilantro

Whip the butter and cilantro together until smooth and creamy. Chill until ready to use.

This spectacular Victorian inn has received so many accolades, it's impossible to list them all. Carter House's most recent distinction was the prestigious "Best Inn in America" award for 1989. It is located in the small, culturally rich seaport town of Eureka in the heart of the Redwood Empire. Carter House's style and hospitality, and its insistence on quality, creativity, friendliness, and taste, have impressed travelers, authors, and chefs from coast to coast and around the world.

Carter House Country Inn

301 L Street
Eureka, California 95501
(707)445-1390

In the historic heart of downtown St. George are nine pioneer homes—beautifully restored and elegantly decorated, and known as The Greene Gate Village Inn. The complex includes a swimming pool and an old-fashioned candy store and soda fountain.

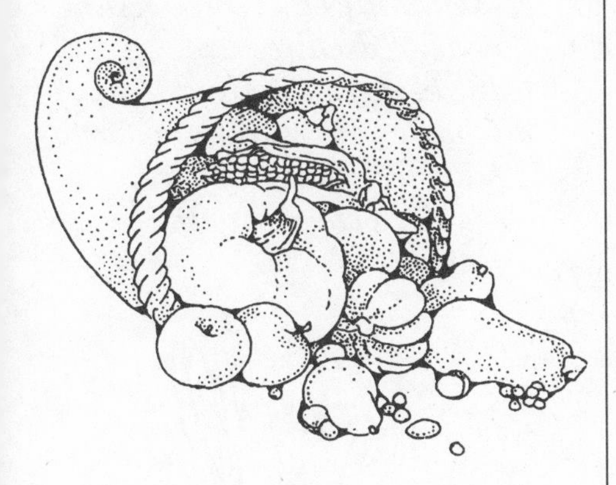

Quick Granola

1/2 cup vegetable oil
1/3 cup honey
1/2 cup peanut butter (optional)
1 teaspoon vanilla
1/4 teaspoon ground cinnamon
3 cups rolled oats
1/2 cup wheat germ
1/2 cup almonds
1/2 cup pecans
1/2 cup sunflower seeds
1/2 cup coconut
1 cup raisins

Heat the oil, honey, peanut butter, vanilla, and cinnamon together over low heat. Mix together all other ingredients except the raisins. Pour the heated mixture over the other ingredients and spread on cookie sheets. Bake at 300 degrees F. for 20 minutes. Stir in the raisins and store in an airtight container. Makes 8 cups.

Greene Gate Village Inn

76 West Tabernacle
St. George, Utah 84770
(801) 628-6999

Oat Bran Granola

8 cups rolled oats (not quick-cooking)
1 1/2 cups unprocessed oat bran
1/2 cup walnut pieces
1/2 cup raw sunflower seeds
1/2 cup vegetable oil
3/4 cup honey
2 teaspoons honey
2 teaspoons vanilla extract
1 cup dark raisins
1 cup golden raisins
1 to 2 cups puffed millet

Mix the oats, oat bran, nuts, and seeds. In a small saucepan heat the oil, honey, and vanilla, stirring until bubbly. Thoroughly mix the liquids with the dry ingredients. Divide the mixture between two jelly roll pans and bake at 325 degrees F. for 30 minutes, stirring every 10 minutes for even browning. Stir again as the mixture cools, to prevent clumping. When the mixture is thoroughly cool, add the raisins and millet. Store in an airtight container. Makes about 16 cups.

Queen Anne Inn

2147 Tremont Place
Denver, Colorado 80205
(303) 296-6666

Step into Denver's 19th Century at the Queen Anne Inn. Enjoy the grand oak staircase, the quaint rooms, the many elegant period furnishings, the art, music and greenery throughout, and the hospitality for which the West is famous. This beautiful three-story structure, built in 1879, exemplifies the Queen Anne style of architecture. Innkeepers Ann and Charles Hillestad are world travelers who treasure small hostelries with local flavor.

Conover's Bay Head Inn was built in 1912 as a summer cottage for the L. Hastings Alexander family. The original architectural drawings for the house are framed and show the reconstruction in 1916 as an inn. A massive cut-stone fireplace, family photographs, and well-placed antiques add to the guest's pleasure. The views from the inn are impressive, including the ocean, bay, marina, and yacht club. Shapely old homes make the rest of the scenic landscape. Guests can dine in the sunny dining room, on the manicured lawn, or on the front porch.

Overnight Apple Oatmeal

2 cups milk
1/4 cup brown sugar
1 tablespoon melted butter
1/4 teaspoon salt
1/2 teaspoon cinnamon
1 cup rolled oats
1 cup chopped apple
1/2 cup raisins
1/2 cup chopped walnuts

Grease the inside surface of a slow cooker crock pot. Measure into it the milk, brown sugar, melted butter, salt, and cinnamon. Stir to combine with a wire whisk. Add the oats, chopped apple, raisins, and nuts; mix well. Cover. Just before going to bed, turn on the crock pot, at "low" speed. The cereal will be ready for morning. Serve with milk. Serves 4.

Conover's Bay Head Inn

646 Main Avenue
Bay Head, New Jersey 06742
(908) 842-4664

Maine Crabmeat Breakfast Pie

8 eggs
1 bunch green onions, chopped
1 large red bell pepper, chopped
6 ounces crabmeat
1 cup grated Swiss cheese
1 cup grated Cheddar cheese
2 cups half-and-half
1 teaspoon salt
1/2 teaspoon pepper
1 cup fresh bread crumbs

Butter a 10-inch quiche pan. Beat the eggs. Mix all the remaining ingredients together and add to the eggs. Pour into the pan, and bake at 350 degrees F. until set, 30 to 45 minutes. Cut in wedges, and serve hot. Serve for breakfast, lunch, or supper with a salad. Serves 8.

The Arundel Meadows Inn

P.O. Box 1129
Kennebunk, Maine 04043
(207) 985-3770

Located two miles north of Kennebunk, Maine on Route 1 and five miles from Kennebunkport, this 165-year-old farmhouse offers seven guest rooms, each uniquely decorated with art and antiques. Three of the rooms feature fireplaces for the winter months. A stay at the Inn includes a full breakfast and afternoon tea prepared by the proprietor, Mark Bachelder, who was professionally trained by Madeleine Kamman, the renowned chef, teacher, author, and television personality.

This lovely inn was opened in 1987; it has grown to a thriving business providing comfortable accommodations and delicious food. There is an English Tea Room on the premises serving country breakfasts, bountiful luncheons, and romantic candlelit dinners. A fabulous five course feast is served at dinner. The inn has its own English bakehouse featuring pies, breads and cakes.

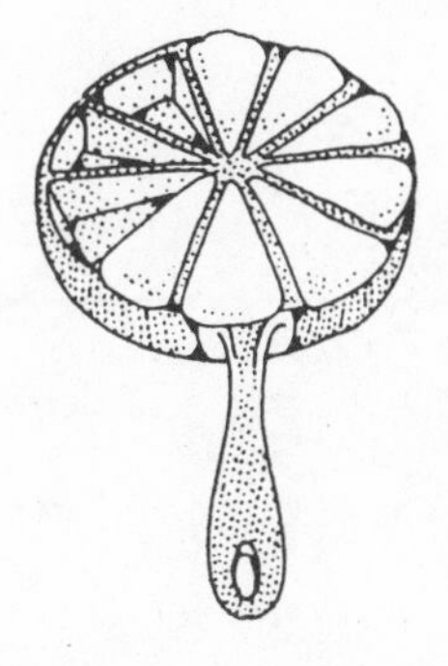

Crab Quiche

1 9-inch pie crust
1/2 cup mayonnaise
2 tablespoons flour
2 eggs, beaten
1/4 cup milk
1/2 pound fresh or frozen crabmeat
1/2 pound Swiss cheese, grated
1/2 cup chopped green onion
2 cups sliced mushrooms

Prebake the pie crust at 450 degrees for 10 minutes and let cool. Mix together the mayonnaise, flour, eggs, and milk. Stir in the crabmeat, cheese, green onion, and mushrooms. Spoon the quiche mixture into the cooled pie crust and bake at 350 degrees for 35 to 40 minutes, until the custard is set. Serve warm or at room temperature. Serves 4 to 6.

Country Fare Guest House

904 Main Street
Lander, Wyoming 82520
(307) 332-9604

Lo-Cal Zucchini Quiche

4 cups thinly sliced unpeeled zucchini (about 7)
1 onion, chopped
1/4 to 1/2 cup butter or margarine
1/2 cup chopped fresh parsley
1/2 teaspoon salt
1/2 teaspoon freshly ground pepper
1/4 teaspoon garlic powder
1/4 teaspoon dried basil
1/4 teaspoon dried oregano
2 eggs, well beaten
2 cups grated Swiss cheese

Saute the zucchini and onion in the butter until the onion is translucent. Add the parsley and seasonings. Remove from the heat and add the eggs and cheese. Pour into a greased casserole. Bake at 375 degrees F. for 25 minutes. Let stand for 15 minutes before cutting into squares. Serves 4 to 6.

The Corners

601 Klein Street
Vicksburg, Mississippi 39180
(601) 636-7421

Bettye and Cliff Whitney's beautiful home reflects the romance and elegant charm of the 1873 era in which it was built, taking the visitors back to the unhurried times of the Old South. With its flower gardens and 65-foot verandas overlooking the Mississippi River, The Corners symbolizes a gentler way of life.

very good

Dairy Hollow House occupies a restored turn-of-the-century farmhouse. Its welcome is heartfelt and the cuisine is world-class. On an Ozark hillside in the much-loved Victorian resort town of Eureka Springs, Dairy Hollow House is visited by guests from all over the world. Its legendary fare is lovingly prepared by Crescent Dragonwagon and Jan Brown. The recipe included here was taken from The Dairy Hollow House Cookbook.

Hashed Brown Quiche

2 tablespoons vegetable oil
1 onion, finely chopped
5 potatoes, unpeeled, grated
3 eggs
1 1/2 cups heavy cream or 1 12-ounce can evaporated milk
1/2 teaspoon soy sauce
1/2 teaspoon dry mustard
Freshly ground pepper
1 cup grated sharp Cheddar cheese
3 tablespoons chopped fresh parsley
Paprika
Grated Parmesan cheese
Sliced tomato, for garnish
Parsley sprigs, for garnish

In a cast-iron skillet, heat the vegetable oil and saute the onion. When the onion is translucent, add the grated potatoes. Cover the skillet with a lid and cook over low heat until the potatoes are translucent and slightly browned, about 5 minutes.

In a food processor or blender place the eggs, cream, soy sauce, mustard, and pepper. Blend until smooth.

When the potatoes are done, remove from the heat. Press the cooked potatoes to the bottom and edges of the skillet with the back of a wooden spoon, shaping into a crust. Pour the egg and cheese mixture into the crust. Sprinkle with the Cheddar cheese, chopped parsley, paprika, and Parmesan cheese. Bake at 350 degrees for 35 to 40 minutes, or until the filling is set, the potato crust browned, and the cheese bubbly. Cut into wedges and serve. Garnish each plate with a slice of tomato and a sprig of parsley. Serves 6.

Note: If the grated potatoes are to sit for any length of time, place in a bowl and cover with cold water. Drain and squeeze dry before proceeding with the recipe.

The Dairy Hollow House

515 Spring Street
Eureka Springs, Arkansas 72632
(501) 253-7444

Ham and Cheese Quiche

1 partially baked pie shell, cooled
1/2 cup Swiss cheese, grated
1/2 cup Cheddar cheese, grated
2 cups half-and-half
1/2 teaspoon curry powder
Dash of hot pepper sauce
1/4 teaspoon salt
4 eggs, beaten slightly
1/2 cup finely diced ham

Add the cheeses to the pie shell. Mix together the cream and seasonings in a 4-cup measuring cup. Microwave on high for 2 minutes. Stir a small amount of hot cream into the eggs, then stir the egg mixture into the remaining cream. Pour gently into the pie shell. Sprinkle with the ham. Bake at 400 degrees for about 35 minutes or until the custard is set. Serves 6.

The Bellmore House

1500 North Main
Hutchinson, Kansas 67501
(316) 663-5824

Bellmore House is a turn-of-the-century mansion set apart by the impressive wrought-iron fence surrounding the property and the austere decorative lions guarding the front steps. The art work of Pat Buckley Moss, depicting the Amish and the Mennonite people at work and at play, sets the mood. Her artistry is used as a theme for each guest room. Delicious breakfasts are served in the formal dining room with soft lighting from the antique brass fixtures.

The Barrows House grounds are part of a parcel of land that originally belonged to the Dorset church in 1784. The main inn's front rooms and those above were built in 1804. Much energy and time have been spent restoring and redecorating this lovely building and the surrounding corrages by Sally and Tim Brown, who bought the property in 1986. Chefs Tim Blackwell and Gary Walker provide the culinary expertise to prepare hearty breakfasts and full gourmet dinners daily.

Spinach and Leek Tart

2 pounds fresh spinach, chopped (or 2 10-ounce packages frozen spinach, thawed and drained well)
2 cups chopped leeks, or green onions
1 1/2 cups finely chopped Italian parsley
10 tablespoons butter
Juice of 1/2 lemon
Pinch of sugar (optional)
8 eggs, well-beaten
Salt, pepper, and nutmeg to taste
Plain yogurt and/or sour cream

Combine the spinach, leeks, and parsley. In a large , heavy skillet, melt 8 tablespoons of the butter and cook the vegetables over medium heat until tender, about 1/2 hour. Be careful not to brown. Remove to a bowl and stir in the lemon juice and sugar. When cool, stir in the beaten eggs. Add salt, pepper, and nutmeg. Heat the remaining 2 tablespoons of butter in a heavy 10-inch skillet. Add the spinach-egg mixture and saute over very low heat. Cook, tightly covered, until the eggs are set and the bottom is slightly browned, about 20 minutes. Brown the top under a preheated broiler. Serve warm or at room temperature, cut in wedges. Plain yogurt or a mixture of yogurt and sour cream makes an excellent sauce for these vegetarian tartlets. Serves 8 to 10.

Note: The tart may also be cut in small pieces and served as an hors d'oeuvre.

Barrows House

Dorset, Vermont 05251
(802) 867-4455

Sugar Plum Bacon

1/2 pound sliced bacon
1/2 cup packed brown sugar
1 teaspoon ground cinnamon

Let the bacon warm to room temperature. Cut each slice in half crosswise. Combine the sugar and cinnamon. Coat each bacon slice with the sugar-cinnamon mixture. Twist and place in a shallow baking pan. Bake at 350 degrees for 15 to 20 minutes or until the bacon is crisp and the sugar is bubbly (watch closely; sugar burns easily). Place the cooked bacon slices on foil to cool. Serve at room temperature. Serves 8.

This inn's culinary reputation is such that the innkeepers, Jim and Marilyn Westerfield, often teach cooking classes locally and at the Dierbergs School in naerby St. Louis. The structure is built of rough-hewn logs with a look of colonial frontier times. In the evenings, the guests indulge in seven course dinners amid the glow of 100 candles. Antique furnishings, some dating back to before the American Revolution, abound.

The Westerfield House

8059 Jefferson Boulevard
Freeburg, Illinois 62243
(618) 539-5643

The Heartstone Inn is decorated with a mix of interesting antiques and cozy country accents, including an abundance of grapevine wreaths, old lace, painted furniture, and hand-crafted accessories. It has ten lovely guest rooms, all with private baths. Porches both upstairs and down are popular gathering places on summer nights. A large comfortable parlor invites guests to meet and share their Eureka Springs discoveries. The following recipes are taken from the inn's own cookbook, The Heartstone Inn Breakfast Cookbook *written by innkeepers Iris and Bell Simantel.*

Italian Sausage Skillet

2 pounds Italian sausage, cut in 1-inch pieces
1 tablespoon olive oil
4-ounces mushrooms, sliced
1 large red onion, cut in half then cut into 1/8-inch slices
1 green bell pepper, chopped

Cook the sausage in the oil in a 12-inch skillet over medium heat until brown and no longer pink inside, 20 to 25 minutes. Add the mushrooms and onion; reduce the heat. Cover and simmer, stirring occasionally, until the vegetables are tender, about 10 minutes. Add the green pepper. Cover and simmer until the green pepper is tender, about 5 minutes. Serves 8 to 10.

Heartstone Inn

35 Kings Highway
Eureka Springs, Arkansas 72632
(501) 253-8916

Country Pork Sausage

3 pounds lean ground pork
1 tablespoon coarse salt
1 teaspoon freshly ground pepper
2 teaspoons caraway seeds
6 tablespoons sage
1 1/4 cups chopped fresh parsley
1 1/4 green onion
2 tablespoons dill
2 tablespoons marjoram
2 tablespoons thyme
2 tablespoons oregano
2 tablespoons rosemary

Combine all ingredients, mix well with the hands, and form into 2-to 3-ounce patties. Fry until browned and cooked through and serve warm. Makes 16 to 24 patties.

Cheat Mountain Club

P.O. Box 28
Durbin, West Virginia 26264
(304) 456-4627

Here is a snug mountain inn offering the finest in accommodations, good food, and West Virginia style hospitality at its best. Everything is picture-perfect here: the inn itself, the surrounding country-side, and views for miles. People return again and just relax and enjoy.

Visitors to this lovely inn, which is owned and operated by Elizabeth Farrell, have a magnificent view of Lake Geneva right across the road. The inn is one of the few places around the lake that offers private, personal accomodations. The stately, Victorian structure was built in 1903. Finely crafted antique furniture is placed throughout the house, accented by appropriate wallpapers and lacy curtains.

Sausage Apple Ring with Cheese Scrambled Eggs

2 pounds bulk pork sausage meat
1 1/2 cups cracker meal
2 eggs, slightly beaten
1/2 cup milk
1/4 cup minced onion
1 cup finely chopped apple
Scrambled eggs with Cheddar cheese

Combine all ingredients for the sausage ring and mix thoroughly with a fork. Press lightly into an oiled 6-cup ring mold. Turn out onto a shallow baking pan. Bake at 350 degrees for 1 hour. Drain the excess fat from the pan. Fill the center with scrambled eggs to which grated Cheddar cheese has been added. Serves 6 to 8.

Note: The Sausage Ring may be partially baked (for 30 minutes) the day before it is to be served. Refrigerate overnight, then bring to room temperature before baking for an additional 30 minutes just before serving.

Elizabethian Inn

463 Wrigley Drive
Lake Geneva, Wisconsin 53147
(414) 248-9131

Phyllo Roll

Here's a delicious breakfast treat from RiverSong in Colorado.

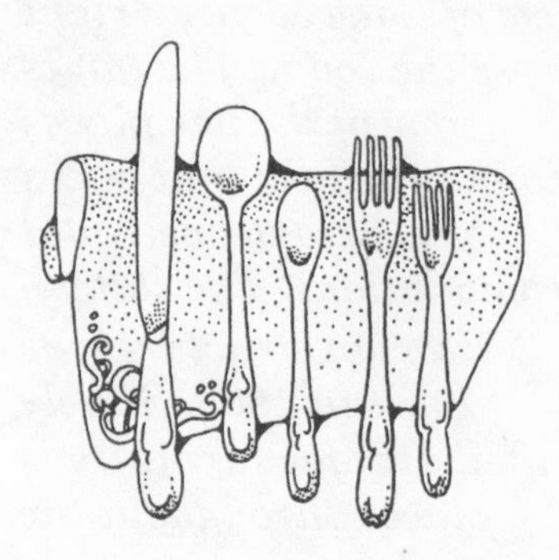

Oil
1/3 cup chopped celery
1/3 cup chopped green pepper
1/4 cup sliced green onion
6 ounces mushrooms, chopped
2 tablespoons Dijon mustard
1 1/2 cups diced cooked ham
1 tablespoon flour
1/2 cup grated Cheddar cheese
Pepper
Butter
8 sheets phyllo dough
Bread crumbs
Cranberry sauce

In a large saucepan, cook the celery, green pepper, onions, and mushrooms until tender; add the mustard. Stir in the ham, flour, cheese, and pepper. Melt the butter and brush each layer of phyllo dough, sprinkle bread crumbs between layers, using all eight sheets. Mound the ham mixture onto the phyllo, fold over about 1 1/2 inches on each end and roll up, starting at one of the long sides. Brush the top with butter and make several diagonal cuts. Cover and chill for up to 24 hours. Bake at 400 degrees for 25 to 30 minutes, until brown. Serve with cooked cranberry sauce. Serves 3 to 4.

RiverSong

Estes Park, Colorado 80517
(303)586-4666

The Hope-Bosworth is a charming Queen Anne style Victorian inn built in 1904 by an early Geyserville pioneer, George M. Bosworth. the house, built entirely of heart redwood, is a "pattern book house." During the 1906 earthquake the brick chimneys toppled to the ground and plaster fell from the walls, but the house withstood the quake.

Savory Ham Loaf with Creamed Eggs

1 pound ham, coarsely ground in a food processor
1/2 pound fresh pork, coarsely ground in a food processor
2 teaspoons Dijon mustard
1 tablespoon brown sugar
2 eggs
1 small onion, finely chopped
3/4 cup fresh bread crumbs
1/2 cup tomato sauce
1/2 teaspoon pepper
Creamed eggs (recipe below)
Paprika, for garnish

Thoroughly mix all ingredients, using the hands or a large spoon. Press into a greased 8 1/2 by 4-inch loaf pan. Place the pan inside a shallow pan; fill the outer pan with water to reach 1 inch up the side of the loaf pan. Bake at 350 degrees for 1 hour. Drain off any accumulated grease; let the loaf pan sit in the pan for 1/2 hour before unmolding. Unmold and cut into 1-inch slices. Serve hot with Creamed Eggs; garnish with sprinkle of paprika. Serves 8.

Creamed Eggs
2 cups Basic White Sauce (recipe below)
1 teaspoon Dijon mustard
1/4 teaspoon cayenne pepper
1/2 teaspoon paprika
6 hard-cooked eggs, shelled
Paprika, for garnish

Season the hot white sauce with the mustard, cayenne, and paprika. Slice the eggs into sauce and stir gently to combine.

Basic White Sauce
2 tablespoons butter
2 tablespoons flour
1 cup milk
Salt and white pepper to taste
Nutmeg to taste
Cayenne pepper to taste

In a small saucepan, melt the butter over medium high heat; stir in the flour and cook, stirring occasionally, for 4 minutes. Whisk in the milk gradually, cooking until thickened. Add the seasonings. Makes about 1 cup.

Hope Merrill House
P.O. Box 42
Geyserville, California 95441
(707) 857-3356

Almond Chicken Hash

Chicken for breakfast? Keep an open mind. This is one of the favorites at the Inn at Coit Mountain.

1 cup sliced mushrooms
1/2 cup sliced almonds
2 tablespoons butter
2 cups diced, cooked chicken
2 1/2 cups Cream Sauce (recipe below)
Salt, freshly ground pepper to taste
8 eggs
Paprika, to taste

Saute the mushrooms and almonds in the butter. Add the chicken and cream sauce. Add salt and pepper to taste and turn into a shallow baking dish. Chill until needed or bake at 350 degrees until heated through (about 30 minutes). The eggs may be baked in "wells" on the hash or done in a pan and placed alongside the hash on the serving plate. Sprinkle with paprika as desired. Serves 4.

Cream Sauce
6 tablespoons butter
6 tablespoons flour
2 cups light cream
1/2 cup chicken broth
1/4 teaspoon nutmeg
Salt and freshly ground pepper to taste
Melt the butter and stir in the flour. Gradually add the milk and chicken stock, stirring and heating until thick.

Inn at Coit Mountain

HCR63, Box 3
Newport, New Hampshire 03773
(800) 367-2364

Four years after their honeymoon in Bayfield, Wisconsin, Mary and Jerry Phillips fell in love all over again. The object of their affection: a gracious Queen Anne style mansion atop a grassy green knoll in the village of Bayfield on Lake Superior's south shore. Built in 1890, the inn features elegant Victorian dining and lodging at its very best.

Lake Superior Trout Meuniere

8 small fresh trout or 4 pounds of fresh fillets
2 cups milk
1/2 to 3/4 cup flour
1 teaspoon salt
1/2 teaspoon coarse-ground black pepper
1/2 teaspoon chopped fresh dill
Vegetable oil
4 tablespoons butter
Lemon slices, for garnish
Sprigs of parsley, for garnish

Clean the fish and rinse well under cold running water. Place the fish in a shallow pan, cover with milk, and let stand for 30 to 45 minutes. Remove from the milk; drain but do not dry. Coat one fish or fillet at a time in flour seasoned with salt, pepper, and dill (using additional flour as needed).

Pour enough vegetable oil into a deep heavy skillet to fill to 1/2 inch deep. Heat over medium heat. Add the trout and cook until golden brown on the underside; turn, and brown the second side. Transfer the fish to a serving platter. Pour the oil from the skillet and wipe dry with pepper toweling. Add the butter to the skillet and heat to sizzling. Pour the butter over the trout. garnish with thin slices of lemon and sprigs of fresh parsley. Serves 8.

Old Rittenhouse Inn

P.O. Box 584
Bayfield, Wisconsin 54814
(715) 779-5111

8
Desserts

The Matlick is a lovely country inn in an equally lovely area of California. Owner/Innkeeper Nanette Robidart is a gracious hostess who welcomes her many guests with warmth and gives them great food to satisfy the heartiest of appetites. Visitors flock here over and over again.

Harvest Cake

2 cups sugar
3/4 cup vegetable oil
2 eggs
1 teaspoon vanilla extract
1/2 cup chopped walnuts
1 cup chopped dates
2 cups flour
1 cup coconut
2 teaspoons ground cinnamon
1 teaspoon baking soda
1 teaspoon salt
4 or 5 Granny Smith apples, chopped

Combine the sugar, oil, eggs, and vanilla in a large mixing bowl. Blend well. Stir in the walnuts, dates, and coconut. Sift the flour, cinnamon, baking soda, and salt into a bowl. Add to the sugar and egg mixture and blend thoroughly. Stir in the chopped apples. The batter will be gummy. Transfer to a 12-cup bundt pan greased and dusted with flour. Bake until a cake tester inserted in the center comes out clean, about one hour. Allow the cake to cool in the pan for 10 minutes. Turn out on a rack or cake plate. Serve warm with vanilla ice cream or whipped cream. Serves 12.

The Matlick House

1313 Rowan
Bishop, California 93514
(619) 873-3133

Blueberry Bundt Cake

2 cups sifted cake flour (not selfrising)
3 tablespoons instant nonfat dry milk
2 1/2 teaspoons baking soda
1/2 teaspoon salt
1 teaspoon ground cinnamon
1/2 teaspoon ground nutmeg
1/4 teaspoon ground cloves
1/2 cup chopped walnuts
1 1/2 cups sugar
3/4 cup lowfat plain yogurt
3 eggs, beaten
3/4 cup corn oil
1/2 teaspoon lemon extract
1 cup blueberries
Confectioners' sugar, for garnish

Grease and flour a 12 cup bundt ban. Combine the flour, dry milk, baking soda, salt, cinnamon, nutmeg, and cloves. Add the nuts. In a separate bowl, combine the sugar and the yogurt. Beat in the eggs, corn oil, and lemon extract. Fold in the blueberries. Combine the dry and liquid ingredients, mixing just enough to blend. Pour into the prepared bundt pan. Bake for 50 to 60 minutes, until a cake tester inserted into the center comes out clean. Cool for 15 minutes in the pan, then turn out on a rack to cool completely. Sprinkle with confectioners' sugar before serving. Serves 12.

Conover's Bay Head Inn

646 Main Avenue
Bay Head, New Jersey 06742
(908) 892-4664

Beverly Conover's Bay Head Inn was built in 1912 as a summer cottage for the L. Hastings Alexander family. The architectural drawings for the house are framed and show the reconstruction in 1916 as an inn. A delicate sense of color will embrace you as you step inside. The massive cut stone fireplace, family photographs, and well-placed antiques add to the guests' pleasure. The views from the inn are impressive, including the ocean, bay, marina, and yacht club. Shapely old homes comprise the rest of the scenic landscape.

The Fairfield Inn was originally the plantation home of Squire William Miller, who settled in Fairfield in 1755. In the "olden days", the highway through Fairfield was known as the "Great Road" from New-York to Hagerstown, so the inn was a stagecoach stop as well as a drover's tavern. It has been in continuous operation since 1823. Patrick Henry is said to have stayed at the inn. During the Civil War, the famous Confederate General, Jeb Stuart, visited the Inn in 1862 and again in 1863 when the confederates occupied the town for ten days during the Battle of Gettysburg. Delightful suppers and dinners are served at this historic retreat.

Chocolate Chip Applesauce Cake

1 1/2 cups sugar
1/2 cup vegetable oil
2 eggs
2 cups applesauce
2 cups flour
1 1/2 teaspoons baking soda
1/2 teaspoon salt
1/2 teaspoon ground cinnamon
2 tablespoons unsweetened cocoa powder
Topping
2 tablespoons sugar
1/2 cup chopped nuts
1 cup semisweet chocolate chips

Cream the sugar, oil, and eggs. Add the applesauce; then add the flour, baking soda, salt, cinnamon, and cocoa. Pour into a greased and floured 9 by 13-inch pan. Combine the ingredients for topping and sprinkle over the batter. Bake at 350 degrees F. for 40 minutes. Serves 12.

The Fairfield Inn

Main Street
Fairfield, Pennsylvania 17320
(717) 642-5410

Jam Cake

3 cups flour
1 tablespoon unsweetened cocoa powder
1 teaspoon salt
1 teaspoon ground cinnamon
1 teaspoon allspice
1 teaspoon ground cloves
1 teaspoon baking soda
1/2 teaspoon ground nutmeg
1 1/2 cups sugar
3/4 cup vegetable shortening
1 cup buttermilk
3 eggs
1 cup jam
1 cup chopped nuts
Icing (recipe below)

Combine all the dry ingredients. Add the vegetable shortening and buttermilk and beat for 2 minutes. Add the eggs and beat for 2 minutes. Fold in the jam and nuts. Pour into two greased 9-inch cake pans. Bake at 350 degrees F. for about 25 minutes or until a cake tester inserted in the center comes out clean. Let the layers cool in the pans, then turn out and frost. Serves 8 to 10.

Icing
1/2 cup margarine or butter
1 cup brown sugar
1/4 cup milk
2 cups confectioners' sugar
1 teaspoon vanilla extract

Combine the margarine and brown sugar in a saucepan, bring to a boil, and boil until thick. Remove from the heat and add the milk; boil again. Add the confectioners' sugar and beat well. Stir in the vanilla.

The Olde Wayside Inn

222 West Main Street
West Union, Ohio 46593
(513) 544-7103

The Olde Wayside Inn was built in 1804, and the original log framework still stands. Adams County is the fourth oldest county in Ohio and before the railroads was the main thoroughfare from the southwest to the east. This is the route over which early congressmen and statesmen passed on their way to the national capital, and this old inn became historic as the stopping place of President Andrew Jackson, Henry Clay, Thomas H. Benton and other notable men in the pioneer days of our country. Even Santa Anna, after his defeat by General Sam Houston, was a guest at The Olde Wayside Inn.

Virginia Whiskey Cake

Here is a delightful eighteenth century-style building of unique charm, completely decorated in the old manner. The visitor is carried back to the times of the Randolphs, the Masons, the Fairfaxes, the Jeffersons and the Washingtons. Antique furniture and primitive cooking utensils are prevalent and are displayed in an authentic and useful manner. In the scenic main dining room you will see hand-hewn beams of huge proportions, old sconces, early samplers, corner cupboards, and much much more. Excellent meals are served country-style.

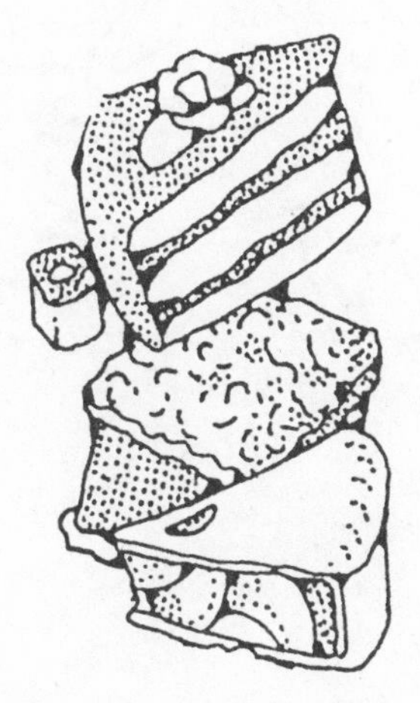

This recipe is adapted from the eighteenth century files of Helen Duprey Bullock, author of The Williamsburg Cook Book.

1 cup sugar
1 cup firmly packed brown sugar
1 cup butter
3 eggs, beaten
3 cups sifted cake flour
1/2 teaspoon baking powder
1/2 teaspoon mace
1 cup 100 proof bourbon whiskey
2 cups broken pecan meats

Combine the sugars and cream with the butter. Add the beaten eggs. Sift together the flour, baking powder, and mace; add alternately with the whiskey. Add the nuts. Bake in a well-greased or paper-lined tube pan at 250 degrees F. for 2 1/2 to 3 hours. The cake should have a moist crumbly texture similar to a macaroon. Wrap in aluminum foil and store in a cool place. (Do not freeze.) The cake cuts easier when cold, but should be served at room temperature. It will keep for two weeks or longer. Slices about 1/2 inch thick are best. Serves 12.

Note: Save the crumbs for parfaits or sundae topping. For added flavor, add 1 tablespoon of whiskey sauce (1/2 cup light corn syrup, 1 tablespoon rum, 2 tablespoons whiskey) to the cake about half an hour before serving. Whipped cream topping is optional.

Evans Farm Inn

1696 Chain Bridge Road
McLean, Virginia 22101
(703) 356-8000

Raspberry Linzer Torte

6 ounces almonds, toasted and ground
4 tablespoons sugar
3/4 cup unsalted butter
3/4 cup flour
1 egg yolk
Juice of 1 lemon
1 teaspoon ground cinnamon
3/4 cup high-quality raspberry preserves

Combine all ingredients except the preserves to make the crust. Chill until firm. Divide the crust mixture in half. Roll out the first half and line a 10-inch fluted tart pan, bottom and sides. Spread the raspberry preserves on the bottom of the crust. Roll out the remaining crust mixture. Cut it into strips and form a lattice crust on top of the preserves. Brush the latticework with an egg wash. Bake at 350 degrees F. until golden brown. Serves 8 to 10.

Note: Peach or apricot preserves may be substituted, though raspberry is traditional for a Linzer Torte.

The Inn At Millrace Pond

P.O. Box 359
Hope, New Jersey 07844
(908) 459-4884

Here is a gracious country inn situated on 23 acres along Beaver Brook in historic Hope. Founded in 1769 by Moravian pioneers, this tiny village is now listed on that state and national registers of historic sites. Restored to Colonial grandeur, the complex of buildings that comprise the inn, offer a splendid variety of fine accommodations. The inn reflects the Colonial traditions of hospitality—food, spirits, and lodging. Dick Gooding and Gloria Carrigan are the hospitable innkeepers.

The Hotel Wilber, where time comes to a standstill, or even backs up a bit, is noted for serving Czech as well as American cuisine.

Svitek

3 eggs
3/4 cup milk
1/2 teaspoon salt
1 cup flour
1/4 cup melted butter or margarine

Beat the eggs well. Add the milk, salt, and flour and mix thoroughly. Grease a 5 by 10-inch jelly roll pan with the melted butter. Bake at 400 degrees F. for 20 minutes, then cut into squares. Serve with jelly, honey, or syrup. Serves 6 to 8.

Hotel Wilber

203 South Wilson
Wilber, Nebraska 68465
(402) 821-9807

Almond Cake

1/2 cup butter
3/4 cup sugar
8 ounces almond paste
3 eggs
1 tablespoon Grand Marnier
1/4 teaspoon almond extract
1/4 cup flour
1/3 teaspoon baking powder

Mix the butter, sugar, and almond paste together well. Beat in the eggs, Grand Marnier, and almond extract. Add the flour and baking powder, without overmixing. Bake for 40 to 50 minutes at 350 degrees F. in an 8-inch buttered springform pan. Serve with a raspberry sauce and softly whipped cream. Serves 8.

Castine Inn

P.O. Box 41
Castine, Maine 04421
(207) 326-4365

The Castine Inn has practiced the art of hospitality ever since it was built in 1898. Guests arriving by car today are greeted as warmly as those who once disembarked from the town wharf (some still do) or stepped out of carriages at the nearest station.

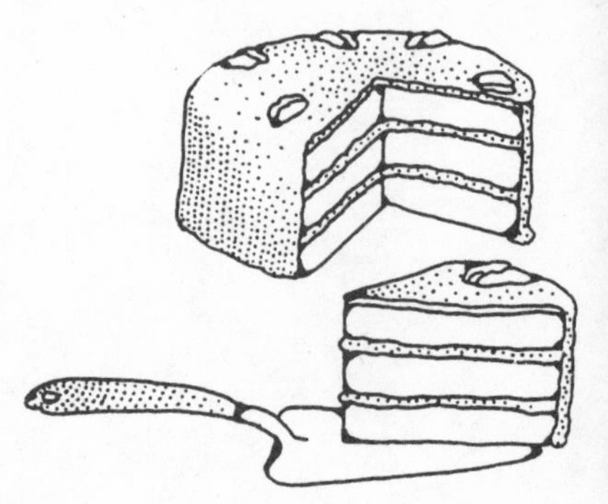

Early settlers named Heald built this homestead in the heart of the White Mountains in 1805 as a two-story structure. Eckley T. Stearns, an appointed governor of Florida, transformed the house into its present Mississippi steamboat appearance by the addition of a third floor to remind him of his antebellum days in the South. The structure became Center Lovell Inn in May 1975 and was restored according to a philosophy of life that says we are all caretakers of our world. Bill and Susie Mosca continue the ongoing work of restoring the homestead.

Cranberry Ice Cream Cake

6 tablespoons butter
1/4 cup sugar
1/2 cup chopped pecans (optional)
1 1/2 cup graham cracker crumbs

Melt the butter in a saucepan, add the sugar, pecans if desired, and graham cracker crumbs. Mix well and press into the bottom and sides of an 8-inch springform pan. Freeze.

Ice Cream
2 egg whites
1 cup heavy cream
1 cup sugar
1 tablespoon orange juice concentrate
1 teaspoon vanilla extract
Pinch of salt
1/2 cup ground cranberries

Beat the egg whites until stiff and set aside. In a separate bowl, whip the cream and slowly add the sugar. Then gently fold in the orange juice concentrate, vanilla, salt, egg whites, and cranberries. Pour into the frozen graham cracker crust and freeze for several hours before cutting into wedges and serving. Serves 6 to 8.

Center Lovell Inn

Route 5
Center Lovell, Maine 04016
(207) 925-1575

Hot Fudge Cake

2 cups flour
4 teaspoons baking powder
1 teaspoon salt
1 1/3 cups sugar
6 tablespoons plus 1/2 cup unsweetened cocoa powder
1 cup milk
2 teaspoons vanilla
4 tablespoons melted margarine or butter
1 cup chopped walnuts
2 cups packed brown sugar
3 cups boiling water

Combine the flour, baking powder, salt, sugar, and the 6 tablespoons cocoa in a bowl. Add the milk, vanilla, and margarine and beat until smooth. Add the nuts. Spread in a greased 9 by 13-inch Pyrex baking dish.

Mix together the brown sugar and the 1/2 cup cocoa. Sprinkle over the batter. Pour the boiling water over the batter. Bake at 350 degrees for 50 minutes. The top layer will be cake and the bottom pudding. Serves 10 to 12.

Silas Griffith Inn

Rural Route 1
Box 66-F
Danby, Vermont 05739
(802) 293-5567

Silas Griffith, lumber baron and Vermont's first millionaire, built a gracious Victorian mansion in 1891 for his new bride. The mansion overlooks the idyllic small town of Danby which lies in a valley surrounded by the beautiful Green Mountains of Vermont. Today the mansion and carriage house have been carefully renovated, appointed with modern conveniences and furnished lovingly with fine antiques. The handcarved cherry woodwork, embossed tin ceilings, and stained glass windows capture the history and elegance of the Victorian period. The restaurant and lounge are informal and specialize in fine wines and the eclectic gourmet cooking of the owner-chef, Paul Dansereau.

Travelers enjoy old fashioned comfort and luxury at this the oldest operating hotel west of the Rocky Mountains. Upon arrival, one steps back into the Victorian era with sumptuous suites furnished with antiques from the Gold Rush days. Hospitality comes naturally here; the National has had more than 130 years of experience in making guests feel welcome. The cocktail hour is enhanced by the ornate back bar, which was originally the dining room buffet in the Spreckels mansion in San Francisco. In the Victorian Dining Room, tables are softly lighted with coal oil lamps.

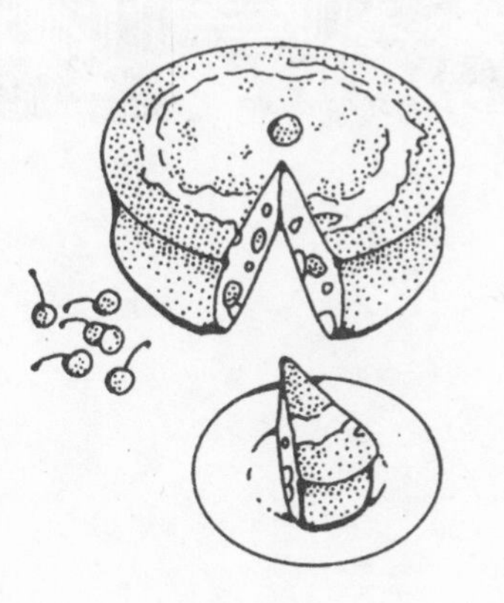

National Hotel's Famous Cheesecake

1 cup butter, softened
2 cups graham cracker crumbs
1 1/2 pounds cream cheese, softened
4 eggs, beaten well
1 cup sugar
2 teaspoons vanilla extract
Dash of lemon juice

Topping
2 cups sour cream
4 tablespoons sugar
1 teaspoon vanilla extract

To make the crust, blend together the butter and graham cracker crumbs and press into a 9 or 10-inch springform pan. Blend together the cream cheese, eggs, 1 cup sugar, 2 teaspoons vanilla, and lemon juice and pour into the crust. Bake for 25 minutes at 350 degrees or until firm. Let cool for 30 minutes.

To make the topping, combine the sour cream with the sugar and vanilla. Pour over the filling and bake at 450 degrees for 10 minutes or until firm. Serves 12 to 15.

National Hotel

211 Broad Street
Nevada City, California 95959
(916) 295-4551

Lemon Chiffon Cheesecake

4 cups graham crackers, crushed
1 cup butter, melted

Blend the crumbs and melted butter in a bowl. Reserve 1/3 cup of the crumb mixture for the top of the cheesecake. Press the remainder on the bottom and sides of a 10-inch springform pan. Bake for 12 to 15 minutes at 325 degrees F. Cool.

Filling
1/4 cup cold water
2 tablespoons unflavored gelatin
3/4 cup and 1/2 cup sugar
5 eggs, at room temperature, separated
Pinch of salt
1/3 cup milk, scalded
1 1/2 pounds cream cheese, softened
1/3 cup fresh lemon juice
2 drops vanilla extract
1/4 cup Grand Marnier or other orange flavored liqueur
Finely grated rind of 2 lemons

Pour the cold water into a cup. Sprinkle with gelatin. Let stand until soft, about 5 minutes. Combine the 3/4 cup sugar, the egg yolks, and salt in the top of a double boiler. Beat well. Set over gently boiling water. Add the milk and beat constantly until thick (about 5 minutes.) Remove from heat. Add the gelatin and stir to dissolve. Cool to lukewarm.

Beat the egg whites until soft peaks form. Add the 1/2 cup sugar gradually. Beat until stiff peaks form. Set aside. With the same beater, beat the cream cheese. Add a small amount of the egg mixture, then fold in the remaining egg mixture. Fold in the lemon juice, vanilla, and liqueur. Fold the egg whites into the cream cheese mixture. Pour into the pan. Sprinkle with the reserved crumbs mixed with the lemon rind. Refrigerate for 6 hours at least or overnight before eating, or freeze. Defrost in the refrigerator. Serves 12 to 15.

Eagle's Landing

Box 1510
Blue Jay, California 92317
(714) 336-2642

Located on the exclusive west shore of Lake Arrowhead, this lovely inn reflects Jack and Dorothy Stone's love of art. The innkeepers have used antiques and objets d'art from different parts of the world, baskets and a wonderful collection of ceramic pieces, to bring warmth and beauty to every nook of their mountain lodge. High in the treetops, with a view of the lake, the atmosphere invites guests to relax and unwind.

The Montague Inn is a small luxury hotel in the European tradition offering elegance and excellence. A restored Georgian mansion, centered on eight beautifully landscaped acres, with 18 guest rooms, the inn invites guests to enjoy the peaceful pleasure of strolling among the gardens and relaxing near Lake Linton. The dining room offers fine cuisine in an intimate atmosphere overlooking the spacious grounds. Dining is by reservation only.

Hazelnut Cheesecake

2 1/4 pounds cream cheese, softened
1 tablespoon vanilla extract
1/3 tablespoon almond extract
1 1/2 cups sugar
6 eggs
3/4 cup toasted chopped hazelnuts, ground
1/4 cup Frangelico (Hazelnut liqueur)
Whipped cream flavored with Frangelico, for topping

Beat the cream cheese until smooth, add the vanilla and almond extract. Add the sugar gradually. When completely mixed, add the eggs, one at a time. Add the ground hazelnuts. Pour the mixture into a 10-inch round cake pan with parchment paper lining the bottom. Grease the paper and the sides of the pan. Drizzle the Frangelico over the mixture and stir it in with a toothpick. Place the pan in a water bath and bake at 450 degrees F. for 15 minutes, then 300 degrees F. for 1 hour (or until a knife inserted in the center comes out almost clean). Let cool completely and turn the pan upside down on a cake plate. Peel off the parchment paper. You may invert the cheesecake back onto another cake plate if you would like it top side up. Refrigerate until ready to use. Top with whipped cream flavored with Frangelico. Serves 12 to 15.

Montague Inn

1561 South Washington Avenue
Saginaw, Michigan 48601
(517) 752-3939

Peanut Butter Cheesecake

Graham cracker crust

2 cups creamy peanut butter
1 pound cream cheese softened
2 tablespoons melted butter
2 teaspoons vanilla extract
1 1/2 cups heavy cream

Topping
6 ounces semisweet chocolate
4 tablespoons hot coffee

Press the graham cracker crust into a 10-inch springform pan and bake at 325 degrees F. for 10 minutes. Cool. To make the filling, beat the peanut butter, sugar, cream cheese, butter, and vanilla until smooth and creamy. Beat the heavy cream until soft peaks form. Fold the whipped cream into the peanut butter mixture. Spoon into the crust. Refrigerate for at least six hours.

To make the topping, melt the chocolate, add the coffee, and mix well. Cool, then spread over the chilled cheesecake. Refrigerate until the chocolate sets. Serves 12 to 15.

The Gregory House

P.O. Box 401
Averill Park, New York 12018
(518) 674-3774

Over a century ago the hand-crafted iron gate in front of The Gregory House welcomed family and friends of the Gregorys' to their cottage in the country. Today, the gate stills stands as a graceful symbol of hospitality to world travelers, welcoming them to an unpretentious but comfortable country inn. The cottage now serves 70 dinner guests in four candlelit dining rooms and houses overnight guests in immaculate bed-rooms. As with the old iron gate, dining is, in effect, "hand-crafted" to provide the kind of food many travelers have come to expect and appreciate from country inns.

This half-timbered hotel was built in 1939 to accommodate train crews who serviced the Great Northern Railway. Bordering Glacier National Park, the comfortable inn is a favorite year-round retreat. Hikers, cross-country skiers, and other guests still enjoy the flavor of the nostalgic railroad past during their stay. The Inn is listed on the National Register of Historic Places.

Pumpkin Brandy Cheesecake

1 1/2 cups ginger snap cookie crumbs
1/3 cup sliced almonds
1/3 cup melted margarine
1/2 teaspoon ground cinnamon
2 pounds cream cheese, softened
1 1/4 cups sugar
1 1/2 teaspoons pumpkin pie spice
1/2 teaspoon ground ginger
4 eggs
1 cup mashed pumpkin
1/4 cup brandy
3 tablespoons half-and-half

Topping
2 cups sour cream
1/4 cup sugar
2 tablespoons brandy
Sliced almonds, for garnish

To make the crust, mix together the cookie crumbs, almonds, melted margarine, and cinnamon and press into a 10-inch springform pan. Bake at 325 degrees F. for 10 minutes.

To make the filling, in the large bowl of an electric mixer combine the remaining ingredients (except those for the topping). Blend well. Pour over the crust and bake at 325 degrees F. for 40 minutes. Turn off the oven and let the cake cool completely without opening the oven door.

To make the topping, combine the sour cream, sugar, and brandy and pour over the cooled cake. Bake at 400 degrees F. for 10 minutes. Cool and refrigerate. Remove from the pan and press sliced almonds onto the sides. Serves 12 to 15.

Izaak Walton Inn

P.O. Box 653
Essex, Montana 59916
(406) 888-5700

Shaker Sugar Pie

1 9-inch unbaked pie shell
1/3 cup flour
1 cup brown sugar
2 cups light cream
1 teaspoon vanilla extract
4 tablespoons butter
Nutmeg

Thoroughly mix the flour and brown sugar and spread evenly on the bottom of the unbaked pie shell. Add cream and vanilla. Slice the butter into pieces and distribute evenly over top of pie. Sprinkle with nutmeg. Bake at 350 degrees F. for 40 to 45 minutes or until firm. Serves 6.

The Golden Lamb

27 South Broadway
Lebanon, Ohio 45036
(513) 932-5065

Ohio's oldest inn, established in 1815, has served the finest foods for more than 150 years. Rustic woods and bricks form the surroundings for a unique dining experience. Guests may choose from among 17 guest rooms and nine dining rooms. Since Lebanon was the site of a major Shaker Community, the inn has a large collection of Shaker furniture and accessories. There is a Shaker dining room, as well as three museum rooms on the fourth floor. Each bedroom is decorated differently, using Shaker and other unique furniture.

The Sedgwick Inn is located on 12 acres in the beautiful Taconic Valley just west of the Berkshire Mountains. The main house dates back to 1791 and both the common rooms and guest rooms are furnished with antiques. The atmosphere is formal but comfortable. The Hancock Shaker Village, Tanglewood (summer home of the Boston Symphony Orchestra), and Williamstown Theatre Festival are nearby. Both downhill and cross-country skiing are within a short drive. The dining room's menu changes weekly and is considered one of the finest in the area.

Ginger Lime Pie

Ginger snaps
2 tablespoons butter
Juice and grated rind of 2 limes
4 tablespoons sweetened condensed milk
2 cups heavy cream
1/2 cup superfine sugar

To make the crust for a 9 or 10-inch pie, process 12 to 14 ginger snaps, toss with 2 tablespoons of melted butter, and press into a pie tin and up the sides. Put in freezer until ready to use. To make the filling, place all other ingredients in a chilled mixing bowl and beat until stiff. Pour into the pie crust. Chill until firm. The pie is especially good served with raspberry sauce. Serves 6 to 8.

The Sedgwick Inn

P.O. Box 250
Berlin, New York 12022
(518) 658-2334

Chess Pie

2 1/2 cups sugar
1/2 cup margarine
1/8 cup self-rising flour
Pinch of salt
4 eggs
1 1/2 teaspoons vanilla extract
1 cup milk
2 9-inch unbaked pie shells

Cream together the sugar and margarine, gradually add the flour, salt, and eggs. Add the vanilla and milk and beat only until the ingredients are mixed. Pour into the crust and bake for 1 hour and 25 minutes at 375 degrees F. Makes 2 9-inch pies.

The Historic Old Talbott Tavern

107 West Stephen Foster
Bardstown, Kentucky 40004
(502) 348-3494

Settlers first began arriving in Bardstown around 1775. It was incorporated as a town in 1782. The first permanent building erected was a stone, all-purpose public house now known as the Talbott Tavern. To this day, the tavern still stands as the oldest western stagecoach stop in America. It was licensed under Patrick Henry, then Governor of Virginia, over two centuries ago. As mid-America's oldest restaurant, the inn's dining room features nationally recognized recipes. The Chicago Tribune has called its food "indescribably delicious."

Chesapeake House is a converted private home about 75 years old. Delightful meals are prepared from old family recipes by a kitchen staff of island homemakers. The word "commercial" could never be applied to the food here since everything is prepared from scratch. This unusual and famous hotel is the only one on the island, which is reached only by mail boat. The ride is an adventure in itself; the sky is full of ducks and geese or seagulls, depending upon the season. There is definitely an "I would like to stay forever" atmosphere about this wonderful place.

Lemon Pie

2/3 cup cornstarch
2 1/2 cups plus 3/4 cup sugar
1/2 teaspoon salt
3 cups boiling water
6 eggs, separated
2/3 cup lemon juice
4 tablespoons butter
1 teaspoon grated lemon rind
1 baked 9-inch pie shell

Mix the cornstarch, sugar, and salt in the top of a double boiler. Add the boiling water and mix thoroughly. Cook until thick and clear. Beat the egg yolks, stir in a little of the hot mixture, pour back into the double boiler, and cook for approximately 2 minutes longer. Remove from the heat, add the lemon juice, butter, and lemon rind, and mix well. Cool and pour into the baked pie shell. Beat the egg whites until barely stiff; add the 3/4 cup sugar gradually and beat until stiff. Swirl over the pie filling, touching the edges all around. Bake at 425 degrees F. until golden brown, about 6 minutes. Serves 6.

Crockett's Chesapeake House

Tangier Island, Virginia 23440
(804) 891-2331

Lemon Shaker Pie

5 lemons, peeled, sliced thin, and seeds removed
2 cups sugar
Pastry for a 2-crust 9-inch pie
5 eggs
Melted butter

Place the sliced lemons in a large bowl, add the sugar, and mix until the sugar is dissolved. Let sit overnight, covered. Roll out the pastry for a 2-crust pie. Transfer the bottom of the crust to a 9-inch pie tin. Beat the eggs until well mixed, then add the lemon-sugar mixture. Mix well and pour into the crust. Fit the top crust over the filling and seal the edges well. Make small slits in the top crust to allow steam to escape. Bake at 300 degrees F. for 1 hour and 10 minutes, until light brown. Let cool completely, to thicken the filling, and reheat to warm before serving. Serves 6.

The New Harmony Inn

P.O. Box 581
New Harmony, Indiana 47631
(813) 682-4491

Here is a delightful inn in a peaceful, picturesque town of less than 1000 residents. New Harmony was the site of two nineteenth century Utopian settlements, and many buildings from those days remain open to the public. The New Harmony Inn was built in 1974, but invites the visitor to explore the legacies from the past while enjoying comforts of the present. There are 90 guest rooms, many with working fireplaces. Its Geranium is one of Indiana's most popular, with an exceptional menu boasting regional as well as continental favorites. The Shaker lemon pie is irresistible.

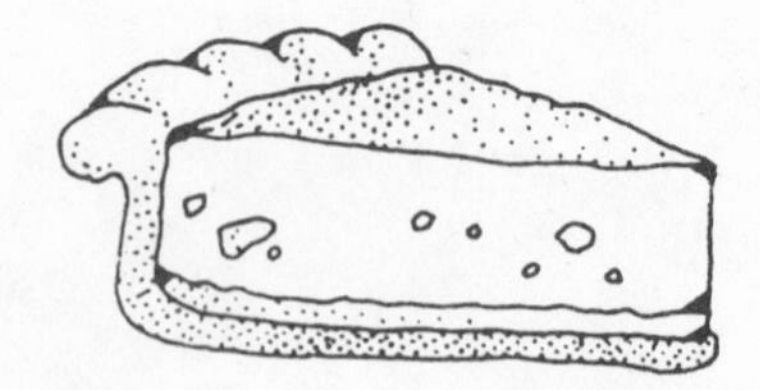

Hill's Resort is located 80 miles from Spokane amid towering trees and overlooking beautiful Priest Lake.

Huckleberry Pie

1 baked 9-inch pie shell
4 cups huckleberries, washed and drained
3/4 cup water
3 tablespoons cornstarch
1 cup sugar
Fresh lemon juice
Whipped cream or ice cream

Simmer 1 cup of the berries with the water for 3 to 4 minutes. Combine the cornstarch and sugar and add to the cooking fruit. Simmer slowly until the syrup is thick and clear ruby red, stirring constantly. When thickened, add lemon juice (1 teaspoon to 1 tablespoon, depending on the sweetness of the huckleberries). Cool slightly.

Line the baked pastry shell with 3 cups of fresh huckleberries. Pour the slightly cooled glaze over the raw berries. Mix very gently with a fork to coat the fresh berries. Chill thoroughly. Serve with whipped cream or ice cream. Serves 6.

Hill's

Route 5
Priest Lake, Idaho 83856
(208) 443-2551

Tarte Tatin with Mango

This is a tropical version of the classic French Tarte Tatin, an upside-down apple pie.

1 cup flour
1/3 cup plus 2 tablespoons butter, softened
1 egg
6 tablespoons ice water
2 tablespoons sugar
Pinch of salt
2 tablespoons raw sugar
8 large mangoes

To make the dough, place the flour in a large bowl and make a well in the center. Add the 1/3 cup butter, the egg, ice water, sugar, and salt. Mix well and let rest for 1 hour.

Combine the raw sugar and the 2 tablespoons of butter in a saucepan and heat, stirring, until the sugar caramelizes. Pour into a 9-inch pie plate. Peel and cut the mango in large wedges. Arrange the wedges on top of the caramelized sugar and butter.

Roll out the dough to a 1/8-inch thickness in a circle large enough to cover the pie plate filled with mango. Bake for 30 minutes at 450 degrees F. Invert the tart onto a serving plate and serve warm. Serves 8.

The Plantation Inn and Famous Gerard's Restaurant

174 Lahainaluna Road
Lahaina, Maui, Hawaii 96761
(808) 667-9225

Here, combined, are one of America's finest inns and very finest restaurants. Gerard's changing menu and award-winning creations have earned it a rating as one of Hawaii's top 10 restaurants by Sheldon Landwehr's prestigious Who's Who in America's Restaurants. *This elegant, intimate French restaurant at the inn is a favorite fine dining spot for Hawaiian residents and visitors alike. The unique country inn blends an elegant turn-of-the-century ambience with the first-class amenities of the finest hotels: Antiques, stained glass, hardwood floors, brass and poster beds, extensive wood trim, and sprawling verandas evoke the charm of old Hawaii. The inn is in a quiet country setting, just a block from the ocean, in the historic whaling town of Lahaina.*

The peaceful and verdant Ojai Valley is 90 minutes northwest of Los Angeles and 30 minutes east of Santa Barbara. The inn reflects the genteel Southern California lifestyle of the early days of this century. The beauty of the surroundings and the artistry of the inn's staff assures one's visit will become a special memory. The same can be said of dining at the Ojai Valley Inn, one of the very finest inns in the world.

Chocolate Pecan Pie

4 eggs
1 cup golden brown sugar
3/4 cup light corn syrup
Pinch of salt
1/4 cup unsalted butter, melted
1 teaspoon vanilla extract
2 1/4 cups chopped pecans
3 ounces unsweetened chocolate, melted and cooled
1 unbaked 9-inch pie shell

Beat the eggs in a bowl, then add the brown sugar, corn syrup, salt, butter, and vanilla. Whisk together. Mix one-half of the mixture into the chocolate with a wooden paddle. Fold in the pecans and the remaining butter and sugar mixture. Pour into the pie shell and bake at 300 degrees until the mixture is set, 45 minutes to 1 hour. Serves 6 to 8.

Ojai Valley Inn

P.O. Box 1866
Ojai, California 93023
(805) 646-5511

Chocolate Mousse Pie

Crust
3 cups chocolate wafer crumbs
1 stick unsalted butter (approximately), melted

Filling
1 pound semisweet chocolate, melted
4 eggs, separated
2 whole eggs
2 cups heavy cream
6 tablespoons confectioners' sugar
1 1/2 teaspoons vanilla extract (Mexican if available)

To make the crust, mix the melted butter with the chocolate wafer crumbs in a bowl. Enough butter should be used so the crumbs stay together when pressed into the pan. Press into a 10- or 12-inch springform pan, along the bottom and sides. Chill.

To make the filling, melt the chocolate in the top of a double boiler over simmering water. Separate the 4 eggs. Place the egg whites in a large bowl and beat until soft peaks form. Beat the heavy cream with the confectioners' sugar and vanilla until stiff. When the chocolate is melted, cool slightly. Then add the four egg yolks and blend well. The chocolate will become hard to stir. Continue to blend and add the two whole eggs. Fold in some of the whipped cream (about 3/4 cup) into the chocolate mixture, then fold in some of the egg white. Pour the chocolate mixture into a larger bowl and fold in the remainder of the whipped cream and egg whites, alternating between the two. Make sure to fold gently so as not to deflate the mixture.

When the mixture is completely blended, pour into the prepared crust. Chill for at least 6 hours, preferably overnight, or freeze until ready to serve. Serves about 12.

DeHaven Valley Farm is located in Northern Mendocino County, on twenty acres of meadows, hills, and streams, across from the Pacific Ocean. The Victorian farmhouse, built in 1875, has been beautifully restored, and two cottages offer spacious seclusion and fireplaces. Guests enjoy exploring tidepools, a variety of farm animals, and soaking in the hot tub. The Farm is also ideally located to visit the gigantic redwoods twenty-five miles to the North and the artist colony of Mendocino twenty-five miles south.

DeHaven Valley Farm

39247 North Highway 1
Westport, California 95488
(707) 961-1660

Tucked away in the Skylands of northwestern New Jersey, you will find the Whistling Swan Inn, a ten-bedroom family home built circa 1900. All the rooms have private baths; a full buffet style breakfast is served in the dining room. Nearby are wineries to tour, ski slopes, antiquing, and a variety of wonderful restaurants. Historic Waterloo Village is minutes away.

Green Tomato Pie

Pastry for one 9-inch two-crust pie
4 cups fresh green (unripened) tomatoes, thinly sliced
1 cup brown sugar
1/2 teaspoon cinnamon
1/2 teaspoon salt
1/2 teaspoon ground nutmeg
1/2 teaspoon ground cloves
2 tablespoons flour
4 tablespoons fresh lemon juice
6 pats butter or margarine

Make pastry for a 9-inch two-crust pie, using the recipe of your preference. Roll out and place the bottom crust in a 9-inch pie pan. Combine all ingredients for the filling so that the tomatoes are well covered with sugar and spices. Put the mixture into the bottom crust and dot the top with the pats of butter. Cover with the top crust and crimp the edges to seal.

Bake at 425 degrees for 30 minutes, then lower the temperature to 350 degrees for 30 minutes or until the top crust is golden brown. Serves 6.

Whistling Swan Inn

P.O. Box 791
Stanhope, New Jersey 07874
(201) 347-6369

Arkansas Derby Pie

3 eggs
3/4 cup sugar
1 cup dark corn syrup
1 tablespoon melted butter
2 tablespoons Southern Comfort
1 teaspoon vanilla extract
1/4 cup coconut
1/2 cup semisweet chocolate chips
1/2 cup pecans
Pinch of salt
Unbaked 9-inch pie shell

Beat the eggs slightly with an electric mixer; add the sugar and mix well. Add the corn syrup and mix well; then add the butter, Southern Comfort, vanilla, coconut, chocolate chips, pecans, and salt. Mix well and pour into the pie shell. Bake at 375 degrees for 45 minutes. Serves 6 to 8.

This inn has garnered for itself a reputation for being a "hotel of homelike atmosphere." Southern cuisine is served in the Victorian Tea Room.

The Great Southern Hotel

127 West Cedar
Brinkley, Arkansas 72021
(501) 734-4955

In central Louisiana, overlooking historic Bayou Beouf, the traveler will find Walnut Grove Plantation. Built during the 1830s, it represents Louisiana at its grandest. Guests are invited to browse the beautiful gardens with their brick walks, and bird sanctuaries. The mansion is filled with fine furnishings. Sunnyside Cottage and Buttercup House offer cozy comfort to overnight guests.

Sweet Potato Pie

2 cups cooked and mashed yams
1 cup sugar
3 eggs
4 tablespoons margarine
1 teaspoon vanilla extract
1/2 cup bourbon
1 tablespoon flour
1 teaspoon ground nutmeg
1 tablespoon fresh lemon juice
1 unbaked 9-inch pie shell
Whipped cream, for garnish
Chopped pecans, for garnish

Combine all ingredients except the pecans and whipped cream. Mix together with an electric mixer until well blended. Fill the pie shell with the potato mixture and bake at 325 degrees for about 45 minutes. Serve topped with whipped cream and sprinkled with chopped pecans. Serves 6.

Walnut Grove Plantation House

Route 1, Box 41
Cheneyville, Louisiana 71325
(318) 2203

Buttermilk Coconut Custard Pie

2 9-inch pie shells
1/2 cup butter or margarine, melted
1 1/2 cups sugar
3/4 cup buttermilk
4 ounces coconut (fresh or frozen)
5 eggs
1 1/2 teaspoon vanilla extract
Pinch of salt (optional)

Prebake the pie shells for 4 minutes at 350 degrees. Set aside to cool. Combine the butter, sugar, buttermilk, eggs, coconut, and vanilla. Pour into the pie shells. Bake at 325 degrees. on a cookie sheet for 40 to 45 minutes. Cool. Serve at room temperature. Cover with meringue or serve with whipped cream if desired. Serves 6.

Randolph House Country Inn

P.O. Box 816
Fryemont Road
Bryson City, North Carolina 28713
(704) 488-3472

In the heart of the quaint town of Bryson City, at the gateway to the Smoky Mountain National Park, one finds an historic inn known locally as the Mansion or the White House. The building is listed on The National Register of Historic Places as the Frye-Randolph House. The house was built by timber baron Amos Frye in 1895 and has 12 gables and more than 50 windows to make it exceptionally light and airy. All rooms contain the original furnishings. Co-proprietor Ruth Randolph Adams, a relative of the original owner, is known internationally for her southern gourmet cooking. She and her husband Bill maintain the traditional high standards of southern hospitality.

This is one of the loveliest inns in America. An indoor pool and resident theatre company are only two of its drawing cards. Beautiful hardwood floors, a country decor, and warm cornbread made from meal ground at a water-driven mill make a visit here memorable.

Persimmon Pecan Pie

3 eggs, slightly beaten
1 cup persimmon pulp
1 cup sugar
1/2 teaspoon ground cinnamon
1/4 teaspoon salt
1/2 cup dark corn syrup
1 teaspoon vanilla extract
1 unbaked 9-inch pie shell
1 cup chopped pecans
Whipped cream, for garnish

In a small mixing bowl, combine the eggs, persimmon pulp, sugar, cinnamon, salt, corn syrup, and vanilla; mix well. Pour into the unbaked pastry shell. Top with the pecans. Bake at 350 degrees for about 40 minutes, or until a knife inserted into the center comes out clean. Chill and serve with whipped cream. Serves 6.

Spring Mill Inn

Spring Mill State Park
Rural Route 2, Box 68
Mitchell, Indiana 47446
(812) 849-4081

Autumn Harvest Apple Pie

Crust
2 cups flour
3/4 cup butter
2 tablespoons vegetable shortening
1/2 cup sugar
Pinch of salt
1 egg, lightly beaten

Filling
1/3 cup canned pumpkin
1/2 cup sugar
1 tablespoon fresh lemon juice
1 teaspoon flour
1/2 teaspoon ground ginger
1/2 teaspoon ground cinnamon
1/4 teaspoon ground cloves
1/4 teaspoon allspice
3 cups thinly sliced assorted apples (2 cups firm, 1 cup soft)
1 1/2 cups cranberries
1 cup thinly sliced fresh pumpkin (1 or 2 slices)
3 tablespoons butter, cut in small pieces

Egg wash made by mixing 1 egg yolk with 2 tablespoons water.
To make the crust, combine the flour, salt, and sugar, cut in the butter and shortening (using a pastry blender or two knives), and add the egg. Mix only until combined. Chill for 1/2 hour. Roll out into two circles to fit a 9-inch pie pan. To make the filling, combine the first 8 ingredients in a large bowl. Add the apples, cranberries, and pumpkin and toss to blend. Pour into the pie crust, then dot the butter over the filling. Top with the remaining pie crust. Brush the top with an egg wash and bake for 1 hour and 15 minutes at 350 degrees. Serves 6.

Nathaniel Porter Inn

125 Water Street
Warren, Rhode Island 02885
(401) 245-6622

Paulette and Robert Lynch are innkeepers at this handsome country inn named after Nathaniel Porter who, at the age of twelve, was among the 77 Minute Men who stood on Lexington Green and fired the first shots of the American Revolution in 1775. Nathaniel Porter is a direct ancestor of the current owners. The building is listed on The National Register of Historical Places. The rear of the structure dates to 1750, and the main house was built by a wealthy sea captain in 1795. The interior is an exceptional example of colonial American architecture.

Here is a historic country inn offering good food, good friends, good lodging. It was built in 1898 with a wide old staircase and spacious halls to welcome visitors to its attractive parlors. All rooms have private baths; there are also family suites. The inn serves regional New England cuisine in its large, attractive, dining room. Connie and Tom Mazol are the innkeepers.

Peach Praline Pie

3/4 cup sugar
3 tablespoons plus 1/4 cup flour
4 cups peeled and sliced fresh peaches
1 1/2 teaspoons fresh lemon juice
1/3 cup firmly packed brown sugar
1/2 cup chopped pecans
3 tablespoons butter
1 unbaked 9-inch pie shell

In a large mixing bowl, combine the sugar, and the 3 tablespoons flour. Mix well. Add the peaches and lemon juice. In a small bowl, combine the brown sugar, 1/4 cup flour, and pecans. Cut in the butter until the mixture becomes crumbly. Sprinkle one third of the nut mixture in the unbaked pie shell to form a layer on the bottom. Cover with the peach mixture and sprinkle the remaining nut mixture over the peaches. Bake at 400 degrees or until peaches are tender; about 30 minutes. Serves 6.

Note: If the pie browns too quickly, lower the oven temperature immediately.

The Bradford Inn

Main Street
Bradford, New Hampshire 03221
(603) 938-5309

Fresh Blueberry Pie

1 baked 9-inch pie shell, cooled
4 cups fresh or frozen blueberries
1 cup sugar
2 tablespoons cornstarch
1/4 teaspoon salt
1/4 cup water
1 tablespoon butter or margarine

Line the cooled pie shell with 2 cups of the blueberries. To make the sauce, cook the remaining berries with the sugar, cornstarch, salt, and water over medium heat until thickened. Remove from the heat, add the butter, and cool. Pour the sauce over the berries in the shell. Chill until ready to serve. If desired, serve with whipped cream. Serves 6.

Middlebury Inn

P.O. Box 798
Middlebury, Vermont 05753
(802) 388-4961

This graciously appointed inn is over 150 years old, having provided food, drink, and lodging since 1827. It really had its genesis in 1794 as Mattock's Tavern, not much more than a a clearing in a dense forest. Both the Morgan Room Cocktail Lounge and the dining room serve excellent cuisine. Buffets, a favorite repast in the Middlebury tradition, are offered frequently. In the summer, country fair booths are set up in the old ballroom.

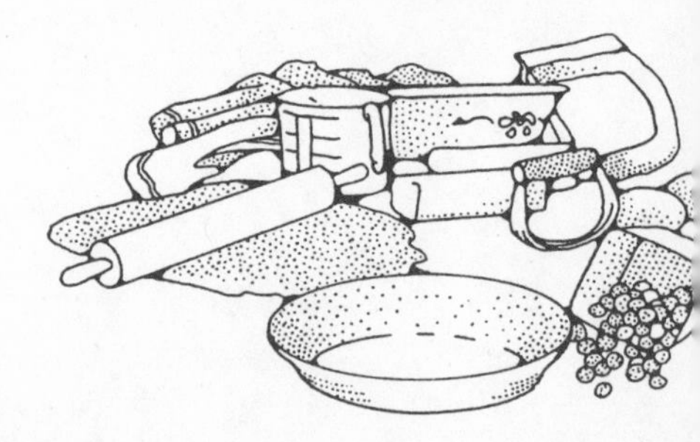

Said by many to serve the best food in Vermont, Green Mountain Inn offers a wide choice of popular New England dishes. It is located at the foot of the road to Mount Mansfield and Smuggler's Notch, and is listed on the National Register of Historic Places. Built in 1833, it has 50 rooms, all with private baths. Jan S. Wadds is the owner/innkeeper; Keith Martin is the celebrated chef.

Blueberry Apple Crumb Pie

3 cups wild Maine blueberries
3 Granny Smith Apples, peeled and sliced
2/3 cup sugar
2 tablespoons flour
2 tablespoons cornstarch
1 tablespoon fresh lemon juice
1/2 teaspoon ground cinnamon
Dash of ground nutmeg
1 unbaked 9-inch pie shell, brushed with an egg wash

Crumb Topping
1 1/8 cups sugar
1 cup flour
1/3 cup ground walnuts
1/2 cup butter, softened

Thoroughly mix all the ingredients for the filling. Pour into the pie shell. Mix the ingredients for the topping with the fingertips to a coarse meal. Cover the pie with the topping and bake at 400 degrees for 15 minutes; lower the heat to 350 degrees and bake for 30 to 40 minutes longer. Serves 6.

Green Mountain Inn

P.O. Box 60
Stowe, Vermont 05672
(802) 253-7301

Lemon Almond Tart

Crust
1/2 cup unsalted butter, cut into pieces, at room temperature
1/4 cup sugar
1 egg
1 1/2 cups flour
1 teaspoon grated lemon rind

Filling
1 1/4 cups coarsely ground almonds
1 cup sugar
3 egg whites, at room temperature
Dash of cream of tartar

Custard
5 egg yolks
1/2 cup sugar
Juice of 2 or 3 lemons
Grated rind of 1 lemon
1 cup unsalted butter, at room temperature
8 to 10 sliced almonds, for garnish

To make the crust, beat the butter and sugar in a medium-sized bowl with an electric mixer on medium speed until light and fluffy, about 2 minutes. Add the egg, lemon rind, and flour and mix until a smooth dough is formed. Shape the dough into a ball and flatten. Wrap in plastic wrap and refrigerate until chilled. Before using, let the dough stand at room temperature until it is soft enough to roll but still cold. Press the pastry evenly over the bottom and one inch up the sides of a 9 by 3-inch springform pan. Set aside.
(Continued on following page)

The Vermont Marble Inn

On The Town Green
Fair Haven, Vermont 05743
(802) 265-8383

The elegant Vermont Marble Inn stands proudly on the village green in the sleepy town of Fair Haven. At first sight, the Victorian mansion, built in 1867 of Vermont golden marble, is breathtaking --- one step through the towering walnut doors reveals luxury and charm unique to this magnificent country inn.

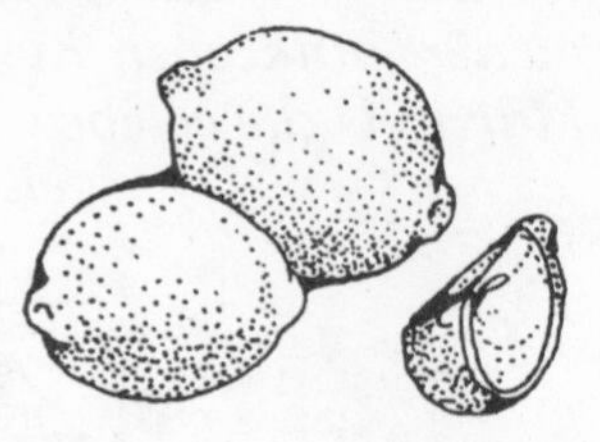

Dining at the inn is a delight. Great care has been taken to create an intimate and romantic atmosphere in the two stately dining rooms.

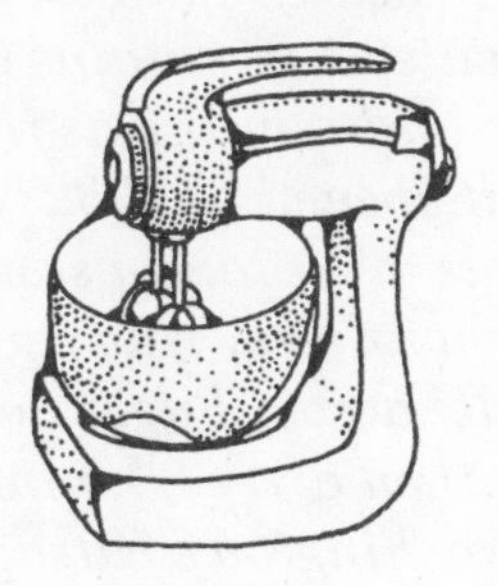

(Continued from previous page) Reserve 3 tablespoons ground almonds for a garnish. To make the filling, stir together the remaining almonds and the sugar in a small bowl and set aside. Beat the egg whites in a large bowl with an electric mixer on low speed until foamy. Add the cream of tartar and beat on high speed until stiff peaks form. Gently fold the almond mixture into the egg whites. Pour into the prepared crust. Bake for 30-40 minutes at 350 degrees, until the top is golden brown. Remove to a wire rack and cool at room temperature.

Meanwhile, to make the custard, whisk the egg yolks and sugar in a double boiler until thick and creamy. Whisk in the lemon juice and rind. Cook over simmering water, whisking constantly, until mixture becomes thick enough to hold its shape and mound when dropped from a spoon, about 10 to 15 minutes.

Do not bring to a boil. Remove from the heat and pour into a bowl. Whisk in the butter a little at a time. Cool at room temperature. Spread over the filling in the crust. Before serving, sprinkle reserved ground almonds around the top of the tart, making a 1-inch border. Place sliced almonds in the center. Remove the sides from the springform pan. Serve at room temperature. Serves 8.

The Vermont Marble Inn

On the Town Green

Fair Haven, Vermont 05743

(802) 265-8383

Apple Blackberry Crumble

4 cups sliced apples
1 cup blackberries
1 to 1 1/2 cups brown sugar
2 teaspoons ground cinnamon

Topping
3/4 cup lightly packed brown sugar
3/4 cup flour
3/4 cup rolled oats
1/2 cup chopped walnuts
1/2 cup butter
1/2 teaspoon ground cinnamon

Toss together the apples, blackberries, brown sugar, and cinnamon and place in a greased 9 by 13-inch baking dish. Blend the ingredients for the topping and sprinkle evenly on top of the fruit. Bake at 375 degrees for 1 hour. Serves 9 to 12.

The Manor Farm Inn

26069 Big Valley Road, N.E.
Poulsbo, Washington 98370
(206) 779-4628

This well-known inn has been featured in many national magazines, including Architectural Digest, Sunset, House and Garden, Esquire, Gourmet, *and* Bon Appetit. *Thanks to its off-the-beaten-path location in Poulsbo, it remains as fresh and inviting as the day it opened in 1982. Guests must take a scenic half-hour ferry ride from Seattle across Puget Sound, and then drive 20 minutes up Washington's Kitsap Peninsula. Innkeepers Robin and Jill Hughes offer visitors acres of lush farmland in which to roam, trout-stocked lakes, and fine cooking. White walls and light woods provide a serene backdrop for the chef's five-course dinners and sumptuous breakfasts. The menu changes daily, emphasizing the Northwest's justly famous seafood and produce.*

The village of Wakefield is the perfect setting for a family-run country inn. As the center of South Kingstown, Wakefield has kept pace with the twentieth century without sacrificing its rural beauty and traditions. Larchwood Inn, located at the quiet end of the village, has also survived the necessities of modernization while preserving the charm of its 150 years of history. The three-story manor is surrounded by a wide expanse of beautifully landscaped grounds while, inside, the inn offers guest accommodations plus four dining rooms and a lounge. Larchwood Inn has a fine reputation for its excellent food and drink.

Pompadour Pudding

1 quart milk
3/4 cup sugar
2 tablespoon cornstarch
1/3 teaspoon salt
3 eggs, separated
2 teaspoons vanilla extract
2 squares unsweetened chocolate, melted
3/4 cup sugar
4 tablespoons milk

Scald the milk; add the sugar, cornstarch, and salt and cook for 15 minutes. Beat the egg yolks, and cook for 5 minutes. Add the vanilla and fill six custard cups three-fourths full.

To prepare the topping, combine the chocolate, sugar, and milk. Beat the three egg whites until stiff and dry; add to the chocolate mixture. Place the topping on pudding, dividing the mixture among the custard cups until level. Place the custard cups in a pan filled with hot water. Bake at 325 degrees for 45 minutes. Serves 6.

Larchwood Inn

176 Main Street
Wakefield, Rhode Island 02879
(401) 783-5454

Berry Clafouti

4 cups fruit (blueberries or peaches and blueberries)
1 cup sliced almonds
3/4 cup flour
2/3 cup plus 1 tablespoon sugar
1/2 teaspoon baking powder
1/2 teaspoon ground cinnamon
1/8 teaspoon salt
3 eggs
3/4 cup milk
2 tablespoons butter or margarine
2 teaspoons vanilla extract

Butter a casserole or quiche dish and distribute the fruit on the bottom. Grind 1/2 cup of the almonds; add the flour, 2/3 cup sugar, baking powder, cinnamon, and salt. Add the eggs, milk, butter, and vanilla and stir until blended. Pour the batter over the fruit. Sprinkle with the remaining 1/2 cup almonds and the 1 tablespoon sugar. Bake at 350 degrees for 50 to 60 minutes or until browned. Serve with whipped cream, if desired. Serves 6 to 8.

Riversong

P.O. Box 1910
Estes Park, Colorado 80517
(303) 586-4666

Riversong is a small mountain country inn at the foot of Giant Track Mountain in Estes Park, Colorado. Once a luxurious summer home of the wealthy, Riversong is now a very special and inviting bed and breakfast inn. The inn is at the end of a country lane on twenty-seven wooded acres and offers a rushing trout stream, a rustic gazebo reflected in the inn's own pond, gentle hiking trails with rock benches to enjoy the breathtaking panorama of snow-capped peaks in adjacent Rocky Mountain National Park.

A visit to Heritage Manor is like stepping back in time. Guests have a choice of two structures, one built in 1903, and the other in 1907, the year Oklahoma became a state. Both homes have been restored to their original beauty. Heritage Manor is located in the northwest portion of Oklahoma, where the famous land run of 1893 opened the area to homesteaders. Delicious food is served in the handsome dining room. A.J. and Carolyn Rexroat are the innkeepers at this delightful retreat.

Date and Walnut Dessert

1 cup brown sugar
1 1/2 cups water
1 cup sugar
1 cup flour
2 teaspoons baking powder
1 cup milk
1 teaspoon vanilla extract
1 cup chopped walnuts
1/2 cup chopped dates
Whipped cream, for garnish
Dash of nutmeg, for garnish

Dissolve the brown sugar in the water in a deep baking dish. Make a batter of the white sugar, flour, baking powder, milk, vanilla, walnuts, and dates. Pour the batter over the dissolved brown sugar (*do not* stir the batter), and bake at 350 degrees for approximately 40 minutes. Serve with whipped cream on top and a sprinkle of nutmeg. Serves 4 to 6.

Heritage Manor

Rural Route 1
P.O. Box 33
Aline, Oklahoma 73716
(405) 463-2563

9 Breads, Muffins, and Cookies

There is no such thing as a one-time visitor to The Keeper's House, a delightful island lighthouse inn boasting a magnificent setting on the rockbound coast of Maine. Guests return over and over again. Delicious goodies seem to flow endlessly from innkeeper Judith Burke's aromatic kitchen. This recipe was taken from her popular cookbook, Kitchen With a View.

Oat Wheat Bread

1/2 cup warm water
4 teaspoons active dry yeast
1 teaspoon sugar
1/4 teaspoon ground ginger
3 cups rolled oats
3 1/2 cups boiling water
3 tablespoons butter or margarine
1/2 cup molasses
1 tablespoon salt
1 cup bran or bran cereal
2 cups whole-wheat flour
4 to 5 cups white flour

Place the warm water in a small bowl. Add the yeast, sugar, and ginger. Pour the boiling water over the oats. Add the butter, molasses, and salt. Add the bran, whole-wheat flour, and yeast mixture. Add the white flour. Knead for 10 minutes. Let rise in a greased bowl for 90 minutes. Punch down. Place in three greased loaf pans. Let rise. Bake for 40 minutes at 350 degrees. Makes 3 loaves.

The Keeper's House

P.O. Box 26
Isle de Haut, Maine 04645
(207) 367-2261

Sprouted Herb Bread

2 cups flour
1 package active dry yeast
3/4 cup milk
2 tablespoons shortening
1 tablespoon honey
1/2 teaspoon salt
1 egg
1 cup snipped sprouts
1/2 cup wheat germ
1/2 teaspoon crushed basil

In a mixing bowl, combine 1 cup of the flour and the yeast. Heat the milk, shortening, honey, and salt until warm. Add to the flour mixture, then add the egg. Beat on low speed for 1/2 minute, then on high for 3 minutes. Add the remaining ingredients. Cover and let rise for 1 hour. Beat the dough down and let rest for 10 minutes. Spoon into a pan and let rise again until doubled in bulk. Bake at 375 degrees for 20 minutes for small loaves, 40 minutes for large loaf. Makes 1 loaf.

The Applebutter Inn

152 Apple Wood Lane
Slippery Rock, Pennsylvania 16057
(412) 794-1844

Nestled in the rolling green meadows of rural western Pennsylvania, The Applebutter Inn offers a window to the past. Guests can still experience the elegance of a more gracious bygone era and still enjoy the luxury of today's comforts and pleasures. Built by Michael Christley in 1844, on land granted to encourage westward settlement, the original structure was built of bricks formed and fired on the premises. Twelve-inch brick walls set on an 18-inch solid, hand-cut stone foundation have stood the test of time.

High Meadows is considered Virginia's vineyard inn, minutes south of Charlottesville and just north of historic Scottsville. The inn occupies a grand house, where guests stay in beautifully appointed rooms, each furnished with individually collected period antiques, original botanicals, and steel engravings. Twenty-two acres of gardens, footpaths, forests, and ponds guarantee peace and quiet. High Meadows was recently placed on the National Register of Historic Places. The recipe we include here was selected from the inn's own cookbook, written by the chef-owner, Peter Sushka, The Best of High Meadows.

No Knead and Never Fail Bread

(Honey and Wheat Loaves)

4 1/3 cups whole-wheat and white flour (half-and-half)
2 packages active dry yeast
2 tablespoons honey
1 3/4 cups warm water (110 degrees F.)
1/3 cup salad oil
1 1/2 teaspoons salt
1/3 cup wheat germ

Put the flour in a bowl and place in a warm (150 degrees) oven for 15 minutes. In a large bowl, dissolve the yeast and honey in 3/4 cup of the warm water and let stand until bubbly (15 minutes). Stir in the remaining 1 cup of water, the oil, salt, and wheat germ and add the warmed flour, 1 cup at a time, beating well by hand after each addition. When the dough begins to cling to the sides of the bowl, turn out onto a floured board and shape into a smooth loaf. Place in a greased 9 by 5-inch loaf pan and cover with plastic wrap. Let rise in a warm place until the dough rises 1 inch above the rim of the bowl (35 minutes). Bake at 400 degrees for 35 minutes. Makes 1 loaf.

High Meadows Inn

Route 4 Box 6
Scottsville, Virginia 24590
(804) 286-2218

Norwegian Rye Bread

2 packages active dry yeast
1 cup warm water
1 cup plus 2 1/2 cups white flour
1 teaspoon sugar
3 tablespoons caraway seed
1 tablespoon fennel seed
1 cup warm water
1 1/2 cups rye flour
2/3 cup brown sugar
3 1/2 tablespoons molasses
3 tablespoons melted butter
1 tablespoon grated orange rind
1 teaspoon salt
1 teaspoon vinegar

Soften the yeast in the warm water. Combine 1 cup of the white flour and the sugar in a bowl and combine with the yeast mixture. Let stand for 5 minutes. Add the remaining ingredients. Knead for 15 to 20 minutes on a floured surface. Place the dough in a greased bowl and let rise to double in bulk (1 hour). Knead for 10 minutes. Divide in half and place in loaf pans to rise again. Bake for 25 to 30 minutes at 350 degrees. Makes 2 loaves.

Cheat Mountain Club

P.O. Box 28
Durbin, West Virginia 26264
(304) 456-4627

Here is a snug mountain inn offering the finest in accommodations, good food, and West Virginia-style hospitality at its best. Everything is picture-perfect here: the inn itself, the surrounding countryside, and views for miles. People flock here again and again to relax and enjoy.

From the moment guests enter the lobby of the Hotel Alex Johnson, they are taken back to times when horse-drawn buggies, herds of bison, and old-fashioned trains were commonplace. Several signs of earlier days and expert craftsmanship are immediately evident—a fireplace made of native fieldstone, eight hand-carved Sioux Indian busts used as beam supports, a magnificent chandelier formed of lances, and ceilings decorated with intricate Sioux beadwork. Fine dining is available in the Landmark Restaurant.

Dilly Casserole Bread

2 packages active dry yeast
1/2 cup warm water
2 cups lukewarm cream style cottage cheese
1/4 cup sugar
2 tablespoons minced onion
2 tablespoons butter
4 teaspoons dill seed
2 teaspoons salt
1/2 teaspoon baking soda
2 eggs
4 1/2 to 5 cups flour
Melted butter, for garnish
Salt, for garnish

Soften the yeast in the warm water. Combine in a mixing bowl the cottage cheese, sugar, onion, butter, dill seed, salt, baking soda, eggs, and softened yeast. Add the flour and form a stiff dough, beating well after each addition. Cover and let rise in a warm place until doubled in bulk. Stir down and place in an 8-inch casserole dish. Let sit in a warm place for 30 to 40 minutes. Bake at 350 degrees for 40 to 50 minutes or until golden brown. Brush with butter and sprinkle with salt. Makes 1 loaf.

Note: If rolls are desired, this recipe makes approximately 35 1 1/2-ounce rolls.

Hotel Alex Johnson

523 6th Street
Rapid City, South Dakota 57701
(605) 342-1210

All Bran Bread

2 packages active dry yeast
1 cup lukewarm water
1 cup All Bran cereal
1 cup shortening
3/4 cup sugar
1 cup boiling water
2 eggs, beaten
6 cups flour
1 teaspoon salt

Mix together the yeast and lukewarm water and set aside. Combine the All Bran, shortening, sugar, boiling water and let sit until lukewarm. Add the eggs. Combine the flour and salt. Add 2 cups of the flour to the egg and All Bran mixture. Beat. Add the yeast mixture and then the rest of the flour. Mix well. Let rise until doubled in bulk. Punch down and form into loaves or rolls. Let rise until doubled in bulk. Bake at 400 degrees for 30 to 40 minutes, until golden brown. Makes 2 loaves.

Monjeau Shadows Country Inn

Bonito Route
Nogal, New Mexico 88341
(505) 336-4191

Located in southern New Mexico, Monjeau Shadows is an inn built in the 1980s in the style of a charming Victorian era farm house. Each graceful and traditionally appointed room affords a restful ambiance with maximum privacy. Breakfast is served on the manicured grounds, or in the sunny breakfast nook with a view of the surrounding mountains. While the inn specializes in delicious breakfasts, reservations are taken for lunch and dinner.

Located on the beautiful campus of Dartmouth College, the history of The Hanover Inn reflects the growth and changes of the college. Eleven years after Dartmouth was founded in 1769 via a charter granted by King George III, General Ebenezer Brewster arrived in Hanover to accept a position as College Steward. His home occupied the present site of the inn. The General redesigned his home in 1780, converting it into a tavern. The Inn's 101 rooms can accommodate more than 200 persons quite comfortably. It boasts three distinctive restaurants.

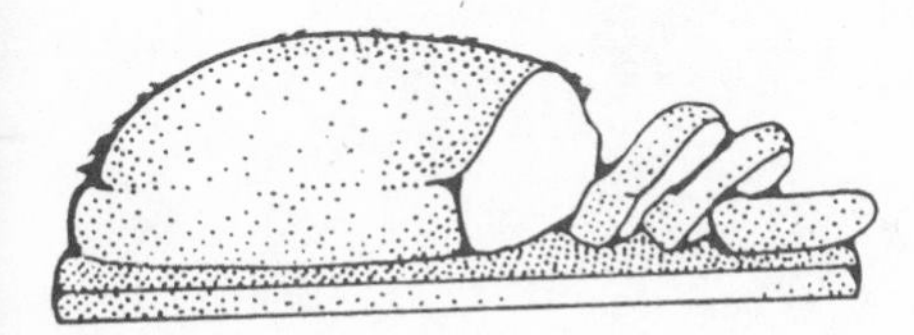

Cumin Seed Bread

1 cup milk
1/2 cup honey
6 tablespoons butter
2 teaspoons salt
1 cup orange juice
4 teaspoons ground cumin
2 1/2 cups whole-wheat flour
2 1/2 cups bread flour (all purpose if bread is not available)
2 packages active dry yeast

In a saucepan warm the milk, honey, butter, salt, orange juice, and cumin until just warm to the touch and the butter is soft.

In a large mixing bowl put 1 cup each of the flours and sprinkle on the yeast. Pour on the milk mixture and beat with a wooden spoon or the flat beater attachment of a mixer, for about 3 minutes, until the batter is smooth. Add another 1/2 cup of each flour, blend, and continue adding flour a little at a time until the dough is firm enough to knead. Knead by hand or machine until the dough is smooth and elastic.

Place the dough in a greased bowl and cover with plastic wrap, set aside until dough doubles in bulk (about 1 hour). Punch the dough back down and cover again. Allow the dough to rise a second time, until doubled, about 45 minutes.

Punch the dough down again, cut into halves, and shape into slightly flattened balls to make free-formed round loaves. Place the loaves on a baking sheet, cover lightly with plastic wrap or a damp cloth, and let rise until almost doubled again. Slash the tops three times, and bake at 375 degrees F. until golden on top and the loaves sound hollow when tapped on the bottom. Makes 2 loaves.

Hanover Inn

P.O. Box 151
Hanover, New Hampshire 03755
(603) 643-4300

Bread Sticks

1 1/2 cups hot water
2 tablespoons sugar
1 heaping tablespoon active dry yeast
3 cups flour
1 1/2 teaspoons salt
1/2 cup butter or margarine
Cinnamon sugar
Herb salt
Pizza salt
Grated Parmesan cheese
Italian blend seasonings

Combine the hot water and sugar and let cool to warm. Add the yeast, then add the flour and salt. Mix well and knead for 3 minutes. Let the dough rest for 10 minutes. Melt the butter. Roll the dough into a rectangle on a floured board. Cut into 1/2 to 1-inch strips. Fold each strip in half (and in half again if you wish) and twist several times. Dip into the melted butter and place on a greased baking sheet. Sprinkle with one of the topping. Let rise for 15 to 20 minutes. Bake at 350 degrees F. until golden, 12 to 15 minutes.

Green Gate Village Inn

76 West Tabernacle
St. George, Utah 628-6999
(801) 628-6999

In the historic heart of downtown St. George are nine pioneer homes—beautifully restored and elegantly decorated and known as the Green Gate Village Inn. The complex includes a swimmimg pool and an old-fashioned candy store and soda fountain.

The Baldpate is just what you would expect in a classic mountain lodge. Built from native materials in 1917, the rustic lodge has a tradition of providing the best in western style hospitality and comfort to all its guests. The novel Seven Keys to the Baldpate *gave the inn its name--and inspired a Broadway play, radio play, and movie. The story plot--seven people who each believe they hold the only key to an isolated mountain hotel--was the basis for the famous key collection. This collection, the largest in the world, now contains thousands of keys. Nestled on the side of Twin Sisters Mountain, the inn has commanding views from its windows and porch. Mike, Lois, Jenn, and MacKenzie Smith are the caring innkeepers.*

Georgia's Spanish Breakfast Pastry

Bottom Layer
1 cup flour
1/2 cup butter, softened
1 tablespoon water

Mix all ingredients with a fork until well blended. Round into a ball and divide in half. Pat each half into a long strip, 12 inches by 3 inches on an ungreased cookie sheet. Place the strips at least two inches apart.

Second Layer
1/2 cup butter
1 cup water
1 cup flour
3 eggs
1 teaspoon almond extract

Place the butter and water in a small saucepan, and heat to boiling. Remove from the heat and immediately mix in the flour, stirring briskly to prevent lumps. Return to the heat, and stir in the eggs one at a time, beating until smooth after each addition. Remove from the heat, and add the almond extract. Divide mixture in half and carefully spread each half over the unbaked bottom layer. Be certain to spread completely to the edges of each strip. Bake at 350 degrees for 50 to 60 minutes, just until barely golden. The pastry will fall slightly when removed from the oven. Cool for several minutes before frosting.

Top Frosting Layer
2 tablespoons butter
1 1/2 cups confectioners' sugar
1 teaspoon vanilla extract
1/8 teaspoon salt
2 tablespoons milk
1/2 cup sliced almonds

Blend all ingredients except the almonds. Spread half of the mixture over each strip of pastry, then sprinkle with sliced almonds. Slice 1 inch wide on the diagonal. Serves 10 to 12 as breakfast or dessert or, if cut into smaller diamond shapes, serves 20 to 24 as afternoon teacake.

The Baldpate Inn

4900 South Highway 7, P.O. Box 4445
Estes Park, Colorado 80517
(303)586-5668

Norwegian Toast

1 cup margarine
1 1/2 cups sugar
2 eggs
3 3/4 cups flour
1 teaspoon baking soda
1 teaspoon ground cardamom

Cream the margarine and sugar. Add the eggs. Add the flour, baking soda, and cardamom. Form ten balls and flatten them on two ungreased baking sheets. Bake at 350 degrees F. for 35 to 40 minutes. Cut into strips. Spread out and toast for 7 minutes at 375 degrees, turning once. Makes about 50 pieces of toast.

Built in 1908, the Greenbriar is Coeur d'Aline's only nationally registered historic mansion. During most of its history, the structure was used as a boardinghouse. (Some say it was also a bordello at one time.) The third floor, with its gracefully arched windows, was once a dance hall. A four-course gourmet breakfast is served to house guests and a dining facility has been added for both guests and the public to enjoy.

The Greenbriar Inn

315 Wallace Avenue
Coeur d'Alene, Idaho 83814
(208) 667-9660

This three-story building was built in 1912 as a boardinghouse for miners. Later, it became a roominghouse and now is the only inn of its kind remaining in this area of Idaho. Local activities include fishing, hiking, boating, rafting, gold-panning and visiting the many interesting attractions in the area.

Cinnamon Rolls

1/2 cup lukewarm milk
1/2 cup sugar
1 teaspoon salt
2 packages active dry yeast
1/2 cup lukewarm water
2 eggs
1/2 cup shortening
4 1/2 to 5 cups flour
Cinnamon sugar
Brown sugar
Frosting (recipe below)

Mix together the milk, sugar, and salt and set aside. Place the yeast in the water and let sit for 5 minutes. Mix well and add to the milk mixture. Add the eggs and shortening and blend. Add flour until the dough has the proper consistency. Place the dough on a floured board and knead until smooth and elastic, about 5 minutes. Place the dough in a greased bowl and turn so that the greased side is up. Cover with a damp cloth and let rise until double in bulk, about 1 1/2 hours. Punch the dough down, turn over, and let rise until double in bulk, about 30 minutes. Roll the dough into a rectangle with 1/2-inch thickness, or less. Brush with butter. Sprinkle with cinnamon sugar and brown sugar. Roll up as for a jelly roll, but not too tight. Brush water along the seam and press the edges together. Slice the roll into 1-inch slices. Place on a greased baking sheet. Let rise until double in bulk. Bake at 375 degrees for 25 minutes. Remove from the oven and place on wire racks to cool. Frost. Makes about 18.

Frosting
3 cups confectioners' sugar
1/4 cup melted butter
1/4 cup lukewarm water
1/2 teaspoon vanilla

Combine all ingredients and mix well.

The Montgomery Inn

Coeur d'Alene, Idaho

Angel Biscuits

1 1/2 teaspoons active dry yeast
1/4 cup warm water
1 tablespoon honey
2 1/2 cups sifted flour
2 tablespoons sugar
1 1/2 teaspoons baking powder
1/2 teaspoon baking soda
1/4 teaspoon salt
1/3 cup vegetable shortening
1 cup buttermilk

Let the yeast soak in a mixture of the water and honey. Meanwhile, sift together the flour, sugar, baking powder, baking soda, and salt. Using two knives or a pastry blender, cut in the shortening until the mixture resembles coarse meal. Stir just until the dough comes together. Turn out onto a lightly floured surface. Knead lightly—for 30 seconds at the most—and place in a greased bowl. Cover and refrigerate for at least 1 hour or up to four days.

When ready to bake, roll out the dough to a 1/2-inch thickness on a lightly floured board. Cut in rounds and place about 1/2 inch apart on a baking sheet sprayed with vegetable oil. Bake at 400 degrees until golden, about 12 minutes. Serve hot. Makes 2 dozen large biscuits.

Dairy Hollow House

515 Spring Street
Eureka Springs, Arkansas 72632
(501) 253-7444

Dairy Hollow House occupies a restored turn-of-the-century farmhouse. Its welcome is heartfelt and the cuisine is world-class. On an Ozark hillside in the much-loved Victorian resort town of Eureka Springs, Dairy Hollow House is visited by guests from all over the world. Its legendary fare is lovingly prepared by Crescent Dragonwagon and Jan Brown. This recipe was taken from The Dairy Hollow House Cookbook.

Easy Cheese Blintzes

Betsy and Frank Kennedy are the efficient innkeepers at this delightful inn. It was built as a mill house around 1780. Originally located on the Fishawak River, it was later moved to its present location on Main Street, and served as a home for the Parrot family for over a century. The visitor enjoys the ambience of a unique colonial residence, and the charm of a bygone era combined with all the conveniences of today.

1 8-ounce package cream cheese, softened
2 egg yolks
1/2 cup sugar
1/2 teaspoon fresh lemon juice
1 large loaf good-quality white bread, sliced
1 1/2 sticks melted margarine
1 1/2 cups brown sugar
3 teaspoons ground cinnamon

Mix the cream cheese, egg yolks, sugar, and lemon juice until smooth. Trim the crusts from the bread and roll out. Brush one side of each slice with melted margarine and place 1 teaspoon of the cream cheese mixture on the unbuttered side. Combine the brown sugar and cinnamon. Roll up each slice of bread, buttered side out, and dip in the brown sugar and cinnamon mixture. Freeze. When needed, bake on a greased baking sheet at 350 degrees for 10 minutes. Makes about 16.

The Parrot Mill Inn

47 Main Street
Chatham, New Jersey 07928
(201) 635-7722

Pecan Nut Roll

1 package active dry yeast
1 teaspoon plus 1/2 cup sugar
1/4 cup lukewarm water
2 cups sifted flour
1/8 teaspoon salt
3/4 cup margarine, cut in pieces
2 eggs, separated, at room temperature
1 teaspoon vanilla extract
1/4 cup chopped pecans
Confectioners' sugar for dusting

Place the yeast and 1 teaspoon sugar in the water for 15 minutes. In a food processor, process the flour, salt, and margarine until crumbly. Add the egg yolks and yeast mixture and process until a ball forms. Halve the dough and on wax paper roll into 13 by 9-inch rectangles. Beat the egg whites until frothy and then beat in the 1/2 cup sugar, a little at a time. until stiff peaks form. Add the vanilla. Spread half of the egg whites on each rectangle, leaving a 1/2-inch border, and sprinkle pecans on top. From the long end, roll up like a jelly roll. Transfer to a greased baking sheet, seam side down. With a knife, make a 1/4-inch slit down the center of each roll. Bake at 375 degrees for 25 minutes. Cool and dust with sifted confectioner' sugar. Slice and serve. Serves 8.

Barrow House

P.O. Box 1461
St. Francisville, Louisiana 70775
(504) 635-4791

Shaded by a 200-year-old live oak, Barrow House stands in the heart of the historic district of the quaint town of St. Francisville. The original house was a saltbox structure built in 1809 with a Greek Revival wing added just before the Civil War. A large screened porch is "the place to be" for coffee in the morning and drinks in the evening. Rooms are furnished in antiques dating from 1840 to 1870. The inn's candlelight dinners, featuring New Orleans style food, are well-known in the area. Six plantations open to the public are close by.

Redfish Lake Lodge is located at the headwaters of the main fork of the Salmon River in the heart of Sawtooth National Forest and bordering the Sawtooth wilderness area. The dining room offers an excellent menu with a mountain atmosphere. The inn was built for the sportsman, nature lover, photographer, horseback rider, and naturalist—for the person who wants to turn his back upon the grinding roar of the civilized world and seek peace and quiet in untouched mountain country.

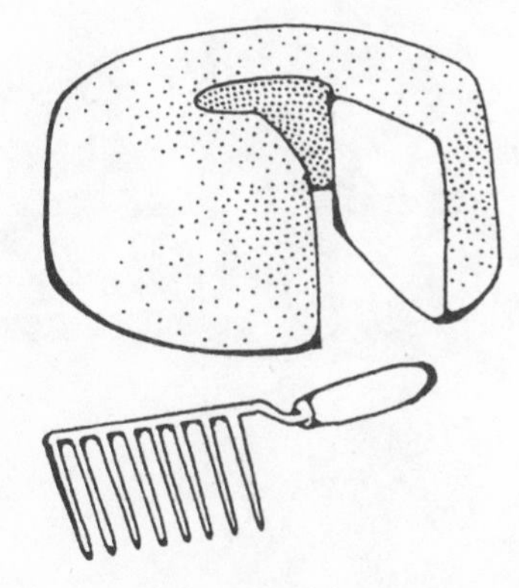

Yogurt Poppy Seed Coffee Cake

1 2-ounce package poppy seeds
1 cup yogurt (vanilla preferred)
1 cup butter
1 1/2 cups sugar
4 eggs separated
2 cups plus 2 tablespoons flour
2 teaspoons vanilla extract
2 teaspoons baking soda
Confectioners' sugar, for garnish

Grease an angel food cake pan and dust with flour. Soak the poppy seeds in the yogurt. Cream the butter and add sugar. Blend into the yogurt mixture. Beat the egg yolks and add to the mixture. Add the vanilla, flour, and baking soda. Beat the egg whites until stiff and fold in. Pour the batter into the pan and bake at 375 degrees for 45 minutes. Let cool and sprinkle with powdered sugar. Serves 10 to 12.

Redfish Lake Lodge

P.O. Box 9
Stanley, Idaho 83278
(208) 774-3536

Raspberry Cream Cheese Coffee Cake

2 1/4 cups flour
3/4 cup plus 1/4 cup sugar
3/4 cup butter
1/2 teaspoon baking powder
1/2 teaspoon baking soda
1/4 teaspoon salt
2 eggs
3/4 cup sour cream
1 teaspoon almond extract
1 8-ounce package cream cheese
1/2 cup raspberry preserves
1/2 cup sliced almonds

Grease and flour the bottom and sides of a 9 or 10-inch springform pan. In a large bowl, combine the flour and 3/4 cup of sugar. Cut in the butter until the mixture resembles coarse crumbs. Reserve 1 cup of the crumb mixture. To the remaining mixture, add the baking powder, baking soda, salt, one of the eggs, the sour cream, and almond extract; blend well. Spread batter over the bottom and 2 inches up the sides of the pan.

Combine the cream cheese, 1/4 cup sugar, and the remaining egg; blend. Pour over the batter in the pan. Carefully spoon the preserves over the cheese filling

In a small bowl, combine the reserved crumb mixture and the sliced almonds. Sprinkle over the top of the preserves. Bake at 350 degrees for 45 to 55 minutes. Serve warm or cool. Cut into wedges. Serves 16.

Beechwood Inn

2839 Main Street
Barnstable Village, Massachusetts 02630
(508) 362-6618

Located along the Old King's Highway historic district in picturesque Barnstable Village, Beechwood Inn offers a central location from which to enjoy the many pleasures of Cape Cod. A mile away is Barnstable Harbor for sport fishing and whale watching, and nearby are Mill Way Beach for swimming and the dunes at Sandy Neck. Elegant antiques abound at Beechwood Inn, as do good food and gracious service.

Quiet, intimate, romantic, special; these are just a few of the adjectives that describe The Glenborough Inn. One steps back into a graceful era when courting was an art. Visitors are surrounded by historic antiques, hand crocheted treasures, and Victorian lace. Each room is individually designed, with comfortable beds and large pillows. Chef Judy Groom's gourmet specialties are a highlight. The aecluded gardens invite leisurely strolls.

Buttermilk Coffee Cake

2 1/4 cups flour
1 cup firmly packed brown sugar
3/4 cup sugar
3/4 cup vegetable oil
1/2 teaspoon plus 1 1/4 teaspoons ground cinnamon
1/2 cup chopped walnuts
1 cup buttermilk
1 egg, beaten
1 teaspoon baking soda
1 teaspoon baking powder

Blend the flour, sugars, oil, and 1/2 teaspoon cinnamon in a large bowl. Transfer 3/4 cup of the mixture to a medium bowl. Stir in the walnuts and 1 1/4 teaspoons cinnamon. Combine the buttermilk, egg, baking soda, and baking powder in a small bowl. Blend into the flour mixture until thoroughly incorporated. Spoon the batter into a greased 9 by 13-inch pan, spreading evenly. Sprinkle the nut mixture over the top, then press it into the batter with the back of a spoon. Bake until a cake tester inserted in the center comes out clean, about 30 minutes. Serve warm with butter. Serves 8.

The Glenborough Inn

1327 Bath Street
Santa Barbara, California 93101
(805) 966-0589

Vermont Apple Breakfast Cake

2 cups flour
1 cup sugar
2 teaspoons baking powder
1 teaspoon salt
2/3 cup vegetable oil
1 cup milk
2 eggs
2 to 3 cups sliced apples
1/2 cup sugar mixed with 1 teaspoon cinnamon

Combine the first seven ingredients and beat for 3 minutes. Pour into a greased and floured 9 by 13-inch pan. Arrange the apple slices in top of the batter, then sprinkle with the sugar-cinnamon mixture. Bake at 350 degrees F. for 40 to 50 minutes. Serves 9 to 12.

Note: This recipe may be cut in half and baked in an 8-inch square pan.

The Inn at Woodchuck Hill Farm

Grafton, VT 05146
(802) 843-2398

The Inn at Woodchuck Hill Farm is one of the oldest buildings in Grafton, built circa 1790. It is on a hilltop almost two miles from the village at the end of a country road. It is furnished in beautiful antiques, with accommodations for 18 guests. The visitors enjoy the peace and quiet of rural New England, strolling along country lanes, through fields and woodlands--all within the inn's 200-acre property. Dinner is a four-course, single-entree meal with guests seated at a single large table.

This is an 1830 restored Greek Revival mansion named after The Indian word for "happy home." The home and guest rooms are furnished with 18th and 19th century artifacts. Confederate President Jefferson Davis once addressed the townspeople from the balcony. Adjacent to the main house are landscaped gardens, brick courtyards, and former slave quarters. This home is located in the heart of the Historic District and is on the National Register of Historic Places.

Overnight Coffee Cake

3/4 cup margarine softened
1 cup sugar
2 eggs
1 cup sour cream
2 cups flour
1 teaspoon baking powder
1 teaspoon baking soda
1/2 teaspoon salt
1 teaspoon ground nutmeg
3/4 cup firmly packed brown sugar
1 teaspoon ground cinnamon
1/2 cup chopped pecans

Combine the margarine and sugar and cream until light and fluffy. Add the eggs and sour cream, mixing well. Combine the next five ingredients; add to the batter and mix well. Pour into a greased 13 by 9 by 2-inch pan.

Combine the brown sugar, pecans, and cinnamon, mixing well. Sprinkle evenly over the batter. Cover and chill overnight. Uncover and bake at 350 degrees for 35 to 40 minutes or until a cake tester inserted in the center comes out clean. Serves 9 to 12.

Anchuna

1010 1st East Avenue
Vicksburg, Mississippi 39180
(601) 636-4931

Pumpkin Bread

3 cups sugar
1 cup salad oil
4 eggs, well beaten
1 16-ounce can pumpkin
3 cups flour
2 teaspoons baking soda
1/2 teaspoon baking powder
1 teaspoon ground nutmeg
1 teaspoon ground cinnamon
1 teaspoon ground cloves
1 teaspoon allspice
1 teaspoon salt
1 cup floured raisins (optional)
1 cup chopped pecans (optional)

Mix together the sugar, oil, eggs, and pumpkin. Sift together the dry ingredients and add. Mix just until blended. Fold in the raisins and/or pecans if desired. Pour into two greased and floured 9 by 5-inch loaf pans and bake at 350 degrees for 1 hour. Or use four small loaf pans and bake for approximately 45 minutes. Makes 2 or 4 loaves.

Parish Patch Inn

625 Cortner Road
Normandy, Tennessee 37360
(615) 857-3017

Parish Patch Inn is a blend of the best in country hospitality and city comfort. Situated along the banks of the Duck River, you will be surrounded by corn fields, green meadows and the peaceful majesty of the smokey blue hills of Middle Tennessee. At the Cortner Mill Restaurant the visitor is treated to the finest of regional cuisine.

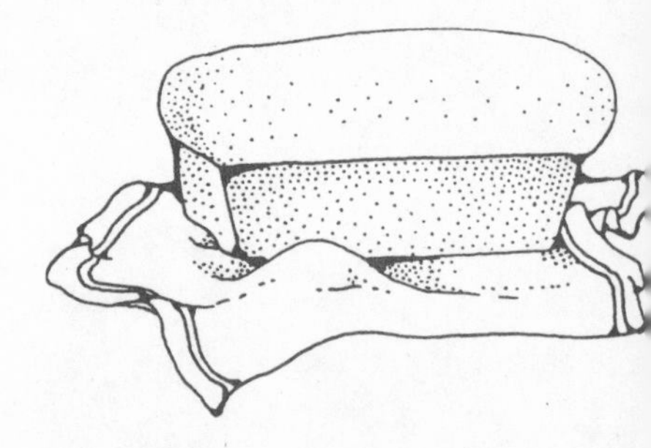

Baird House offers the traveler the warmth and beauty of a turn-of-the-century grand house. It has been attractively restored and furnished with fine antiques, Oriental rugs, and original art. Two of the bedrooms have working fireplaces, which guests may use at their pleasure. Meals at Baird House are hearty and generous.

Poppy Seed Bread

1 1/2 cups sugar
3 eggs, beaten
1 1/2 teaspoons vanilla extract
1 1/2 teaspoons butter flavoring
1 1/2 tablespoons poppy seeds
1 teaspoon almond extract
3 cups flour
1 teaspoon salt
1 1/2 teaspoons baking powder
1 1/2 cups milk
1 cup salad oil
Glaze (recipe below)

Add the sugar to the beaten eggs. Add the flavorings. In a separate bowl, mix the flour salt, and baking powder. Add to the sugar-egg mixture; then add the milk and oil. Grease and flour two small loaf pans. Bake at 350 degrees for 1 hour, until a cake tester inserted in the center comes out clean. Remove from oven and pour over the Glaze. Makes two small loaves.

Glaze
1/4 cup fresh orange juice
3/4 cup confectioners' sugar
1/2 teaspoon vanilla extract

Combine all the ingredients and mix well.

Baird House

P. O. Box 749
Mars Hill, North Carolina 28754
(704) 689-5722

Cranberry Bread

4 1/2 cups flour
2 1/2 cups sugar
1 teaspoon baking soda
3 teaspoons baking powder
2 teaspoons salt
2 eggs
2 cups fresh orange juice
8 tablespoons margarine, melted
1 cup water
2 cups cranberries

Sift together the flour, sugar, baking soda, baking powder, and salt. Make a well in the center of the dry ingredients. Combine the eggs and orange juice, then the margarine and water in a large measuring cup, using only a hand beater. Pour the wet ingredients into the well of the dry ingredients and stir just enough to moisten. Add the cranberries and pour the batter into three greased and floured loaf pans. Bake at 325 degrees F. for 1 hour. Do not overbake. Makes three loaves.

Captain Lord Mansion

P.O. Box 800
Kennebunkport, Maine 04046
(800) 522-3141

This splendid mansion, built by Nathaniel Lord, began as a joyful place where his family and descendants shared relaxing times and created warm memories. When the inn was established, the owners endeavored to preserve the gracious atmosphere that typified life there throughout the Lord family's time. During the latest restoration, the original wallpaper in two rooms was preserved. There are hand-blown windows throughout the mansion. Visitors enjoy climbing the four-story spiral staircase to view the historic neighborhood from the octagonal cupola.

The inviting atmosphere of the Embassy and Windsor Inns, evoking both gentler times and the intimate warmth of European service, reflects a tradition of hospitality which has graced the inns for nearly 70 years. The atmosphere of a warm family home has been preserved. The decor of the 39 rooms of the Embassy Inn recalls the Federalist style of the nineteenth century, popularized by Thomas Jefferson. Graceful Art Deco geometry distinguishes the 37 rooms of the adjoining Windsor Inn, reminiscent of the 1920s when both inns first opened.

Blueberry Bread

1/4 cup vegetable shortening
3/4 cup sugar
1 egg
2 teaspoons vanilla extract
1 1/2 cups flour
1 1/2 teaspoons baking powder
1 cup fresh blueberries

Cream together the shortening, sugar, and vanilla until fluffy. Add the egg and beat well. Add the flour and milk alternately and beat well after each addition. Gently stir in the blueberries, adding extra if you desire. Bake in a greased 8 by 8 by 2-inch pan at 375 degrees for 20 minutes. If a glass pan is used, reduce the temperature to 360 degrees. Serves 6.

The Embassy and Windsor Inns

1627 16th Street, NW
Washington, D.C. 20009
(202) 234-7800

Lemon Bread

1/2 cup butter
1 cup sugar
2 eggs
Grated rind of 1 lemon
1 1/2 cups flour
1 teaspoon baking powder
1/2 teaspoon salt
1/2 cup chopped nuts
1/2 cup milk
Glaze (recipe below)

Cream the butter and the sugar. Add the eggs and lemon rind and combine well. Combine the flour, baking powder, and salt and add. Stir in the nuts. Add the milk and stir until just combined. Bake in a greased loaf pan at 350 degrees for 45 to 50 minutes. While the bread is hot, spoon over the Glaze. Makes 1 large loaf or 2 small.

Glaze
Juice of 1 lemon
1/2 cup sugar

Combine the ingredients and mix well.

Red Lion Inn

Main Street
Stockbridge, Massachusetts 01262
(413) 298-5547

When you step inside the Red Lion Inn, you enter a world of friendly courtesy and hospitality. Situated in a lovely Berkshire Hills town that once was an Indian village, on a street that was once a stagecoach road, the inn was built in 1773 as a small tavern and stagecoach stop for vehicles traveling the Boston, Hartford, and Albany runs. During its life, the inn has sheltered five United States presidents. There is the charm of Straffordshire china, colonial pewter, and furniture. The fare is traditional New England , with many continental specialities also available.

This half-timbered hotel was built in 1939 to accomodate train crews who serviced the Great Northern Railway. Bordering Glacier National Park, the comfortable inn is a favorite year-round retreat. Hikers, cross-country skiers, and other guests still enjoy the flavor of the nostalgic railroad past during their stay. The inn is listed on the National Register of Historic Places.

Rocky Mountain Apple Bread

4 eggs
2 cups sugar
1/2 cup buttermilk
1/2 cup mayonnaise
1 teaspoon vanilla extract
3 1/2 cups flour
1/4 teaspoon salt
1 teaspoon baking powder
1/2 teaspoon baking soda
1 teaspoon ground cinnamon
2 tart green apples, peeled, cored, and chopped
1 cup raisins
1 cup chopped walnuts

In a large bowl, beat the eggs, sugar, buttermilk, mayonnaise, and vanilla until smooth. In another bowl mix the flour, salt, baking powder, baking soda, and cinnamon. Add to the egg mixture and stir just until combined. Add the apples, raisins, and nuts; stir just to mix. Spread the batter evenly in two greased and floured 5 by 9-inch loaf pans. Bake at 375 degrees F. until a cake tester inserted in the center comes out clean, about 1 hour and 10 minutes. Cool in the pan for 10 minutes, then turn out onto a rack to cool completely. Makes 2 loaves.

Izaak Walton Inn

Box 675
Essex, Montana 59916
(406) 888-5700

Apple Raisin Muffins

1 1/2 cups flour
1 1/2 cups whole-wheat flour
3/4 cup sugar
1 tablespoon baking powder
1 teaspoon ground cinnamon
1/2 teaspoon ground nutmeg
2 eggs
2 cups chunky apple sauce
1/2 cup oil
1/2 cup milk
1 cup raisins

Combine all ingredients, mix until just blended, and place in greased muffin tins. Bake at 350 degrees for about 20 minutes. Makes 18.

Asa Ransom House

10529 Main Street
Clarence Hollow, New York 14031
(719) 759-2315

In 1799, the Holland Land Company offered lots ten miles apart in what is now Clarence, New York, to "any proper man who would build and operate a tavern upon it." The first to accept this offer was a young silversmith named Asa Ransom. Mr. Ransom first built a combination log cabin home and tavern. Then in 1801, he built a sawmill near the creek that bears his name, and in 1803, he built a grist mill. The dining rooms were added in 1975; great care was taken to retain the charm of the nineteenth century.

The Washington House Inn can be described as country Victorian in an in-town setting--an experience combining romance, elegance, and comfort. Antique Victorian furniture, marble mantel pieces, and fresh flowers offer a warm reception. The recipes that follow are taken from the inn's cookbook, The Country Bakery Book.

Cranberry Nut Muffins

1 cup cranberries, coarsely chopped
1/2 cup sugar
1 3/4 cup flour
1 tablespoon baking powder
1 teaspoon salt
1/2 teaspoon ground cinnamon
1/4 teaspoon allspice
1 egg, beaten
1/4 teaspoon grated orange rind
3/4 cup fresh orange juice
1/3 cup melted butter
1/4 cup walnuts

Toss the cranberries in 1/4 cup of the sugar; set aside. Thoroughly stir together the flour, the remaining 1/4 cup sugar, the baking powder, salt, and spices. Make a well in the center. Combine the egg, orange rind, orange juice, and melted butter (add all at once to the well); stir until the dry ingredients are moistened. Gently fold in the cranberries and nuts. Fill greased or lined muffin tins two thirds full. Bake at 400 degrees for 20-25 minutes. Makes 1 dozen.

Washington House Inn

Corner of Washington and Center
W62 N573 Washington Avenue
Cedarburg, Wisconsin 53012
(414) 375-3550

Plum Muffins

1 1-pound 13-ounce can purple plums
1/2 cup butter
1 teaspoon baking soda
2 cups sifted flour
1 cup sugar
1/2 teaspoon salt
1/2 teaspoon ground cinnamon
1/2 teaspoon ground cloves
1/2 cup raisins
3/4 cup chopped walnuts

Drain the plums, remove the pits and mash or put through a chopper or blender. In a saucepan, combine the plums with butter and heat until the butter is melted. Remove from the heat and stir in the baking soda. The mixture will turn gray in color and foam. Cool to room temperature, add the flour, sugar, salt, cinnamon, cloves, raisins, and walnuts. Mix well, fill muffin cups, and bake for 30 minutes at 350 degrees.

Rainbow Ranch Guest Lodge

On the Gallatin River near Big Sky
42950 Gallatin Road
Gallatin Gateway, Montana 59730
(406) 995-4132

Rainbow Ranch is on the Gallatin River, a blue ribbon trout stream, and is a short distance from the entrance to Big Sky Resort, with its ski hill and Arnold Palmer Golf Course. It is the only real lodge at Big Sky. Magnificent mountains surround the inn, and a national forest and Yellowstone National Park are 12 miles to the south. The Inn offers family-style dining, with great care taken to insure that every meal is of superior quality and is a memorable dining experience.

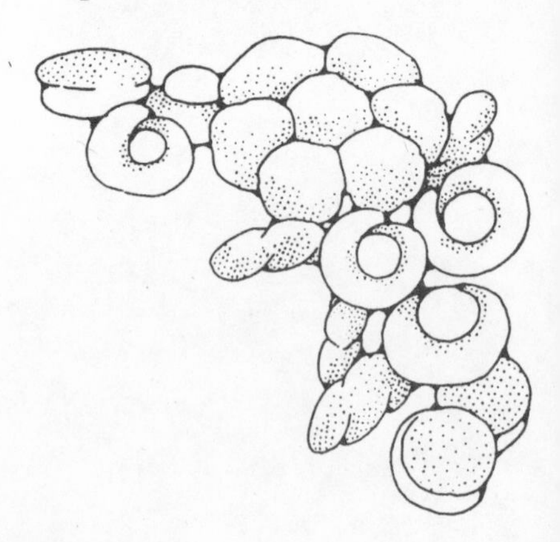

This lovely inn recaptures the warmth of a bygone era. Each room is furnished with fine antiques, and each is named for a person who contibuted to the growth of Cleburne County. Visitors warm themselves by a crackling wood fire and enjoy the charm of planked oak floors. Located in the Ozark foothills, the inn is near some superb trout fishing at Greers Ferry Lake.

Granola Muffins

2 cups flour
1 cup rolled oats
1 1/2 cups granola
2 tablespoons baking powder
2 teaspoons salt
1 cup sugar
1 cup raisins
3 teaspoons cinnamon
2 cups water
2 eggs
1/2 cup vegetable oil

Combine the dry ingredients in a large bowl and blend well. Add the water, eggs, and oil and stir until the dry ingredients are just moistened. Place the batter in greased muffin tins. Bake at 400 degrees for 20 to 30 minutes. Makes about 2 dozen.

Oak Tree Inn

1802 West Main Street
Heber Springs, Arkansas 72543
(501) 362-7731

Bacon Cheese Muffins

5 thick bacon strips
2 cups flour
1 tablespoon sugar
1 tablespoon baking powder
1 teaspoon salt
1/4 teaspoon pepper (or more, to taste)
1 onion, minced (or one bunch green onions, minced)
1 cup grated sharp Cheddar cheese
1 egg
3/4 cup milk

While the bacon is very cold, stack the strips, and cut them into four strips lengthwise; then cut them across into 1/2-inch pieces. Cook the bacon in a small, heavy saucepan until it is light golden brown but not crisp. Pour the fat through a strainer set over a measuring cup; add vegetable oil if needed to bring the fat up to the 1/4 cup level. Drain the bacon on paper toweling.

Mix the flour, sugar, baking powder, salt, and pepper in a large bowl. In a small bowl, whisk the egg, milk, and bacon fat. Add the bacon, onion, and cheese; then pour over the dry ingredients. Fold in with a rubber spatula just until the dry ingredients are moistened. Spoon the batter into greased muffin cups and bake at 400 degrees for 20 to 25 minutes or until golden brown and springy to the touch in the center. Let cool in the pans for 5 minutes and then turn out onto a rack. Serve with salsa for a delicious breakfast treat. Makes about 2 dozen. Note: You may add a pinch of thyme and oregano and use plain yogurt or buttermilk instead of regular milk.

Idaho Rocky Mountain Ranch

HC64 Box 9934
Stanley, Idaho 83278
(208) 774-3544

Here is one of the finest guest ranches in the West, nestled in one of the most spectacular and unexplored regions of America: the Sawtooth and White Cloud mountain ranges of Central Idaho. Established in 1930, the lodge was hand-crafted by carpenters from the same lodgepole pine felled by the basin's pioneers. Surrounding the ranch are hundreds of miles of trails, meandering through the Sawtooth wilderness.

White Mountain Lodge is the oldest building in Greer, a farmhouse built in 1892 by one of the first Mormon families to settle in the area. The external walls of the lodge are formed by 4 by 10-inch timbers held together with wooden nails. An important landmark has been preserved and transformed into a delightful inn where one feels very much at home. Russ and Sophia Majesky are the owners/innkeepers. Sophia delights her guests with the wonderful meals she personally prepares.

Raspberry Muffins

1 2/3 cups flour
3/4 cup sugar
2 teaspoons baking soda
1/2 teaspoon salt
1/2 cup milk
1 egg, well beaten
1/2 cup vegetable or corn oil
1/2 cup raspberries

Blend the dry ingredients together in a medium bowl. Combine the well beaten egg, the milk, and oil and add to the dry ingredients. Stir until no lumps are present, then fold in the raspberries. Fill greased and floured muffin tins two-thirds full. Bake at 375 degrees for about 25 minutes. Makes about 1 dozen.

White Mountain Lodge

P.O. Box 139
Greer, Arizona 85927
(602) 735-7568

Zucchini Muffins

Try these tempting zucchini muffins from the White House Inn in Goliad, Texas.

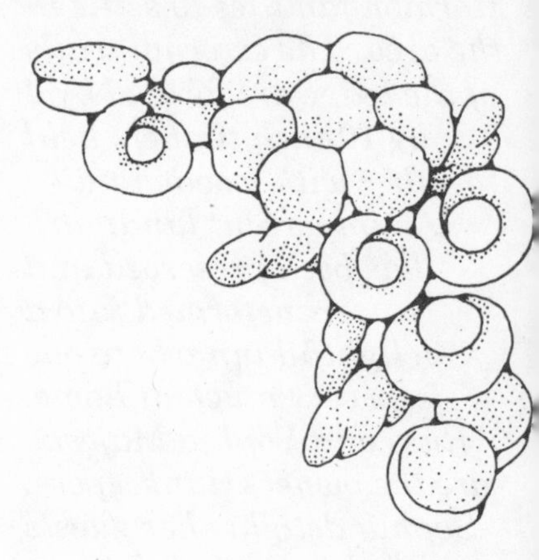

2 cups whole-wheat flour
1 tablespoon baking powder
1/2 teaspoon salt
1 teaspoon ground cinnamon
3/4 cup milk
2 eggs, lightly beaten
1/4 cup oil
1/4 cup honey
1 cup shredded zucchini

Combine the dry ingredients. Mix the remaining ingredients and add to the dry. Stir until barely moistened. The batter will be lumpy. Fill greased muffin tins two-thirds full. Bake at 375 degrees for about 20 minutes. Makes 1 dozen.

White House Inn

Box 922
Goliad, Texas 77963
(512) 645-2701

Pineapple--in bran muffins? It's delicious! This recipe lets you create one of the perennial favorites from Hawaii's Poipu Plantation.

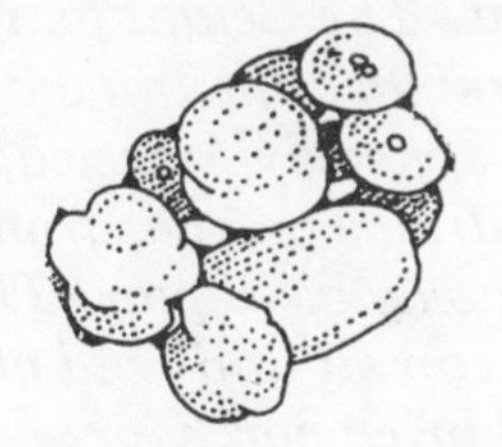

Pineapple Bran Muffins

1 cup Bran Flakes
1 cup milk
1 cup crushed pineapple, drained
1/3 cup vegetable shortening
1/2 cup sugar
1/3 cup honey
2 eggs, well beaten
1 1/3 cups flour, sifted
1/2 teaspoon salt
2 teaspoons baking soda

Soak the bran in the milk and set aside. Cook the crushed pineapple until no liquid remains. Cool. Cream together the shortening, sugar, and honey, then add the eggs. Mix in the bran and pineapple. Add the sifted flour, salt, and baking soda. Bake at 350 degrees for about 15 to 20 minutes. Makes about 16.

Poipu Plantation

1792 Pee Road
Koloa, Kauai, Hawaii 96756
(808) 742-6757

Peach Muffins

2 cups flour
1/3 cup brown sugar
1 tablespoon baking powder
1/4 teaspoon baking soda
1/8 teaspoon allspice
1/2 teaspoon salt
1 egg
1 cup sour cream
1/4 cup milk
1/4 cup oil
1/2 cup chopped peaches

Combine the dry ingredients in a large bowl and make a well in the center. Combine the wet ingredients, pour into the well, and stir until the dry ingredients are just moistened. Fold in the peaches. The batter will be lumpy. Fill greased muffin tins three-fourths full and bake at 400 degrees for 20 to 25 minutes. Makes 8 large muffins.

Country Heritage

64707 Mound Road
Romeo, Michigan 48065
(313) 752-2879

A stay at Country Heritage, a beautifully restored Greek Revival farmhouse surrounded by old sugar maples is a real return to the past. The Celani family has furnished the inn with the look of early America, and it draws patrons from as far away as Japan. The visitor can sit and read on the red brick porch, or wander around the farm's barns and gardens. Country Heritage is famous for its prize-winning muffins. A recipe for one house favorite is shared with us by JoAnn Celani.

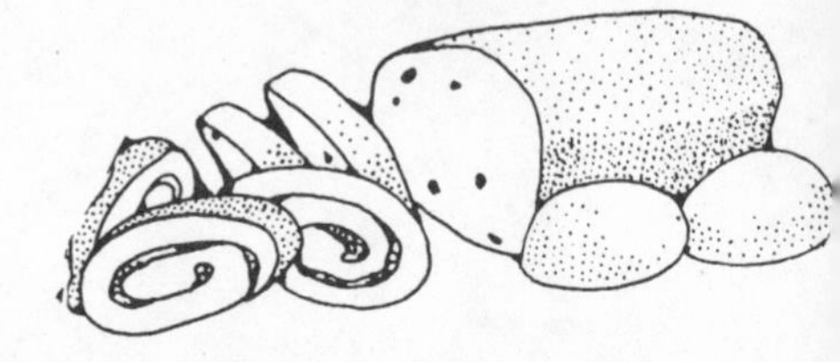

This gracious two-and-a-half story Victorian structure with a gabled hip roof has been offering lodging since 1950. Surrounded by manicured landscaping, including a gazebo, the building features a large veranda with scrolled wood brackets, turned posts and a porte cochere. Hardwood floors, lofty windows, and antique furnishings create a comfortable nineteenth century feeling in each of the bedrooms. The innkeepers have filled their inn with Wedgwood pottery, original art, handmade quilts, and fresh flowers. Delicious foods are served in the sun porch, the gazebo, or in one's bedroom.

Orange Tea Muffins

1 1/2 cups flour
1/2 cup sugar
2 teaspoons baking powder
1/2 teaspoon salt
1/2 cup butter
1/2 cup fresh orange juice
2 eggs
Grated rind of 1 orange
1 cup fresh or frozen raspberries (optional)
1/2 cup coconut (optional)

Combine the flour, sugar, baking powder, and salt; blend well. Melt the butter. Remove from the heat and stir in the orange juice, eggs, and orange rind; beat. Add the raspberries and coconut if desired. Stir the liquid into the dry mixture and blend until just moistened. Spoon into well-greased muffin cups. Bake at 375 degrees for 15 to 20 minutes. Makes 1 dozen .

Wedgwood Inn

111 West Bridge Street
New Hope, Pennsylvania 18938
(215) 862-2570

Pumpkin Muffins

2 1/2 cups flour
2 cups sugar
2 teaspoons ground cinnamon
1/2 teaspoon ground nutmeg
1 teaspoon baking powder
1/2 teaspoon salt
2 eggs, lightly beaten
1 cup cooked or canned pumpkin
1/2 cup vegetable oil
2 cups, finely diced peeled apples

In large bowl, combine the dry ingredients. Set aside. Combine the wet ingredients and add to the bowl of dry ingredients. Mix until the dry ingredients are just moistened. Pour into greased muffin tins and bake at 350 degrees for 30 to 35 minutes. Makes about 18.

Note: If you like streusel topping, mix 2 tablespoons flour, 1 teaspoon cinnamon, 1/4 cup sugar, and 4 tablespoons butter and sprinkle over the muffins before baking.

The Village of Little Britain

P.O. Box 20
Nottingham, Pennsylvania 19362
(717) 529-2862

Fred and Evelyn Crider are innkeepers at this delightful manor. It is accurately billed as "a home away from home." The visitor can relax in a quiet, restful country setting away from city noises, busy crowds, and bustling traffic. The inn is nestled among the beautiful Lancaster County farmlands. Step back in time as you travel through Old Strasburg and historic Lancaster. Learn more about history as you tour nearby Gettysburg.

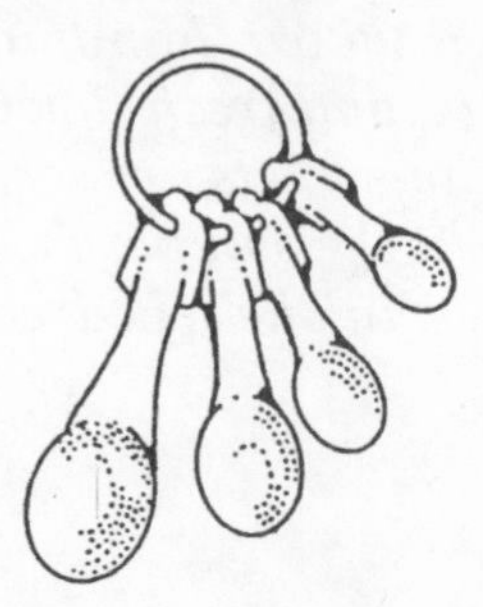

The Sugar Hill Inn, tucked away in the beautiful White Mountains, offers its guests the quiet charm of a true country inn. It was built in 1789 by one of Sugar Hill's original settlers, and converted to an inn in 1929. Much care and thought was given to restoring old beams, floors, and original fireplaces. The ten rooms in the inn and the six country cottages are individually decorated with fine antiques, hand stenciling and delicate wall-papers--enhanced by stenciled Hitchcock chairs, old brass tools, and colorful theorem paintings on velvet.

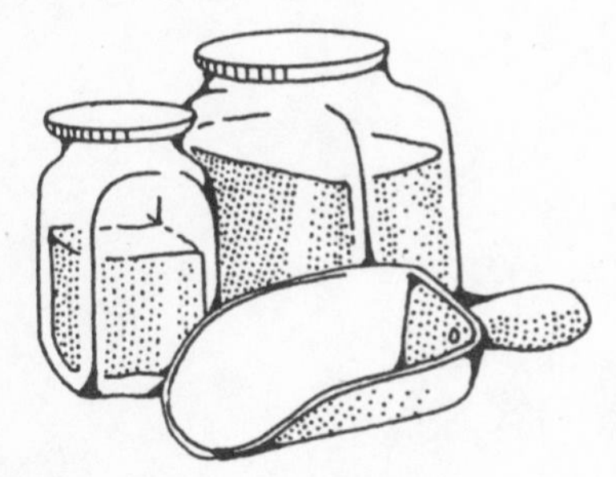

Blueberry Muffins

1 cup flour
1/2 teaspoon salt
1 teaspoon baking powder
1/2 teaspoon baking soda
2 eggs
1 cup sour cream
5 tablespoons butter (melted)
1 cup firmly packed brown sugar
1 cup rolled oats
1 cup blueberries, fresh or frozen (if frozen do not defrost)

In a small bowl combine the flour, salt, baking powder, and baking soda. Set aside 2 tablespoons to coat the blueberries. In a large bowl, beat the eggs; add the sour cream and blend well. Add the melted butter and brown sugar and stir into the egg mixture. Stir in the oats. Fold in the flour mixture, stirring only enough to dampen the flour; the mixture should not be smooth. Toss the blueberries in the reserved flour and stir into the batter. Spoon the mixture into the muffin tin, filling the cups two-thirds full. Bake at 375 degrees for 25 to 30 minutes, until brown, cool in the pans. Makes 1 dozen.

Sugar Hill Inn

Route 117
Franconia, New Hampshire 03580
(603) 823-5621

Bonnie's Lemon Blueberry Muffins

1/2 cup milk
Grated rind of 1 lemon
1 tablespoon chopped lemon balm (optional)
2 cups flour
2 teaspoons baking powder
Pinch of salt
6 tablespoons butter, softened
1 cup sugar
2 eggs, lightly beaten
2 tablespoons fresh lemon juice
2 cups blueberries, fresh or frozen

Glaze
1 tablespoon fresh lemon juice (or more)
Confectioners' sugar

Heat the milk, remove from the heat, and add the lemon zest and lemon balm. Let cool. In a large bowl cream the butter and add the sugar gradually, beating until creamy. Add the eggs slowly and beat well. In a separate bowl combine the flour, baking powder, and salt. Add the milk mixture to the butter mixture, add the lemon juice, and mix well. Add the flour mixture and blend well. Add the blueberries and stir gently until just incorporated. Fill greased or paper-lined muffin cups at least three-fourths full. Bake for 20 to 25 minutes at 400 degrees. Do not overbake. The muffins should be very light in color, not brown. To make the glaze, whisk the confectioner's sugar into the lemon juice until the mixture has the consistency of a thick paste. While the muffins are still a little warm, drizzle the glaze over each muffin. Makes 14 to 16.

White Lace Inn

16 North 5th Avenue
Sturgeon Bay, Wisconsin 54235
(414) 743-1105

This Victorian inn in famous Door County, Wisconsin, offers 15 very special guest rooms in three historic structures, all individually prepared and decorated by Innkeepers Bonnie and Dennis Statz. Every room is complete with the comforts expected at a fine inn. At windows, on dressers, over a bed, or in a frame, you will find the lace from which the White Lace Inn takes it name.

The North Garden Inn is a Queen Anne Victorian on the National Register of Historic Places, superbly suited to attend to the traveler's needs. Many of the beautifully appointed rooms have splendid views of Bellingham Bay. A Steinway grand piano adorns the front hall. Innkeepers Barbara and Frank DeFreytas pride themselves on offering warm personal service to the many who make this their home away from home. Fine dining is offered in the formal dining room.

Chocolate Chip Banana Muffins

4 overripe bananas, mashed
1 cup sugar
1/2 cup butter
1 egg
1 teaspoon vanilla extract
2 cups flour
1 teaspoon baking soda
1/2 teaspoon baking powder
1 cup semisweet chocolate chips

Beat together the bananas, sugar, butter, egg, and vanilla. Mix the dry ingredients and add to the banana mixture. Add the chocolate chips. Spoon into greased muffin tins and bake at 350 degrees for 25 minutes. Makes about 2 dozen.

North Garden Inn

1014 North Garden
Bellingham, Washington 98225
(206) 671-7828

Raisin and Oat Scones

2/3 cup butter or margarine, melted
1/3 cup milk
1 egg
1 1/2 cups flour
1 1/2 cups rolled oats
1/4 cup sugar
1 tablespoon baking powder
1 teaspoon cream of tartar
1/2 teaspoon salt
1/2 cup raisins or dried currants

Combine the dry ingredients and add the melted butter, milk, and egg; mix just until moistened. Stir in the raisins. Drop by teaspoonfuls onto a greased baking sheet. Bake at 425 degrees for 12 to 15 minutes or until a light golden brown. Makes about 1 dozen.

Montague Inn

1561 South Washington Avenue
Saginaw, Michigan 48601
(517) 752-3939

The Montague Inn is a small luxury hotel in the European tradition that offers elegance and excellence. A restored Georgian mansion centered on eight beautifully landscaped acres with 18 guest rooms, the inn invites guests to enjoy the peaceful pleasure of strolling among the gardens and relaxing near Lake Linton. The dining room offers fine cuisine in an intimate atmosphere overlooking the spacious grounds. Dining is by reservation only.

The story behind this elegant inn is one of local interest and color. The building was originally constructed in 1908 as a children's home. Its restoration is the fulfillment of a dream for Francie Morgan, who grew up in the neighborhood and played with many of the children who lived at the home. Overnight guests are served a delightful breakfast in bed, on the balcony, or in the Tea Room. The Sunday Brunch Buffet is a favorite with overnighters as well as short term guests.

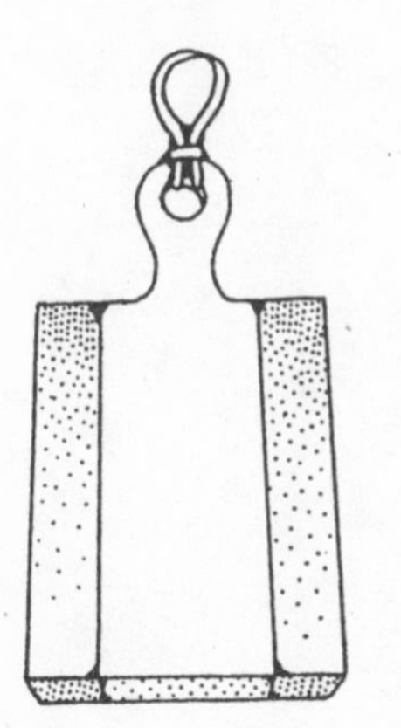

Savory Scones

1 cup self-rising flour
1/2 teaspoon baking powder
Pinch of salt
1 teaspoon mustard
1/4 cup butter or margarine
3 ounces Cheddar cheese, grated
2 ounces diced ham
1/2 cup milk

Sift the flour, baking powder, salt and mustard into a bowl. Rub in the butter until the mixture resembles coarse crumbs, then stir in the cheese and ham. Add enough milk to make a fairly soft dough. Turn onto a lightly floured surface. Knead very gently and roll out to a 3/4-inch thickness. Cut into rounds and place on a floured baking sheet. Brush with milk and bake at 425 degrees for 10 minutes. Cool on a wire rack. Makes 10 to 12.

Note: Francie's serves these scones with strawberry and cinnamon butters which can be made by stirring strawberry jam or cinnamon and sugar into soft butter.

Francie's

104 South Line
De Quoin, Illinois 62832
(618) 542-6686

Bran Scones

1 3/4 cups flour
1 1/2 teaspoons baking powder
1/2 teaspoon baking soda
1/4 cup plus 1 tablespoon sugar
6 tablespoons cold butter, cut bite-size
2 tablespoons plus 2 teaspoons heavy cream
1/2 cup buttermilk
1/3 cup All-Bran cereal

Combine the flour, baking powder, baking soda, and the 1/4 cup sugar in a mixing bowl; cut in the butter until the mixture resembles coarse meal. In another bowl, stir together the buttermilk, 2 tablespoons cream and bran cereal. Pour over the flour and mix with a fork until the dough masses together. On a lightly floured work surface, pat the dough into a disk shape and roll into a circle about 3/4 inch thick. Using a 2-inch biscuit cutter, cut into rounds. Place on a lightly greased baking sheet. Brush the tops with the remaining cream and sprinkle with the remaining sugar. Bake for 20 minutes at 350 degrees or until golden brown. Makes 16.

Note: If you plan to freeze the scones, remove from the oven before they brown, cool and wrap tightly, freeze, thaw, and reheat until brown.

Glen-Ella Springs Inn

Clarkesville, Georgia

This inn remains much as it was in the late 1800s when people visited it for the health benefits of the nearby springs. Barrie and Bobby Aycock have renovated the inn completely to make it a comfortable respite for today's travelers.

Breakfasts served at this wonderful inn are called "sumptuous culinary creations," and guests are seated at a communal table. Making new friends seems to be a high priority. Another special time is gathering in the early evening to share refreshments before dinner. Barnard-Good House is a totally restored inn located in the National Historic Landmark city of Cape May. Here one steps back in time, happily leaving television, telephones, and air-conditioning behind.

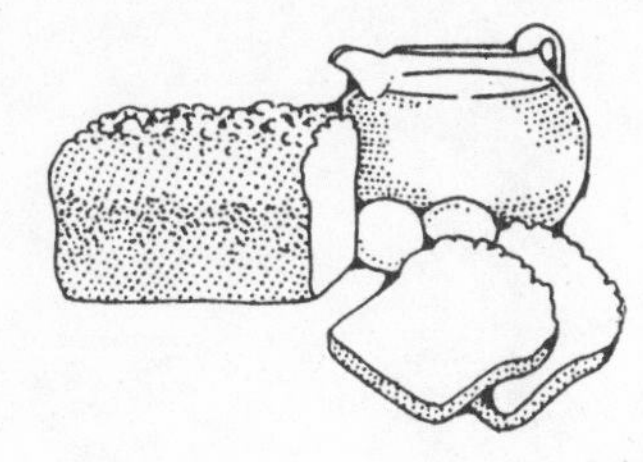

No-Cholesterol Popovers

6 egg whites
1 cup skim milk
2 tablespoons melted margarine
1 cup flour
1/4 teaspoon salt (optional)

Grease twelve 2 1/2-inch muffin tin cups or six custard cups with cooking oil spray. In a large bowl with a mixer set at medium speed, beat the egg whites until frothy. Beat in the milk and margarine until blended. Beat in the flour and salt until the batter is smooth. Fill the muffin cups three-fourths full. Bake for 50 minutes at 375 degrees. Remove immediately and serve. Makes 6 or 12.

Barnard-Good House at Cape May

238 Perry Street
Cape May, NJ 08204
(609) 884-5381

Oatmeal Banana Cookies

Here's a unique cookie recipe from the Mayan Ranch in Bandera, Texas. Give it a try!

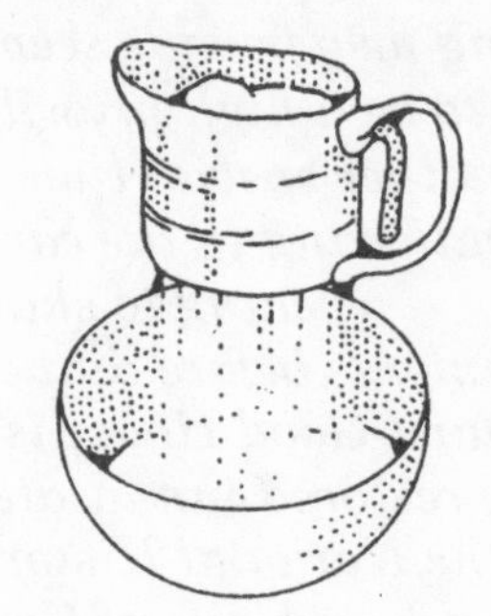

3/4 cup butter, softened
1 cup sugar
1 egg
1 cup mashed banana
1 teaspoon vanilla extract
1 1/2 cups sifted flour
1 teaspoon salt
1/2 teaspoon baking soda
1/2 teaspoon nutmeg
3/4 teaspoon cinnamon
1 1/2 cups uncooked quick-cooking oatmeal
1/2 cup chopped walnuts

Cream the butter and sugar. Add the egg, banana, and vanilla and blend well. Combine the dry ingredients and add to the butter-sugar mixture. Stir just until combined. Stir in the walnuts. Bake on a greased baking sheet at 400 degrees for 12 to 15 minutes. Makes about 4 dozen.

Mayan Ranch

P.O. Box 577
Bandera, Texas
(512) 796-3312

Three Deer Inn is nestled at the base of Black Mountain and is surrounded by forest. It is constructed of cedar and stone and exhibits fine workmanship. The innkeepers want their guests to learn firsthand about the beauty, splendor, and hospitality found in the mountains of eastern Kentucky, gladly sharing good food, clean surroundings, and friendliness. The Little Shepard Trail nearby is a mountaintop road that offers tremendous views of eastern Kentucky.

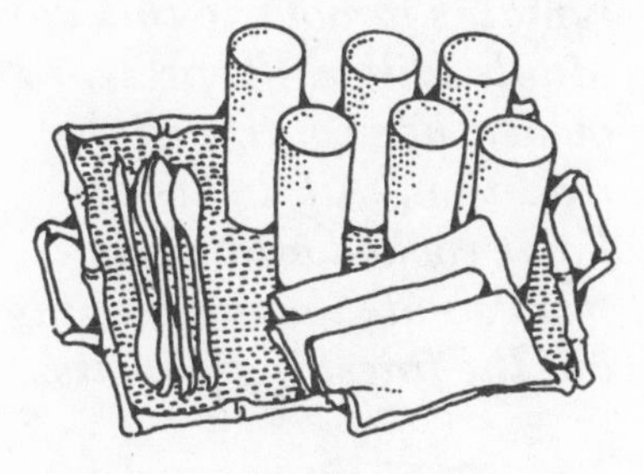

Hunter Cookies

1 cup vegetable shortening (or half butter)
2 cups sugar
1 1/2 cups packed brown sugar
2 eggs
2 teaspoons vanilla extract
1 cup raisins
1 cup nuts
2 cups flour
2 teaspoons baking powder
2 teaspoons baking soda
1 teaspoon salt
1/2 teaspoon ground nutmeg
1 teaspoon ground cinnamon
2 cups rolled oats
2 cups cornflakes

Mix the shortening with the sugars. Add the eggs, vanilla, and raisins, then the nuts. Combine the flour, baking powder, baking soda, salt, nutmeg, and cinnamon. Add to the shortening mixture. Stir in the oatmeal and cornflakes. Drop by tablespoonsful onto a greased baking sheet. Bake at 350 degree F. for 10 to 15 minutes. Makes 4 dozen.

Three Deer Inn

P.O. Drawer 299
Gray's Knob, Kentucky 40829
(606) 573-6666

Sugar Cookies

1 pound margarine
1 cup sugar
1 cup confectioners' sugar
2 eggs
1 teaspoon vanilla extract
4 cups flour
1 teaspoon cream of tartar
1 teaspoon baking soda
Sugar for dipping

Mix the margarine, sugars, eggs, and vanilla. Combine the flour, cream of tartar, and baking soda. Add to the sugar and egg mixture and stir to blend. Roll the dough in balls, dip in sugar, and flatten with a glass. Bake for just 12 minutes at 350 degrees. Makes 3 dozen.

Hotel Manning

P.O. Box 98
100 Van Buren
Keosauqua, Iowa 52565
(319) 293-3232

Edwin Manning came chugging up the Des Moines River in 1837 on a sidewheel riverboat, disembarking at a romantic bend of the river where he founded the town of Keosauqua. The first floor of what is now the hotel was built in 1854 as a general store. Manning added the second and third stories in the late 1890s and turned the building into a hotel and restaurant serving the riverboat trade. It immediately became famous for its food and warm hospitality, and remains famous to this day. Mable Miller, the present owner, has continued the tradition. All dishes are home cooked and made from scratch using nothing but the finest ingredients.

Mason House was built in 1846 on the Des Moines River as a steamboat inn by Mormons trekking to Utah. Travelers received superb hospitality then, and that tradition continues today. Over half of the original furnishings remain. A large state park and state forest are nearby.

Old-fashioned Cinnamon Cookies

(At the Mason House Inn, every guestroom has a cookie jar.)

1 cup margarine
3 cups plus 1/4 cup sugar
2 teaspoons vanilla extract
4 eggs
5 1/2 cups flour
2 teaspoons cream of tartar
1 teaspoon baking soda
1/2 teaspoon salt
1/4 cup sugar
1 tablespoon ground cinnamon

Cream the butter and sugar. Add the vanilla and eggs and blend well. Combine the flour, cream of tartar, baking soda, and salt. Gradually add to the butter-sugar-egg mixture, blending well after each addition. Combine the 1/4 cup sugar and the cinnamon. Drop the dough by teaspoonful into the cinnamon-sugar mixture, then place on an ungreased baking sheet. Bake at 400 degrees for 8 to 10 minutes until set.

Mason House Inn

Bentonsport, Iowa 52565
(319) 592-3133

Oatmeal Chocolate Chip Cookies

4 eggs
1 cup vegetable shortening
1 cup margarine or butter
1 1/2 cups sugar
1 1/2 cups packed brown sugar
3 teaspoons vanilla
2 teaspoons salt
2 teaspoons baking soda mixed with 2 teaspoons hot water
3 cups flour
12 ounces semisweet chocolate chips
4 cups rolled oats

Cream together the shortening, butter, sugars, eggs, and vanilla until light and fluffy. Add the dry ingredients to the creamed mixture and blend well. Add the chocolate chips and rolled oats. Drop from tablespoons 3 inches apart on a greased baking sheet. Bake at 350 degrees for 8 minutes. Let the cookies cool on the sheet for a couple of minutes before moving. They will look uncooked in the middle, but that is the secret of their delicious taste. Makes 7 dozen.

Billed as Kittitas County, Washington's finest country inn, The Moore House was originally built by the Chicago, Milwaukee, St. Paul and Pacific railroad to house men who had the job of getting trains over some of the most hazardous track in the country. Constructed in 1909 and recently placed on the National Register of Historic Places, The Moore House has been lovingly renovated. Hearty food served on Olympian Hiawatha dining car china from another era greets guests as they enter the large and friendly dining room.

The Moore House

P.O. Box 861
South Cle Elum, Washington 98943
(509) 674-5939

Coconut Chocolate Chip Cookies

2 1/2 cups flour
1 teaspoon baking soda
1 teaspoon salt
3/4 cup plus 2 tablespoons butter
2 tablespoons canned coconut cream
1/2 cup sugar
1 cup firmly packed brown sugar
2 eggs
1 teaspoon vanilla extract
2 1/2 cups semisweet chocolate chips
1 1/2 cups chopped pecans
1/2 cup sweetened flaked coconut

Mix the flour, baking soda, and salt, and set aside. In a large bowl, cream the butter and coconut cream. Add the sugars and beat until well mixed. Beat in the eggs and vanilla until the mixture is creamy. Stir the dry ingredients into the creamed mixture just until the flour is completely blended in. Stir in the chocolate chips, pecans, and coconut until combined. Drop by rounded tablespoonfuls onto greased baking sheets. Bake at 375 degrees for 8 to 9 minutes. Makes 5 dozen.

Here is a majestic turn-of-the-century mansion of 42 rooms romantically nestled on a hillside high in the Colorado Rockies. It was the home of John Cleveland Osgood, built to impress and outdo his peers John D. Rockefeller, J.P. Morgan, Jay Gould, John W. "Bet a Million" Gates, President Teddy Roosevelt and other nineteenth century captains of industry. It is now a retreat for those who long for a sense of history, quality, and luxury that is almost extinct. The Castle was completed around 1900 at a cost of millions.

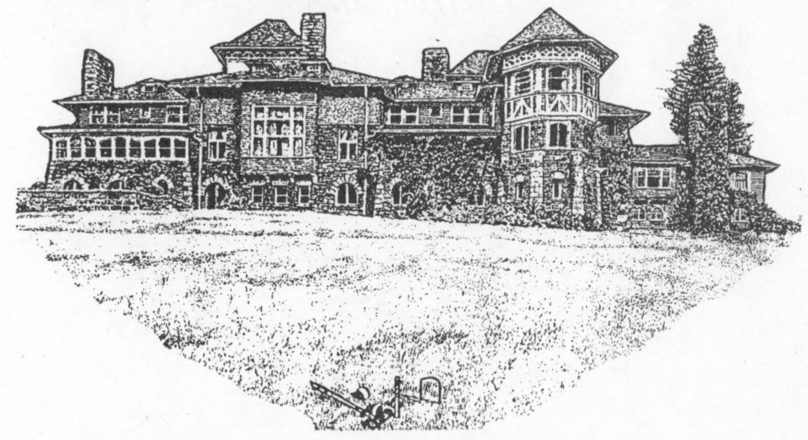

Redstone Castle

58 Redstone Boulevard
Redstone, Colorado 81623
(303) 963-3463

Victorian Vinegar Cookies

Vinegar in cookies--it may seem like a strange idea. But Bob and Marilyn Wiltgen promise these are worth keeping an open mind for.

1/2 cup butter
1/2 cup margarine
3/4 cup sugar
1 tablespoon distilled white vinegar
1 3/4 cup flour
1/2 teaspoon baking soda
1 cup finely chopped walnuts

Cream the butter and margarine. Add the sugar and vinegar; beat until fluffy. Sift the flour and soda and add to the butter and sugar mixture. Stir in the nuts. Drop by teaspoonfuls onto ungreased baking sheets. Bake for 30 minutes at 300 degrees Makes about 4 dozen.

The Lovelander

217 West 4th Street
Loveland, Colorado 80537
(303) 669-0798

A visit to Heritage Manor is like stepping back in time. Guests have a choice of two structures, one built in 1903, the other in 1907, the year Oklahoma became a state. Both homes have been restored to their original beauty. Heritage Manor is located in the northwest portion of Oklahoma, where the famous land run of 1893 opened the area to homesteaders. Delicious food is served in the handsome dining room. A.J. and Carolyn Rextroat are the innkeepers at this delightful retreat.

Swedish Cookies

1 cup butter
1/2 cup confectioners' sugar
1/4 cup cornstarch
1 1/2 cups flour
1/4 teaspoon salt
1/2 teaspoon almond extract
1/2 teaspoon vanilla extract

Beat the butter and confectioners' sugar together. Add the remaining ingredients and beat again. Place the batter in a pastry bag with a tip and squeeze onto ungreased baking sheets. Bake at 350 degrees for 10 to 12 minutes or until slightly brown. Makes about 2 dozen.

Heritage Manor

Rural Route 1
P.O. Box 33
Aline, Oklahoma 73716
(405) 463-2563

Tea Cakes

Try this enticing recipe from Cheneyville, Louisiana's WalnutGrove. The cakes are delicious!

1 1/2 cups sugar
3/4 cup buttermilk
3 cups flour
1/2 cup chopped walnuts
1 teaspoon baking soda
1/2 cup vegetable shortening
2 eggs
1 cup golden raisins
1 teaspoon baking powder
1 1/2 teaspoons vanilla extract

Combine all ingredients and drop by teaspoonfuls onto greased baking sheets. Bake at 350 degrees until done, about 8 minutes. Makes about 4 dozen.

Walnut Grove

Route 1, Box 41
Cheneyville, Louisiana 71325
(318) 279-2203

According to some, Eureka Springs is the Inn Capital of the World. Singleton House is billed "an old- fashioned place with a touch of magic." Sheltering a hidden enchanted garden on a hillside above Eureka Springs' historic district, the restored Victorian style inn is whimsically decorated with an eclectic collection of unexpected treasures. The rooms are uniquely furnished. Hosteler Barbara Gavron delights in pampering guests with Ozark hospitality.

Raspberry Almond Cookies

1 cup almonds
1 cup rolled oats
1 cup pastry flour
1/4 tablespoon ground cinnamon
Pinch of salt
1/2 cup corn oil
1/2 cup maple syrup
4 ounces raspberry jam (sugarless variety best).

Chop the almonds very fine or grind in a blender or food processor into a coarse nut flour. Grind the oats into a coarse flour. Combine the dry ingredients in a bowl. Whip the corn oil and maple syrup together. Add to the dry ingredients. Mix until the dry ingredients are well coated. Form walnut-size balls and place on a greased baking sheet. Press a thumb gently in the center of each ball to create a space for the filling. Fill each cookie with 1/2 tablespoon raspberry jam. Bake at 350 degrees for 10 to 15 minutes or until golden brown. Makes about 16.

Note: Filberts, walnuts, or cashews may be substituted for the almonds and various flavors of preserves may be used for the filling.

Singleton House

11 Singleton
Eureka Springs, Arkansas 72632
(501) 253-9111

Biscotti

1 1/4 cups sugar
3/4 cup vegetable shortening
3 eggs
1/2 cup milk
1 1/2 teaspoons oil of anise
4 cups flour
Scant tablespoon baking powder
Confectioners' sugar, for garnish

Cream the sugar and shortening together. Add the eggs, milk, and oil of anise. Add the flour and baking powder and form into three flat loaves. Bake at 375 degrees for 30 minutes. Slice and toast for 10 minutes more; turn over and do the same. Dust with confectioners' sugar. Makes about 30.

Hickory Grove Inn

State Route 80
Cooperstown, New York 13326
(505) 336-4361

In the early 1800s, Hickory Grove was a popular stagecoach stop for travelers bound from Cooperstown to the Cherry Valley turnpike. The early steamboats, which ferried freight and passengers to the lakeside dwellings, also stopped at the inn to provide for the passengers' refreshment. The area was purchased from local Indians in 1769. The inn was built shortly after 1800 by the Van Ben Schoten family and for the past century and a half has been noted for good food and relaxation. Vince and Karin Diorio are the innkeepers.

These cookies are among the most popular menu items at Cape Mainstay Inn. They're sure to please.

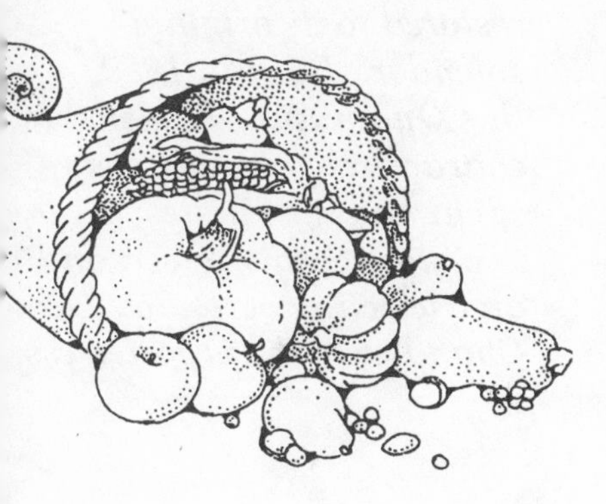

Chocolate Chip Meringue Cookies

2 egg whites
1 teaspoon vanilla
1/4 teaspoon cream of tartar
1/4 teaspoon salt
3/4 cup sugar
6 ounces semisweet chocolate chips

Beat the egg whites, vanilla, cream of tartar and salt until soft peaks form. Gradually beat in the sugar until the mixture is very stiff and glossy. Fold in the chocolate chips. Drop from a teaspoon onto a baking sheet lined with brown paper. Bake at 300 degrees for about 25 minutes. Makes 2 dozen.

Mainstay Inn

635 Columbia Avenue
Cape May, New Jersey 08204
(609) 884-8690

Berry Patch Filled Squares

3/4 cup margarine
1/2 cup sugar
1 teaspoon vanilla extract
1 egg
2 1/2 cups flour
1/2 teaspoon baking powder
2 cups jam, any flavor

Cream the margarine; add the sugar gradually, creaming thoroughly. Add the vanilla and egg; beat well. Sift the flour with the baking powder; add slowly to the creamed mixture, mixing thoroughly after each addition. Press the dough lightly over the bottom and sides of a 13 by 9 by 2-inch baking dish. Bake for 15 to 20 minutes at 400 degrees. Heat the jam in a saucepan over medium heat or in a microwave. Spread the hot jam over the baked cookie dough. Cool before cutting into squares. Store in the refrigerator.

Heritage Park Inn

San Diego, California

Surrounded by 8-acre Victorian Park in the heart of San Diego's historic Old Town, Heritage Park Inn has been completely restored to its original splendor. Built in 1889, this Queen Anne mansion is characterized by a variety of chimneys, shingles, a two-story corner tower, and an encircling veranda. Lori Chandler is the proprietress.

Sundance Inn offers cozy, friendly lodging to travelers desiring to explore the town of Jackson and its surrounding area. The newly remodeled inn, built in the early 1950s and once called the Ideal Lodge, really is an "ideal" place to stay. There is a variety of outings to satisfy any desire, from river rafting the Snake in the summer, to dog sledding, to visiting Granite Hot Springs for a quick dip in the water. Since trapper David Jackson discovered the "Hole" over 150 years ago, travelers have stopped to rest and wonder at the spectacular beauty of the valley and surrounding mountains.

Tom Thumb Tarts

Crust
1/2 cup margarine
1 3-ounce package cream cheese, softened
1 cup flour

Mix all ingredients and form into balls. Press into small muffin cups.

Filling
1 egg, beaten
3/4 cup brown sugar
1 tablespoon melted butter
1 cup chopped nuts
Dash of vanilla extract
Confectioners' sugar, for garnish

Combine all ingredients, except the confectioners' sugar, and mix well. Fill the crusts. Bake at 400 degrees for 18 minutes. Sprinkle with confectioners' sugar when cool. Makes about 1 dozen.

Sundance Inn
P.O. Box I
Jackson, Wyoming 83001
(307) 733-3444

Best in the West Brownies

2 cups flour
2 cups sugar
1 cup margarine
1 cup water
3 1/2 tablespoons unsweetened cocoa powder
1 teaspoon baking soda
1/2 cup buttermilk
2 eggs, beaten well
1 teaspoon vanilla extract
Pinch of salt
Frosting (recipe below)

Combine the flour and sugar and set aside. In a saucepan combine the margarine, water, and cocoa. Heat until the mixture comes to a boil. Pour over the flour-sugar mixture. Add the baking soda to the buttermilk and add to the batter. Add the eggs, vanilla, and salt. Mix with a wire whisk (do not use an electric beater). Bake at 325 degrees for 20 to 30 minutes. Let cool, frost, and cut in squares. Makes 20 to 24.

Frosting
6 tablespoons margarine
6 tablespoons milk
1 1/3 cups sugar
1/2 cup semisweet chocolate chips

Combine the margarine, milk, and sugar in a saucepan. Bring to a boil and boil for 1 minute. Remove from heat and add the chocolate chips. Stir until the chips are melted. Cool.

The Logging Camp Ranch

8 CR 3, Box 27
Bowmar, North Dakota 58623
(701) 279-5501

Above the river, in the pines, there is a North Dakota few have experienced. Four generations of Hansons have owned and operated the 10,000-acre Logging Camp Ranch. This is not a dude ranch. It is a real live, working ranch, much as it was in the 1880s. What it offers is as simple--and as complex--as the nature around it—wilderness, wildlife, and wonder. Log cabins with showers and bathrooms are provided for overnight guests who share bountiful meals with the owners and workers. Seven different unspoiled ecological systems, including North Dakota's only ponderosa pine forest, are part of the land owned by the ranch.

Washington School Inn is a perfect example of what preservationists call "adaptive use." A schoolhouse built in 1889, the building was fully restored as an inn, opening in June 1985. Its location in the old town section of Park City, Utah, puts it close to the magnificent skiing opportunities for which this area is noted. The inn offers its visitors deliciously prepared food, and afternoon goodies are always available to hungry skiers returning from the slopes.

Zucchini Brownies

2 cups flour
1 1/4 cups sugar
1 teaspoon salt
1 1/2 teaspoons baking soda
1/4 cup cocoa
1 egg
1/4 cup oil
2 teaspoons vanilla extract
3 cups grated zucchini
1/4 cup chopped nuts

Stir all ingredients together. Put in a 9 by 13-inch baking pan that has been sprayed with cooking oil spray. Bake for 45 minutes at 350 degrees F. Frost, if desired, perhaps with a cream cheese frosting. Cut in squares. Makes 24.

Washington School Inn

P.O. Box 536
Park City, Utah 84060
(801) 649-3800

10 Country Inn Potpourri

Beverages, Sauces, and Miscellaneous Accompaniments

The history of Balfour House is inextricably meshed with the history of Vicksburg and the Civil War. Many historians agree that it was the fall of Vicksburg on July 4, 1863 that marked the turning point in that great conflict. Frequented during the war by such notable Confederates as Generals Stephen D. Lee, John C. Pemberton, and Martin Luther Smith, Balfour House later became headquarters for Union General James Birdseye McPherson's occupational forces, and business headquarters for the Union army until the war's end. The beautiful structure is considered one of the finest Greek Revival houses in Mississippi. Unaltered since 1850, Balfour House offers a fascinating tour for all ages.

Spicy Peach Marmalade

1 1 3/4-ounce box Sure-Jell
3 pounds ripe peaches, peeled and chopped fine, about 4 cups
Juice of 1 lemon
5 1/2 cups sugar
1/4 teaspoon cinnamon
1/4 teaspoon cloves
1/4 teaspoon nutmeg

Mix Sure-Jell, fruit, and lemon juice and place in a large pot over high heat. Bring to a boil, stirring constantly. Add sugar and bring to a rolling boil. Boil hard for 1 minute, stirring constantly. Remove from heat, and skim off foam with a metal spoon. Add spices. Pour into hot, sterilized jars and seal. Makes 7 half pints.

Balfour House

P.O. Box 1541
Vicksburg, Mississippi 39181
(601) 638-3690

Rhubarb Jam

5 cups rhubarb, washed and cut in 1-inch pieces
4 cups sugar
1 3-ounce package strawberry gelatin dessert

Mix rhubarb and sugar in a large kettle and cook ten minutes, stirring to keep from burning. Remove from heat. Add the Jello and stir to dissolve. Put in small hot sterilized jars and seal, or keep in the refrigerator.

Custer Mansion

35 Centennial Drive
Custer, South Dakota 57730
(605) 673-3333

Custer Mansion is a Victorian Gothic structure built by Newton Tubbs who came to the Black Hills after gold was discovered in 1876. He owned many acres of land and also grew potatoes, sold them or exchanged them at the lumber mill for lumber to build his home. Because of this, the mansion is called "the house that potatoes built." Breakfasts are home cooked, home baked and all you can eat, served by friendly hosts Mill and Carole Seamos. In summer, some guests choose to dine on the slate patio on tables under the huge willow trees.

Strawberry- Rhubarb Jam

Use equal amounts of strawberries, rhubarb, and sugar. Wash and cut rhubarb into small pieces. (Dry strawberries and rhubarb as well as possible since excess water will slow down the "jelling" or thickening of the jam.) Put sugar and rhubarb in a large saucepan and cook until mixture is jelling (runs off the spoon), about 12 to 15 minutes. (The mixture should boil hard, but stir constantly so as not to burn.) Remove from heat and add strawberries. Put back on heat and cook until strawberries are thoroughly heated through, to prevent spoiling. Seal in sterilized jars.

Captain Lord Mansion

P.O. Box 800
Kennebunkport, Maine 04046
(800) 522-3141

This splendid mansion, built by Captain Nathanial Lord, began as a joyful place where his family and decendants shared relaxing times and created warm memories. When the inn was established, the owners endeavored to preserve the gracious atmosphere that typified life there throughout the Lord family's time. During the latest restoration, the original wallpaper in two of the rooms was preserved. There are blown glass windows throughout the mansion. Visitors enjoy climbing the four-story spiral staircase to view the historic neighborhood from the octogonal cupola. Delicious food is served in the lovely dining room.

Cranberry Jelly

8 cups (2 pounds) cranberries
4 cups boiling water
4 cups sugar

Boil cranberries and water 20 minutes. Rub through a sieve. Add sugar and boil 5 minutes. Pour into hot sterile jelly glasses and cover with paraffin. Makes 8 to 10 cups.

Audrie's Cranbury Corner

Rural Route 8
P.O. Box 2400
Rapid City, South Dakota 57708
(605) 342-7788

Here is the perfect place to get away from it all. The inn is the ultimate in charm and old world hospitality. Its spacious rooms are furnished in comfortable European antiques. A delightful Black Hills style breakfast is served to the many appreciative guests who flock here. The inn is located in the Black Hills National Forest, seven miles west of Rapid City.

Janet and Thad May are your hosts at this delightful, romantic country inn featuring elegant accomodations, formal garden and 320 acres of beauty. Guests enjoy a country setting with nature trail, private fish pond, and bird sanctuary, and afternoon tea is served. This is pure Southern hospitality at its best.

Hot Pepper Jelly

1/2 cup ground red hot pepper
3/4 ground red and green bell pepper
6 1/2 cups sugar
1 1/2 cups apple cider vinegar
1 6-ounce bottle liquid pectin

Wash, seed, and grind peppers. Dissolve sugar in vinegar in a large saucepan and add peppers. Remove from saucepan and add peppers. Bring to a full rolling boil. Remove from heat. Cool 10 minutes, stirring occasionally. Add pectin. Seal in sterilized jars. Serve with cream cheese and crackers, or with meats or poultry.

Blue Shadows

Rural Route 2
P.O. Box 432
Greensboro, Alabama 36744
(205) 624-3637

Zucchini Jam

Here's a delicious Zucchini jam recipe from My Blue Heaven in Pawnee City, Nebraska.

6 cups peeled and grated zucchini
1 cup water
6 cups sugar
2 tablespoons lemon juice
20 ounce can crushed pineapple, drained
1/4 teaspoon pineapple flavoring
2 3-ounce packages apricot gelatin dessert

Cook zucchini and water over medium heat. Bring to a boil, reduce heat, and cook six minutes. Add the flavoring. Return to a boil and mix well. Pour into hot, sterile jars and seal with paraffin, or freeze until ready to use. makes 6 to 8 cups.

My Blue Heaven

1041 5th Street
Pawnee City, Nebraska 68420
(402) 852-3131

Step into Denver's 19th century at the Queen Anne Inn. Enjoy the grand oak staircase, the quaint rooms, the many elegant period furnishings, the art, music and greenery throughout, and the hospitality for which the West is famous. This beautiful three-story structure, built in 1879 by Colorado's most famous architect, the inn is an example of the Queen Anne style of Victorian architecture. Owner-innkeepers are Ann and Charles Hillestad. Both are world travelers who treasure small hostelries with local flavor. They have lovingly prepared their delightful inn for their many visitors' enjoyment.

Rasberry Jam Helper

(An inexpensive and simple way to totally transform ordinary raspberry jam.)

2 12-ounce bags cranberries
2 cups water
1 large jar raspberry jam

Wash and pick over cranberries. Heat berries in a large saucepan with the water until the berries "pop.." Add jam and simmer 5 minutes longer, stirring gently. Cool and store in glass jars in the refrigerator.

Queen Anne Inn

2147 Tremont Place
Denver, Colorado 80205
(303) 296-6666

Chunky Apple Chutney

1/2 cup sherry
1/4 cup sugar
3 tablespoons lemon juice
1 cinn amon stick
8 cloves
1/4 cup minced onion
1/4 teaspoon salt
2 medium apples, peeled, cored, and chopped

Mix all ingredients except apples and simmer for 5 minutes. Add apples and 2 tablespoons water. Simmer 5 minutes more. Store in the refrigerator for up to three weeks. Makes about 1 cup.

The Checkerberry Inn

62644 County Road 37
Goshen, Indiana 46526
(219) 642-4445

At the Checkerberry Inn, visitors will find a unique atmosphere, unlike anywhere else in the Midwest. The individually decorated rooms and suites will please even the most discerning guests. Every room has a breathtaking view of unspoiled rolling countryside. A top-rated restaurant serves only the freshest foods, using herbs and other ingredients from the local countryside. The inn is located off a sparsely traveled road in the serenity and seclusion of Amish farmland. Here you will find the uncluttered culture of the Amish, where horses and buggies are still a way of life.

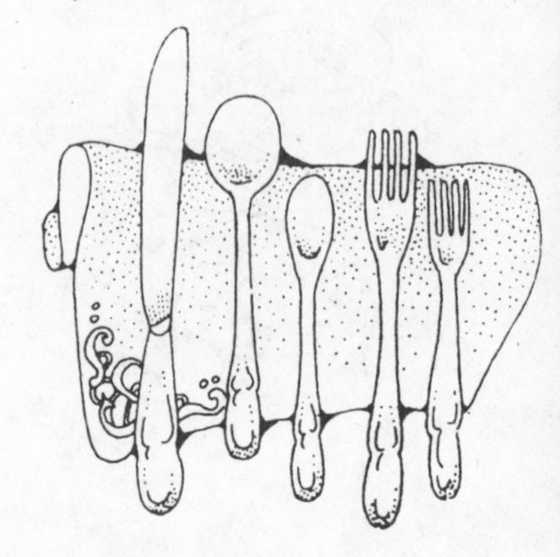

Sand Plum Jelly

(The Sand Plum is a small tart plum that grows wild in the sandy soils of the Midwest.)

Sand plums to make 3 cups juice
1 box fruit pectin
2 3/4 cups honey

Wash plums, cover just barely with with water, and cook. Let juice drip through a bag into another pot. Add the pectin to the juice and bring to a boil, skimming off foam. Add honey and boil 5 to 10 minutes. Pour into hot, sterilized jars and seal with paraffin. Makes 6 cups

A visit to The Harrison is an experience always to be remembered. As one enters through the brass handled double doors into the lobby, one is struck by the beauty of the antique furnishings. The registration desk is an old counter which once stood in the Guthrie Post Office. The lovely light fixtures also came from that post office and are on loan to the inn. All of the fabulous antiques are American Victorian. A delicious, informal breakfast is served in the parlor where linen table coverings and napkins are used. The tableware is china, and the flatware is silver plate in old patterns. Phyllis Murray is the innkeeper/owner. She and her staff are most gracious and eager to please.

Note: Every summer when nature's delightful gift, the Sand Plum, becomes ripe, Guthrie, Oklahoma celebrates with a five-weekend gala that features the visual and performing arts and lots of just plain fun.

Harrison House

124 West Harrison
Guthrie, Oklahoma 73044
(405) 282-1000

Peach Chutney

This lovely inn is a local landmark. Visitors flock here over and over again to partake of the hospitality, deluxe lodgings and great food served in the spacious dining areas. Matthew O'Neill is the chef and inn-keeper. He prepares some of the finest cuisine available, and graciously shares some of his culinary artistry here.

12 peaches, peeled, chopped and pitted
1 cup sugar
1 1/2 cup cider vinegar
1 tablespoon chopped preserved vinegar
1/4 cup chopped citron
3 tablespoons chopped candied lemon peel
1 cinnamon stick
8 whole cloves
1/3 teaspoon coriander seeds

In a saucepan, combine the sugar and vinegar and bring to a boil. Add the peaches, ginger, citron, and lemon peel and a sachet made by tying the cinnamon stick, cloves, and coriander seeds in a square of cheesecloth. Simmer for 5 minutes.

Walden Inn

2 Seminary Square
P.O. Box 490
Greencastle, Indiana 46135-0490
(317)653-2761

The 80 acres of property at the Inn at Cedar Falls are a nature retreat. One can experience a close connection with the out-of-doors in an area abundant with wildlife, birds and whispering trees. The inn is surrounded on three sides by Hocking State Park, and is the only privately operated dining and lodging facility in this area of the Hocking Hills.

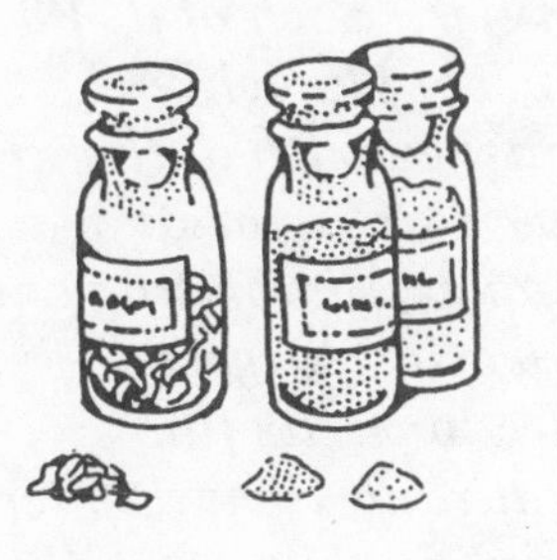

Cranberry Chutney

1/2 cup dried apricots, chopped fine
3/4 cup firmly packed dark brown sugar
3 1/2 cups cranberries, picked over and rinsed
1 Granny Smith apple, peeled, cored, and cut in 1/4 inch pieces
1 teaspoon grated lemon rind
2 tablespoons fresh lemon juice
1/8 cup chopped crystalized ginger
1/8 tablespoon dried hot pepper flakes

In a saucepan, combine the apricots, brown sugar, raisins, and 1 cup water. Bring to a boil while stirring and simmer for five minutes. Add cranberries, apple, and lemon rind. Simmer for 10 minutes. Add lemon juice, ginger, and red pepper flakes. Serve at room temperature or chilled with turkey, chicken, duck, or pork. Makes 3 cups.

The Inn at Cedar Falls

21190 State Route 374
Logan, Ohio 43138
(614)385-7489

Brandied Cranberries

1 pound cranberries
2 cups sugar
1 teaspoon cinnamon
1/2 cup brandy

Place washed berries in a covered glass ovenproof dish with sugar and cinnamon. Bake 1 hour at 350 degrees F. Remove. Pour brandy over the berries and cool. After letting the mixture reach room temperature, chill overnight. Makes about 3 cups.

Strater Hotel

P.O. Drawer E
Durango, Colorado 81302
(800) 427-4431

Authentic Victorian elegance with a hint of the Wild West characterizes the Strater Hotel today, just as it has since 1887. This Durango landmark, located in the heart of the historic entertainment district, is internationally known for its gracious hospitality, charm, and fine service. This four-story brick beauty continues to be owned and operated by one of Durango's pioneer families. Each of its 93 rooms are lavishly furnished with authentic American Victorian walnut antiques, comprising one of the world's largest collections. Its fine restaurant, Henry's offers casual fine dining with great old-world service and fine cuisine, skillfully prepared by an outstanding culinary staff.

The Lodge, built as a home about 100 years ago, has been in operation for over 50 years. Located in the mountains of North Carolina, it offers the variety of all four seasons. The inn is quiet, scenic and restful. It is located on two and one-half acres of rolling land, with its own apple orchards, grape arbors and rhubarb patch. Great food is served family-style in a spacious dining room. The meals are planned and prepared using a variety of locally grown fresh fruits and vegetables.

Cranberry Conserve

1 20-ounce can crushed pineapple
1 6-ounce can frozen orange juice, thawed
1 1/2 cups sugar
3 cinnamon sticks and 1 tablespoon whole cloves, tied in a cheesecloth bag or in a teaball
1 pound fresh cranberries
1 cup whole blanched almonds
1 cup broken pecan pieces

Drain pineapple, reserving juice. Combine the juice with the orange juice concentrate in 2-cup container. Add water to make two cups. In large kettle or dutch oven, combine the juice mixture, sugar, and spices. Bring to a boil, stirring until sugar is disolved. Reduce heat and simmer 10 minutes. Add cranberries and bring to a boil; boil 5 minutes, stirring frequently. Stir in raisins and pineapple; boil 5 minutes, stirring occasionally. Stir in nuts. Pack in hot, sterile jars. Seal with lids and rings. Submerge in hot water bath; simmer for 10 minutes. Remove and store in a cool dry place. Can be stored in refrigerator without water bath. Makes about 3 pints or 6 half pints.

Grandview Lodge

809 Valley View Circle
Waynesville, North Carolina 28786
(704)456-5212

Cinnamon Syrup

1 cup sugar
1/2 cup light corn syrup
1/4 cup water
1 teaspoon cinnamon
1/2 cup heavy cream

In a small saucepan, stir together the sugar, corn syrup, water, and cinnamon. Stirring constantly, bring to a boil over moderate heat; boil for 2 minutes. Syrup will thicken as it cools. Serve warm or at room temperature on french toast, waffles, or pancakes. Makes 1 1/3 cups. Syrup may be refrigerated for several months.

Old Miner's Lodge

516 Woodside Avenue
P.O. Box 2639
Park City, Utah 48060-2639
(801) 645-8068

This inn is a renovated 1863 building located in the national historic district of the colorful resort town of Park City. The lodge was established as housing for local miners seeking their fortunes from the iron-rich hills surrounding town. Today, the spirited warmth and hospitality of Park City's illustrious past remains in this building, which has been lovingly restored to its original splendor.

The Wakefield Inn, which opened in 1803, is a classic stagecoach stop and inn. Early travelers arrived by stagecoach which pulled up to the front door. Passengers would disembark while their luggage was handed up to the second floor. Today, great food is served to the dining public as well as to the guests of the inn.

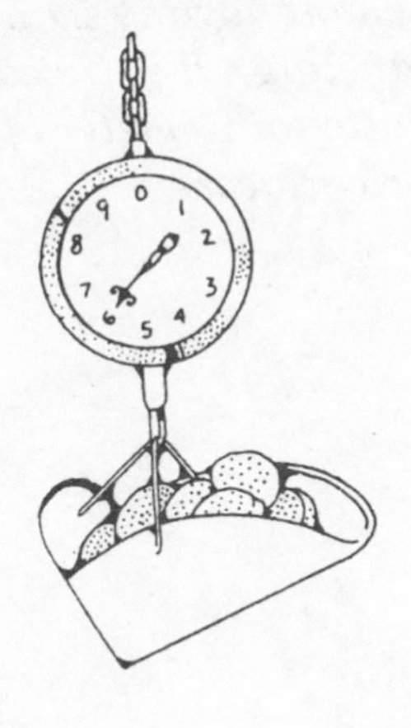

Tangy Corn Relish

1 tablespoon prepared mustard
1 quart cider vinegar
12 cups corn, cut from cob
12 cups shredded cabbage
6 green bell peppers, chopped
6 red bell peppers, chopped
3 cups sugar
3 tablespoons salt

Mix mustard with a little water. Add the remainig ingredients and mix well. Bring to a boil, then reduce heat. and simmer 30 minutes. Seal in hot sterile jars. Makes 9 pints.

The Wakefield Inn

Mountain Laurel Road
Wakefield, New Hampshire 03872
(603) 522-8272

Barbeque Sauce

1 1/2 cups white sugar
1 quart ketchup
1 quart tomato sauce
1 cup molasses
1 cup vinegar
1/4 cup lemon juice
2 cups brown sugar
Tabasco sauce to taste
1/8 teaspoon cayenne pepper
1 teaspoon cinnamon
1 teaspoon cloves
1/4 cup onion salt
1 teaspoon salt
1/4 cup Worcestershire sauce

Mix and heat all ingredients until sugar is melted. Baste on ribs and chicken within the last few minutes of cooking time, or use as a dipping sauce. Makes about 2 1/2 quarts.

The Wells Inn

316 Charles Street
Sisterville, West Virginia 26175
(304) 652-1312

Guests here enjoy the Victorian elegance of a beautifully restored inn with dancing, superb service and charming room accomodations. The inn is located in historic Sisterville on the Ohio River, halfway between Wheeling and Parkersburg. The Wells was established in the rough-and-tumble times of 1894 with a thoroughly elegant interior accented by ornate decoration and deep, rich mahogany trim and paneling. It is listed in the National Register of Historic Places

The White Mountain Lodge, the oldest building in Greer, was built as a farmhouse in 1892 by one of the first Mormon families to settle in the area. Four-by-ten inch timbers are held together with wooden nails to form the external walls of the lodge. A wonderful landmark has been preserved and transformed into a delightful inn where one feels very much at home. Russ and Sophia Majesky are the owner-innkeepers. Sophia delights her guests with the wonderful meals she personally prepares.

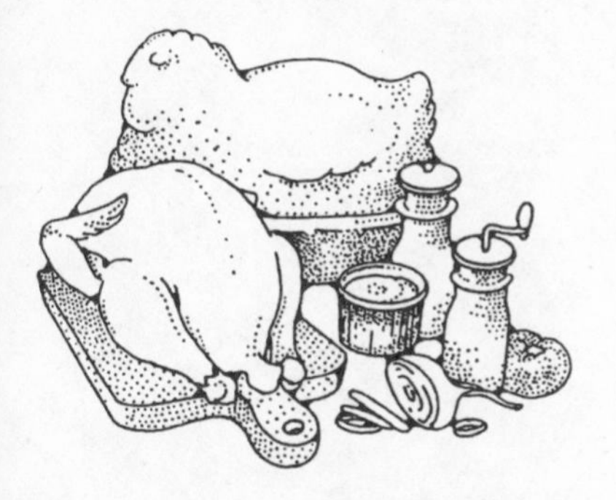

Barbeque Sauce for Fowl

1/2 cup salad oil
1/2 cup lemon juice
1/2 cup wine vinegar
1/4 cup soy sauce
Small amount of sugar if desired
Seasonings as desired (salt, pepper, garlic salt, poultry seasoning)

Combine all ingredients and mix or shake well. Refrigerate for up to 3 weeks. Makes 1 3/4 cups.

White Mountain Lodge

P.O. Box 139
Greer, Arizona 85927
(602) 735-7568

Chocolate Mousse Truffles

Ganache (truffle center)
12 ounces sweet chocolate, broken into small pieces
3/4 cup heavy cream
1/2 stick unsalted butter, quartered
1 egg white, beaten until stiff

Melt chocolate and butter until smooth, stirring occasionally. Scald cream and strain. Mix cream and melted chocolate completely. Gradually stir in beaten egg white. Mixture should be frothy. Cover and refrigerate until ganache is firm.

Dipping
8 ounces semisweet chocolate pieces

Melt chocolate to 110 degrees, stirring occasionally. Remove from heat and bring temperature down to 89 degrees for dipping. Dip each ball in melted chocolate quickly, shaking off excess, and place the truffle on wax paper. When all truffles have been dipped, refrigerate for 30 minutes. Place refrigerated truffles in paper candy cups and then into an airtight container.

Cowslip's Belle

159 North Main
Ashland, Oregon 97520
(503) 488-2901

Cowslip's Belle's craftsman home and newly renovated carriage house were built in 1913, and remain essentially as they were then, with original woodwork and beveled glass. Vintage furniture adds to the comfortable surroundings. Scrumptuous food is served in the sunny dining room. Innkeepers Jon and Carmen Reinhardt will welcome you warmly.

This circa 1899 inn is located on eleven beautiful acres of magnolias and ancient oaks. It is a three story raised French cottage with a 64-foot front porch. There are six elegant fireplaces and wonderful antiques for the visitor's enjoyment. Carl and Claudia Mertz are the owners. Located on the Mississippi Gulf Coast about an hour east of Louisiana, the house was originally built by a retired Italian sea captain to entice his young bride away from her family's home in New Orleans. Claudia Mertz describes the long porch as a spot "where I can eat boiled shrimp and crabs in the shade of magnolias, or just swing to my heart's content, enjoying a tall drink and a thick novel." Delicious cuisine is served in the elegant dining room.

Pecan Divinity

3 cups sugar
1/2 cup white Karo syrup
3/4 cup water
1/2 teaspoon salt
1/2 teaspoon vanilla
1/4 cup egg whites
1 cup pecan pieces

Combine the sugar with the Karo syrup and water. Cook over low heat, stirring until the sugar is dissolved. Increase heat until the mixture boils, then cover the boiling mixture for 3 minutes without stirring. Cook evenly until the mixture reaches 265 degrees or firms up. Separately, add the salt and vanilla to the egg whites and whip until stiff. Slowly pour this mixture into the hot syrup. Continue until the mixture will almost hold its shape, then stir in the pecan pieces. Drop by teaspoons on waxed paper and let set at room temperature. Serves about 30.

Red Creek Colonial Inn

7416 Red Creek Road
Long Beach, Mississippi 39560
(601) 452-3080

Champagne Punch

2 quarts ginger ale
2 quarts sauterne (or dry white wine)
4/5 quart champagne (fifth)
Orange and lemon slices, for garnish

Mix all ingredients in a punch bowl with ice cubes or an ice ring. Garnish with orange and lemon slices. Makes approximately 40 4-ounce servings.

The Old Miner's Lodge

615 Woodside Avenue
P.O. Box 2639
Park City, Utah 48060-2639
(801) 645-8068

This inn is a renovated 1893 building located in the national historic district of Park City. The lodge was built as housing for local miners seeking their fortunes from the ore rich hills surrounding the city. Today, the spirited warmth and hospitality of Park City's illustrious past remains in this lovely building, which has been restored to its original splendor.

The Irma Hotel was built by Colonel William F. "Buffalo Bill" Cody in 1902 and named for his daughter, Irma. The hotel is the grand old lady of downtown Cody, reflecting Buffalo Bill's style and the essence of Western hospitality. The hotel's restaurant serves the tourists traveling to nearby Yellowstone Park as well as locals, and offers a menu to fill the needs of both.

Hot Buttered Rum Mix

1 pound butter, softened
1 pound confectioners sugar
1 pound brown sugar
2 teaspoons nutmeg
1 tablespoon cinammon
1/2 teaspoon ground cloves
1 quart vanilla ice cream

Cream the softened butter, sugars, and spices together (for best results use a mixer). Add softened ice cream and mix thoroughly. Freeze or refrigerate before using. Use 2 teaspoons of above mixture and 1 to 1 1/2 jiggers dark rum. Fill cup with hot water and stir to mix. Serve in Irish coffee mugs.

The Irma

1192 Sheridan
Cody, Wyoming 82414
(307) 587-4221

Holiday Punch

1 3-ounce package cherry gelatin dessert
1 cup boiling water
1 6-ounce can frozen lemonade or pineapple concentrate
3 cups cold water
1 quart cranberry juice cocktail
12 ounces ginger ale (or white wine)
Ice cream, if desired

Dissolve gelatin in boiling water. To this, add the lemonade or pineapple concentrate, cold water, and cranberry juice cocktail. Chill. Just before serving, pour the fruit mixture over ice cubes in a large punch bowl, then add either the ginger ale or white wine. Ice cream dollops can be floated on top of the punch for a frosty effect.

The Brick House

Conklin Dinner Theatre
Box 301
Goodfield, Illinois 61742
(309) 965-2545

The Brick House transports visitors back through history to the inn's origins in 1857, back to the bold, pioneer spirit which was so special to the Illinois heartland when Abraham Lincoln traveled the historic Heritage Trail. Henry Mortimer Robinson, with bricks fashioned by his own hands, built his mansion of walls that in some places measure eighteen inches thick. In 1984, the management of the Conklin Players Dinner Theatre, which is adjacent to the inn, occupying both of the existing barns belonging to the estate, took possession of Brick House, and began much needed restoration and renovation.

*and Thad May are your hosts at
lightful, romantic country inn
ing elegant accomodations,
garden and 320 acres of beauty.
enjoy a country setting with
trail, private fish pond, and
inctuary, and afternoon tea is
. This is pure Southern
ality at its best.*

Southern Comfort Punch

4/5 quart Southern Comfort (fifth)
1 16 ounce can frozen orange juice
1 16 ounce can frozen lemonade
3 quarts lemon-lime carbonated beverage
Red food coloring, optional
Fresh fruit for garnish

Mix liquor, orange juice, and lemonade, then add carbonated beverage. Add a few drops of food coloring if you wish. Add ice an cut up fruit. Makes about one gallon.

Blue Shadows

Rural Route 2
P.O. Box 432
Greensboro, Alabama 36744
(205) 624-3637

Hot Mulled Cider

2 quarts fresh apple cider
1 tsp. grated orange rind, no white membrane
1/2 tsp. whole allspice
1/4 tsp. mace
1/8 tsp. salt, if desired
1/2 tsp. ground coriander
1 tsp. whole cloves
1 tbsp. cinnamon candy (red hots)

Bring all ingredients to boil in large kettle; reduce heat and simmer for 30 minutes. Serve hot with orange slices or whole cinnamon sticks. Yield: 8 one-cup servings.

Patchwork Quilt Country Inn

11748 County Road 2
Middlebury, Indiana 46540
(219) 825-2417

This unusual and delightful restaurant is located on a 340-acre working farm where many of the f[...] served are grown. The inn began ir 1962 as a vacation farm for city pe[...] A few years later a new dining roo[...] The Wood Shed, was added. In it t[...] is a display of antique woodworkin[...] and logging tools and more than 7[...] plates from around the world. Ther[...] a homespun atmosphere at the Patchwork. The kitchen opens into dining room; here grand, family-sty[...] meals are served amid wonderful surroundings. Handmade quilts an[...] patchwork tablecloths are available purchase.

Index of Recipes

C

D

W

Y

Z